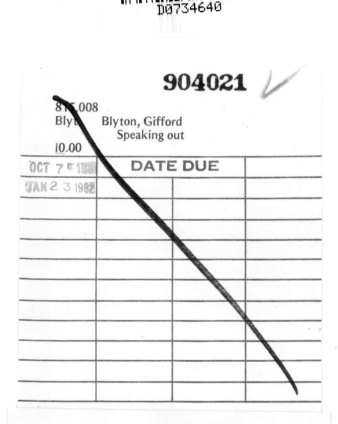

SPEAKING OUT
Two Centuries of
Kentucky Orators

Gifford Blyton
and
Randall Capps

 HUNTER PUBLISHING COMPANY

PREFACE

The inspiration for this book emerged from years of studying public speaking as a fine art. Although most orators speak in something less than an artistic fashion, rhetorical excellence does appear. So it is with famous Kentuckians -- native and transplants -- who spoke on a variety of subjects during various occasions before audiences of all kinds. Perhaps more than "putting the right word in the right place" the speakers discussed here are noted for their impact upon social, political, and religious life in the United States.

The authors are indebted to several persons for assisting in the research and writing of this book. Special thanks are due Dr. Albert D. Kirwan, former President, and Professor of History, University of Kentucky, and Dr. Holman Hamilton, retired Professor of History, University of Kentucky, for advice concerning the selection of personalities. From an original list of eighty speakers, the number was finally reduced to fourteen after long consultations with Drs. Kirwan and Hamilton. Dr. John Nelson, Department of Political Science, University of Iowa, was responsible for much of the basic research at the University of Kentucky. Ms. Colleen Hermann, Ph.D. candidate, Department of English, University of Kentucky, is given a warm thanks for her expert editorial assistance.

Professors Lowell Harrison and Crawford Crowe of the Department of History at Western Kentucky University were generous in reading and commenting on the manuscript. Julia Neal, former director of the Kentucky Library was helpful during the initial stages of the research.

The University of Kentucky Research Foundation support-ed part of the research through a grant. The research was conducted primarily at the Kentucky Library, Western Kentucky University, the Division of Special Collections, University of Kentucky, the Filson Club, Louisville, Kentucky and the Disciples of Christ Historical Society, Nashville, Tennessee. The authors are appreciative for assistance rendered by the librarians at each place. Ester Bennett, niece of Laura Clay, furnished insight about her aunt and allowed the authors the use of a previously unpublished photograph of Miss Clay. The authors gratefully acknowledge the cooperation of former Governor A. B. Chandler for his assistance in locating material pertaining to his oratory.

CONTENTS

CHAPTER I

INTRODUCTION

SPEAKING OUT: TWO CENTURIES OF KENTUCKY ORATORS is not designed primarily as a rhetoric text nor as an anthology of speeches. Instead, it proposes to view the men who spoke and their words. Special attention is given to the personalities, temperaments, mannerisms, and central oratorical characteristics of the men and women whose lives and speeches helped shape or change the course of history during the past two centuries. This personalized approach should be of interest to an audience of almost unlimited variety. While everyone is not fascinated by oratory, *per se*, almost everyone is interested in fascinating people. Since interesting people often create interesting speeches, this collection fulfills a twofold intent: to entertain and to instruct.

It is possible that Kentucky has either produced or nurtured more and better orators than any other state in the Union, yet no significant collection of their speeches has been compiled. Two works exist, but neither reaches beyond a simple presentation of basic biographical material and selected speeches. The first book, *Kentucky Eloquence*, by Bennett Young, published in 1907, contains examples of some early oratory in the Commonwealth. But, of course, it does not include such outstanding later examples as Carry Nation, Alben Barkley or A.B. Chandler. The second work is a master's thesis, entitled "Kentucky Oratory," by Clarke H. Tandy, dated 1903. Again, the date of publication precludes some of Kentucky's best known speakers, and the thesis serves mainly as a rhetorical analysis of particular speeches. These works are useful to an academic audience of teachers and students. However, this book endeavors to reach not only scholars, but also, because of its accent upon the individual, persons interested in great people and their influences.

So that the reader may become acquainted with the orator as well as with his words, biographical insights preface each speech. In each instance the aim is to introduce an important and personable human being, one whom the reader may feel he knows or would like to know. The major thrust is, then, to capture the "essence" of the people behind the words they spoke. For instance, when one learns that Carry Nation's first husband was an alcoholic, her delight in saloon smashing becomes more understandable, and her fanaticism less hostile than her latter-day publicity might lead one to believe.

There are, however, complexities which defy comprehension or simple solutions. John Cabell Breckinridge is an example of such a person: this playmate of Mary Todd became a presidential opponent of Abraham Lincoln, and this Vice-President of the United States became the Secretary of War for the Confederacy. These facts of history accent the difficulty of reducing one man's life to formula, and make for interesting speculation, unproved as it must be.

A variety of career interests permeates both the early and late lives of the orators, but they all held in common a social awareness, a desire for reform, which led each of them to the political arena at one time or another. In the list we find four teachers, eleven lawyers, one hotel owner, a Pulitzer Prize journalist, a suffragette, a bartender, and a baseball commissioner. They represent many sides of life, and some were born into poverty, others into wealth. Yet the force of their personalities, coupled with the demands of their times, placed them in positions of prominence given to very few. The fact that this important mantle was placed upon so many Kentuckians is in itself worth exploration.

From Henry Clay (1777-1852) to A.B. Chandler (1898-present), Kentuckians have been speaking out, and one can only wonder about what unique circumstances of history caused this constellation of oratorical stars. Some scholars have attempted to answer the riddle. Arthur K. Moore in his *The Frontier Mind: A Cultural Analysis of the Kentucky Frontier Hero* touches on some of the possible reasons for the attraction Kentucky held for the idealistically inclined young man. He states: "Kentucky connoted abundance in all desirable things and boundless liberty for all, thus a new life immeasurably superior to that before and equal to the idyllic modes of existence after which the human race has always yearned." Dissatisfied with the *status quo* and anxious for self-improvement, the ambitious moved to the frontier. And while they may have been on the edge of civilization, they brought their earlier culture with them. Here, then, is perhaps a hint of what gives Kentuckians that peculiar flavor of both sophistication and naivete, gentility and aggressiveness, and a determined respect for heritage as well as the energy to strike out in search of new models.

People brought with them their inbred cultural traditions, their interests in literature, history, and the arts, but they applied them to rough surfaces and so learned as much as they taught. The amalgam may well be the present day Kentuckian. By extension, one may see that Kentucky was in its early days a microcosm of the future of the Union itself -- a melting pot, a meeting place for the old and the new, a combination of classes, professions, and tastes.

Perhaps it is not surprising that people desirous of change should travel, concomitantly, with the evangelical spirit of the times. The so-called "Great Revival in the West," beginning in the late 18th century in Logan County, and ending with the frenzy of Cane Ridge in Bourbon County in 1801, added a dimension to Kentucky oratory that has never filtered out. This peculiar blend of learned lawyer and hell-fire preacher is noted in almost all of the speeches of the two-hundred year span.

It may be argued, of course, that there is not any distinctly clear-cut difference between Kentucky orators and those of other States. It is true, however, that Kentucky's early superimposition of Southern, or Virginian, "high culture" upon the rather low tone of the camp meeting may be said to add a special flavor. Also important, in view of the complex of ideas and attitudes which surrounded the Civil War, is the particular status of Kentucky as a border state. As such, the state and its inhabitants were individually and collectively torn by the various happenings and conflicts which the War imposed. The atmosphere was simply different from that of many other states. Kentuckians participated on both sides, and great speeches were made in support of polar positions. Cassius Clay and John Breckinridge were diametrically opposed politically, and their ardor for their separate causes fired them into great and convincing oratory. It is doubtful whether any other state has produced two such orators from such opposing platforms.

Indeed, all of the speeches seem to express a kind of moral fervor that is seldom observed in the "practical politics" usually delivered today. The speeches seemed to be more obviously ideological than current ones. For instance, "either-or" characteristics are more readily seized upon and expressed. The speakers and their audiences were much more certain of specific and mutual moral principles and thus more at ease in couching their arguments and judgments in clearly "moral" terminology. God was invariably invoked and certain to be on the side of the orator, whichever side that was.

Another distinction between the early speeches and those of today is the absence of ghost writers. The fact that a person was the sole author of what was said was important to the kind of oratory prevalent. Perhaps a man had more time then to prepare his material, or perhaps his word counted for more. In addition, it was unnecessary to pare thoughts down to fit the tight scheduling of TV, and, hence, the speeches were normally quite long. Of course, in the absence of modern entertainment media, the speeches themselves became a form of entertainment, full of as much "filler" and flowing asides as the audience could bear.

As a result, there was much repetition and restatement, and much playing to the crowd. Whether on the floor of the Senate or the grass of a picnic, the early orators first captivated listeners by flattery or histrionics, and then drove their points home again and again. But, surprisingly, by the eloquence and use of figurative language, astir with metaphor, alliteration, and allusion, one is never dulled by the rhetoric. Instead, often one is excited by the linguistic beauty and polish of the prose. As a short example, one may point to Henry Clay's comment on the administration of 1834: "It exhibits a state of mind feverish, fretful and fidgety, bounding recklessly from one desperate expedient to another, without any sober or settled purpose." His use of the *f* and *s* sounds fairly hisses his distaste. Ben Hardin, too, delighted in the display of the intricate metaphor:

> *The storms of misfortune and adversity have been threatening us from every quarter -- east, west, north and south. They have gathered over our heads, and threatened every moment to burst upon us, and destroy our liberties forever. I put my hope and trust in God, who has saved us in our trials and difficulties heretofore, that he will preserve us free and independent, and dispel the clouds now lowering over us, and that he will give us once more a clear, serene political sky.*

This rather elaborate, poetic use of imagery was not, however, confined to the early 19th century orators. The speeches of both Alben Barkley and A.B. Chandler abound in the rich and textured uses of symbol and analogy. Barkley addressed the 1948 Democratic National Convention as follows:

> *Destiny itself knocks at our door in behalf of all these and more! Shall we hear the voice and open the door, or shall we slam it in the face of an appealing world, turn our backs upon a divine obligation and refuse to lead the children of men out of the bondage and fear and slavery into a free world and a free life?*

And, in a similar manner, Senator Chandler addressed his peers one month before Pearl Harbor:

We must rely upon a Divine Providence. I believe now, and I have always believed, that Providence usually walks with those who show by their deeds that they merit his protection. There is a destiny which holds the lives of us all in the hollow of its hand.

Of course, the speeches were not without humor. Heavy-handedness weighs on entertainment. However, one orator is remembered solely for a speech so loaded with irony that even he is forgotten in its wake. J. Proctor Knott, with a sense of satire not surpassed by Jonathan Swift, addressed the Senate in 1871 against the building of a railroad which would connect Duluth with expanding commercial centers:

Duluth...I was confident it existed somewhere, and that its discovery would constitute the crowning glory of the present century, if not of all modern times. I knew it was bound to exist in the very nature of things; that the symmetry and perfection of our planetary system would be incomplete without it, that the elements of material nature would long since have resulted from leaving out Duluth...I was convinced that the greatest calamity that ever befell the benighted nations of the ancient world was in their having passed away without a knowledge of the actual existence of Duluth; that their fabled Atlantis, never seen save by the hallowed vision of inspired poesy, was, in fact, but another name for Duluth; that the golden orchard of the Hesperides was but a poetical synonym for the beer gardens in the vicinity of Duluth.

The person of J. Proctor Knott is now difficult to locate; Duluth speaks for itself.

Henry Watterson also engaged in the ironic riposte, as evidenced here:

> *It is given out by those who have investigated the subject, and who think they have got at the facts, that the earth which we inhabit is round. I shall take this for granted, therefore, and observe that its movement is rotary. Hogarth's line of beauty and grace represents a simple, serpentine curve. The rainbow of hope and promise is semi-circular. The broad surface of the ocean, stretching away as far as eye can see in calm or storm -- a dream of peace or a nightmare of horrors -- is one vast oval of wave and sky. And life, which we are told is rounded by a sleep, must conform to nature's laws, or beat itself against the walls within whose rugged circumference nature dwells, for, as nature abhors a vacuum, so she detests an angle, particularly in ideas, engineering, and women.*

Contrasted with the styles of Knott and Watterson one finds sentimentality and folksiness. One fundamental reason for these qualities is to be found in the settings of the speeches. Social gatherings at barbeques or banquets were often occasions for politicking, and the tone of these speeches was far different from that heard on the floor of the Senate. Since the gatherings often did not have public address systems, there was far more intimacy between the speaker and his audience. A speaker felt at home with his crowd. Thus, Cassius Clay may say: "Here in Kentucky, my mother earth, I shall stand unawed by danger, unmoved by denunciation, a living sacrifice for her best prosperity, I shall not fear death itself, if she may but live." This appeal to ethnocentricity is, after all, a fairly sure way to garner both the interest and the votes of a partisan audience.

Whatever the style or tone, there appears to have been much more trust and confidence in rhetoric as a legitimate tool and much more trust that this tool would be used fairly and honestly. The decline of trust in rhetoric we seem now to experience has gone hand in hand with a decline in trust in the political and in particular our own government. Perhaps this development has been a healthy one -- certainly we are much more aware of some of the potential dangers of the application of rhetorical skills. Still, to the extent that such enlivened awareness of potential abuses limits our field of vision to such abuses and thus conditions our approach to rhetoric itself, it represents a distinct loss. Clearly the speakers worried much less than we might today about their addresses being taken as attempts to be demagogic or misleading.

A substantial shift in approaches will be obvious during the long period we are examining. The sheer impact of the Civil War with the realigning of society in its wake was the most powerful instrument of change. Toward the end of the nineteenth century and the beginning of the twentieth, the people in Kentucky, as elsewhere in the United States and the world, were simply not the same people who inhabited these lands in the early parts of the nineteenth century. The different experiences of the different eras made for a different "people" in a collective, cultural sense. Some of the earlier United States "innocence" was gone -- or at least fundamentally diminished. Much of that quality remained, however, to be further desecrated by the wars and other events of the twentieth century. The changes in which the style and importance of oratory were most upset were probably caused by the gradual shift of the medium through which oratory reached the populace at large. Less and less did speeches come from a man personally present to small audiences. The audiences grew larger, the amplification systems grew more powerful, the radio appeared and disembodied the speakers while vastly increasing the audience. Though the old types of speaker-audience relationships continued, as demonstrated in the informal, even colloquial story-telling and anecdotal deliveries of Happy Chandler and others, they were no longer alone and could no longer look forward to comparison to standards appropriate to them. After projecting a dynamic voice on the radio, a person often looked less than "real life" when viewed or heard in person. By contrast, Alben Barkley's "real life" image often overshadowed even the power of his audial performance.

The men and women in this collection were more than simply orators. They were, for the most part, history-makers. Among the group at one time or another were two governors, three senators, five members of the House of Representatives, two Vice-Presidents, two Presidential candidates. Because of their positions of power they helped shape the future of the country, and perhaps of the world. It is hoped that this volume, with its inclusion of photographs, original manuscripts not before published, and whole and excerpted examples of both formal and informal oratory will bring the reader closer to his own roots, and give him pause and comfort in knowing that the problems of today have been around for a long time, and that great men have always faced them, spoken about them, and in most cases solved them.

CHAPTER II

BARTON W. STONE
(1772-1844)

It has been said that if there had not been a God man would have had to invent him. This basic need for an intimate relationship with something grander, stronger, wiser than himself has served as a driving force for man as long as recorded history. Imagine, then, the fervor with which the early settlers of our country greeted the announcement that God would soon send his "glorious deliverance" to them. Beset with hardships, craving release, thirsting for status, these rugged individuals, who carved our country into states, had no grand cathedrals, no men's clubs, no dance halls, and only a few local churches. And out of the combined elements of wanting God's help and approval and needing divergence from their difficult labors, immediately and indigenously, grew the phenomenon of the camp-meeting.

The sites for these revivals were literally "camps," composed of sleeping tents, covered wagons, open bonfires for cooking and heat, all arranged in a square. The major difference between a modern state park layout and the camp-meeting environment is that near the center of the encampment was a rough platform constructed of logs and surrounded by a handrail which served as a pulpit. Around that were rows and rows of roughly hewn logs used as seats for the participants. [1] This was the "church," the entertainment center, the community club for thousands of our ancestors.

When the seats were filled with pioneers who came from as far as a hundred miles for the first of the meetings, the preacher would begin his denouncements of those who were interested in making money, in property, fine clothing and ornaments, liking the bottle (known as "the drunkard's Christ"); those who did not understand the nature and destructiveness of pride. [2] And the frontier folk would swoon in ecstasy at the thought of God's grace and forgiveness, fall on their knees in penance, and leave rejuvenated, renewed, able to continue their labors and their dreams.

Although not the first of the fire and brimstone preachers to conduct a camp-meeting, perhaps the best representative and most controversial was Barton Stone. A devout, sincere Presbyterian minister, Stone attended the regular camp-meeting in the vicinity of Gasper River in July, 1800, where he observed James McGready's extraordinary power over the audience. Stone was greatly distressed at the formal state of religion in his own congregation and was anxious to investigate the work being done by McGready and his associates. He was amazed at what he found, and described the scene as follows:

> *Many, very many fell down as men slain in battle, and continued for hours together in an apparently breathless and motionless state -- sometimes for a few moments reviving, and exhibiting symptoms of life by a deep groan or a piercing shriek, or by a prayer for mercy most fervently uttered.* [3]

Stone concluded that the work being done was good work which was in the interest of furthering God's kingdom on earth, and he found himself in agreement with McGready concerning the preacher's responsibility to the frontier settlers. When he left the Logan County site, he took with him a feeling of strong dedication to make first-hand religious awakening a reality for as many people as he could reach. [4]

Immediately following the meeting, Stone rushed back to his congregations at Cane Ridge and Concord to report the news of the revival. A large crowd gathered at the Cane Ridge log church, and he was inspired to preach from the text: "Go ye into all the world and preach the gospel to every creature. He that believeth and is baptized shall be saved, and he that believeth not shall be damned." These words sent many of the group home weeping. [5]

That same night Stone preached at the Concord church, and, following his sermon, two little girls were struck down under the spell. The emotional responses of the children were similar to those Stone had seen at Gasper River, and the seeds for the still-remembered great Cane Ridge Revival Meeting were sown.

Caught up with the contagion of religious fervor exhibited by his congregation, Stone returned to Cane Ridge the next day, where he was met by a friend shouting the praises of God. Soon a crowd gathered, and in less than twenty minutes of Stone's ardent exhortations, scores had fallen to the ground. They all showed signs of paleness, trembling and anxiety, which would be multiplied thousand-fold near the same place in August, 1801.

The revival spirit of the frontier climaxed with the Cane Ridge meeting. It was a strange phenomenon, partially because of the type of preaching and partially because of the expectation that what had happened in other communities would happen there.[6] But, in sheer excitement, commitment, and wild protestation, it overshadowed its predecessors as a giant does a mouse.

The meeting was called by Presbyterian ministers but was attended by Methodists and Baptists as well. Peter Cartwright, a Methodist revivalist, called it the greatest revival since the days of the Pentecost.[7] The camp was amassed with all segments of society, including "the hunter, the black-leg, the robber, the prostitute -- as well as the devout worshipper." It was also reported that the Governor of Kentucky was present.[8]

Stone's own words convey the general tone of the encampment:

The roads were literally crowded with wagons, carriages, horsemen and footmen, moving to the solemn camp. The sight was affecting. It was judged, by military men on the ground, that there were between twenty and thirty thousand collected. Four or five preachers were frequently speaking at the same time, in different parts of the encampment, without confusion. The Methodist and Baptist preachers aided in the work, and all appeared cordially united in it -- of one mind and soul --

*and the salvation of sinners seemed to be the great ob-
ject of all. We all engaged in singing the same songs of
praise -- all united in prayer -- all preached the same
things -- free salvation urged upon all by faith and re-
pentance.* [9]

News of the Cane Ridge Revival spread throughout the
country. The meeting was unique in several respects, but perhaps
one of the most unusual was the introduction of bodily exercises
into the program. These were of six different types: falling,
rolling, barking, dancing, laughing and singing, and the "jerks."
Apparently it was Barton Stone who promoted and led these
innovations. He did not attempt to explain the cause of the
exercises, but appeared to leave them in the realm of the mysterious. However, he did write of their good effects, which he
said were seen and felt in every neighborhood. [10]

Results of the Cane Ridge Revival are difficult to assess.
Gains in converts were substantial, but it is not clear if the revival
made any inroads in the total unchurched population.[11] The most
far-reaching influence of the Great Revival was the affirmation of
a new form of religious assembly, the camp-meeting.

The revival did, however, have a significant influence on
Stone, and it precipitated a controversy in the Presbyterian
Church which would eventually lead to his withdrawal from that
sect and his formation of a new body. Conflicts arose between the
revival and the anti-revival groups. Representing the revival party
were Scotch-Irish frontier preachers, while leaders in the anti-
revival group were primarily immigrants who had been trained in
Europe.[12]

The final confrontation between the two groups began at
a meeting of the Kentucky Synod in Lexington on September 7,
1803. Here Richard McNemar was condemned for certain teachings, and his own Synod published to its churches that the doctrines of McNemar were dangerous and contrary to the constitution of the church. While the Synod was deliberating on the pro-
cedure to be used against McNemar, Stone and four others presented a paper which was "a protest against the proceedings of

Synod in the affairs of Washington Presbytery, and a declaration that they withdraw from under the jurisdiction of Synod."[13] Following the presentation of the protest, a committee was appointed to confer with Stone and his colleagues to attempt to bring them back to the standards and doctrines of the church. When attempts at reconciliation failed, a motion was introduced to suspend Stone and his associates and declare their churches vacant.

Stone and his friends originally had no intention of leaving the Presbyterian Church. Instead, they met and formed a new presbytery which they called "Springfield." It soon became apparent that Stone and his associates could not continue as an independent presbytery connected with the official Presbyterian Church, and on June 28, 1804, they met to disband. At this meeting they issued *The Last Will and Testament of the Springfield Presbytery*. This document and date mark the beginning of the "reformation," or the birth of the Disciples of Christ movement.

The five who published *The Last Will and Testament* became known by various names: New Lights, Schismatics, Marshallites and Stoneites. The churches with which the five seceding ministers were associated all "held that God and Christ had their abode in the soul of man, and that any exercise that accorded with the inward feelings of love and power and tended to their increase was acceptable to God as worship."[14]

Of those who seceded, only Stone remained true to the views outlined in *The Last Will and Testament*. Finally, in 1832, he joined forces with the Christian Church which had been organized by Alexander Campbell. Two of the original seceders returned to the Presbyterian Church, and the other two joined the Shakers.

Material concerning Stone's activities between 1803 and 1826 when he began publication of the *Christian Messenger* is scarce. It is known that he farmed and taught school in order to support his family, and that he continued to preach at every opportunity. One listener summarized a sermon by Stone in

1805:

> *Stone told them to let no man deceive them about the coming of Christ, for they would all know when he comes, for every eye would see him in the clouds and they would see the graves opening and the bones rising and the saints would rise and meet the Lord in the air....*[15]

Other denominations felt the influence of Stone and his new movement.[16] The Methodist Church was beset with internal struggles between the Northern and Southern segments. While this strife was impeding progress in that church and causing members to leave, Stone and his followers were recruiting disenchanted Methodists. The "Christians" were zealous in their work and the enthusiasm was not limited to the preachers, but church members also were active in espousing the merits of the new movement. Presbyterian ministers felt it necessary to refer to Stone's followers, as evidenced in the following excerpt from a sermon by S.W. Calvert:

> *Yes it is now the fashion of the day to baptize every united Christian effort -- from whatever source it might have originated -- with the name of Presbyterian, and then oppose it, might and main, under the ridiculous pretense that it is one of the measures by which that hated sect is trying to take away our religious liberty, and overturn this great American republic.*[17]

Stone was aware of the controversy surrounding his work, but felt that the Bible was the only sufficient rule of faith and order, and he saw the expression of this conviction as the church's main task. In a statement to his readers he declared: "Let the unity of Christians be our polar star. To this let our eyes be continually turned, and to this let our united efforts be directed -- that the world may believe and be saved."[18]

Reformers come in many sizes, shapes, and temperaments, but usually they are aggressive, physically strong, dramatic, even rough. Not Barton Stone. He was small, thickset, well-proportioned, and, while his voice was bold and commanding, his gestures were natural and easy,[19] almost gentle. He felt a smile was out of place in a pulpit, ever aware of the solemnity of the minister's role. One anecdote serves to highlight both his sweetness and his sobriety: One day, Stone saw a friend driving a horse too hard. He turned and asked the friend if he had heard the horse's prayer to his master. The friend answered that he had not, and Stone then invoked: "On the hill speed me not, down the hill push me not, on the plain spare me not, and in the barn forget me not."[20]

Modest to a fault, Stone felt himself inferior to others. He was extremely melancholy and tended to be apprehensive about the future, and there were indications from his youth that he was emotionally and physically frail.[21] After schooling at David Caldwell's academy at Guilford, North Carolina, Stone spent a year-long struggle trying to determine if he should become a minister. He felt he had no soul-shaking call, and his health broke. However, finally convinced that "God is love," he passed through the crisis, moved to Kentucky, and never wavered again.[22]

Stone, unlike many frontier preachers, had a thorough education. His preparation included training in the classics, theology, sermon writing and delivery. It is probable that he developed an extemporaneous style of delivery, since he was reluctant to write his sermons in advance of preaching them. However, he did much writing for the *Christian Messenger* and frequently published "lectures" such as the four in 1841, entitled: "For Whom Did Jesus Pray That They Might Be One?," "What That Union Is For Which He Prayed," "The Means By Which This Union Is Effected," and "The Happy Consequences Of Such Union." These lectures were based upon a subject dear to Stone's heart throughout his career: the union of Christians.[23]

Stone's reputation as a "good man" was an important factor in his preaching. He knew the Bible well, having read and reread it as a young man, and depended upon the scriptures to support his arguments. He frequently appealed to the emotions of his listeners in order to reach his desired response, but he did not use this tactic until he had established a logical basis for action.[24] He believed that a preacher should balance the use of logic and emotion.

Stone's style was fairly simplistic (as shown by the sermon which follows this chapter) -- the language was so clear as to leave little room for misunderstanding.

Barton Stone died at Jacksonville, Illinois, on November 9, 1844, but in 1847 his body was returned to Cane Ridge, where a monument was erected to his memory. The epitaph on the grave-stone does not mention his greatest contribution, which was in the area of ecumenicity, but it is rather a simple statement of appreci-ation: "Affection and gratitude to Barton W. Stone, a Minister of the Gospel of Christ, and the distinguished reformer of the 19th Century."

2 Cor. XII 15 [25]

And I will gladly spend and be spent for you though the more abundantly I love you, the less I be loved.

What an astonishing thing is the grace of God, what marvelous changes can it produce, and how happy, yea unspeakably felicitous the influence which it exerts on the heart of man, and were we all living under its holy influence; were we all the true and devoted followers of Christ; what happy families should we have, what a lovely congregation would this be, and what a happy world would ours be for righteousness and joy, and peace and love would cover the face thereof as the waters cover the face of the great deep.

Its power can change the Lion into the Lamb -- the blind and deluded pagan idolator into a true worshipper of Christian's God, the sons of Satan into the children of Christ and the bold blasphemer into the tuneful messenger of the tidings of salvation by the work of Christ.

And it was this grace which put into the mouth of the Apostle Paul the language of the text -- in writing to his Christian friends at Corinth --"and I will gladly spend and be spent for you," and said he would give all things and spend all things that he might win them to Christ. His worldly goods did he possess any, his bodily and physical strength, his time, his talents, his life, he would gladly devote to the glory of his God -- and in making them the dove of God.

Behold the change, see the contrast presented in the life of this great apostle. Once he made havoc of the Church of Christ entering into every house and thaling (sic) men and women who dared to profess their love of Christ, and committing them to prison and breathing out threatenings and slaughter against the disciples of the Lord, went unto the high priest and demanded letters to Damascus, that if he found any of this way, whether they were men or women, he might bring them bound into Jerusalem.

But as he journeyed, he came near to Damascus. Suddenly there shined round about him a light from heaven -- and he heard the voice of God address him -- and the spirit of the Lord fell upon him and the grace of God was infused into his soul.

Thus, and thus alone, by the power of that grace, was this bitter persecutor changed into a meek and faithful follower of the Lamb and able defender of his blessed Gospel. "Willing gladly to spend and to be spent for Christ," and to do and suffer anything, to bring honor and glory on his cause. Now, nothing but grace could effect this mighty change and this grace is freely offered to you all -- oh that we all did enjoy it.

The language of the gospel to you all is whosoever willeth, let him come and there is no sinner living who longs to fly to Christ, whom the sacred volume does not invite to seek refuge in him from the wrath to come.

And as the celebrated R. Hill said, I may see amongst you a very wicked man and say that he is on the road to hell. But the very same might have been said of the Apostle Paul when he persecuted the Churches of Christ and longed to be the murderer of every saint. But divine grace subdued his heart and what a wondrous change was completed in him to the praise and glory of God.

This is what has again encouraged me to try to preach the gospel of Christ to you. This is what has brought me to the resolution to spend and to be spent for you, to devote my time to your service and labour again to bring you to Christ, and, although I may be spent and worn out in this service, although it may shorten my life, yet what work is so glorious as working for Christ? What could be made the instrument winning one of you to Christ?

And who can tell but my heart may yet rejoice to see you my dear, for whom I love, and in whom I pray, returning to Jesus and laying hold upon his rich and precious promises. For, blessed be God, it is not decreed that any of you shall be lost because you were born in sin. And yet we cannot understand the mystery of the salvation of some and the condemnation of others.

But I find my way plain; my business is to alarm sinners of their danger, not to bring this man or that man but all to see their awful state and their need of Christ -- not to be looking and searching to see who is elected, but to teach that whoever is willing to come has the sweetest and safest evidence and proof of his decision, for he never would have been willing if God had not made him so.

You who hear the alarming words of warning and still continue hardened and impenitent, give an awful proof that you are rejected of God and your continuing to reject his counsels and his warnings makes your condemnation just, for you must know that all who willfully persist in their disobedience and rebellion are justly condemned of God.

And yet dear fellow sinner, hardened as you may have been, when once your hearts are softened by the power of divine grace, the Lord is ready to blot out your sins by the precious blood of Jesus Christ. It is this alone can preserve you from the anger of God. Take the Bible and examine the ground on which rests the salvation of any sinner and you will find it to be the blood of the Lamb of God.

Are you delivered? It is by his blood. Are you redeemed? It is not by corruptible things as gold and silver, but with the precious blood of Christ, as of a lamb, without blemish and without spots. Are you cleansed from sin? The Bible tells you that the blood of Jesus Christ his son cleanseth you from all sin. Are your robes washed? The Bible tells you that the saints all have their robes washed and made white in the blood of the Lamb. Are you justified? If so, this by the blood of Christ. Are Christians permitted to enter into the Holy of Holies? It is all by the blood of Christ. Do they overcome all things? They overcome by the blood of the Lamb. Do they live? They have life through his blood -- Yes, Fellow Christians, do you not know, do you not feel and find that all the grace and love and money

22

and compassion and kindness and favor of God which you enjoy are ascribed in his work to the blood of Christ, and that all these little streams of joy and comfort which run into your soul are little streams that issue from that glorious fountain, the blood of Christ, the streams whereof make glad the city of our God.

Thus are we lead to contemplate the two great leading doctrines in the gospel of Christ: the fall of man by sin and his recovery by the blood of Christ. And these are the great truths in the enforcement of which the minister should be willing to spend and be spent. And yet there is danger that he who is faithful in those particular to the souls of those who hear him -- may find himself in the position of the apostles when he adds, in the conclusion of our text, "Tho the more abundantly I love you, the less I do love many," is, by nature - proud as well as sinful, and he who takes the liberty of dealing faithfully and honestly with him -- he who plainly points out his faults and his sins, though it be a mark of his love, is generally beloved by him.

Yet let me declare unto you the eternal truths of God. Condemn and abuse the nature of man as that nature deserves, hold you up as guilty helpless sinners walking straight down to the dark regions of eternal night and you will not love me the better for it.

Let me represent you, not only as guilty and criminal in the sight of Heaven, but as utterly unable to deliver yourselves from the penalty of God's violate law or to do anything meritorious in the light of God. That the fundamental cause of your justification is Christ and Christ alone. That it is Jesus Christ, independent altogether of your faith and love and works, and your pride will doubtless be insulted; and yet if anything could conciliate God to man -- ye excruciating agonies of my savior -- Thou perfect satisfaction; Thou bloody death; Thou bleeding, dying Savior -- sacrifice proposed to man after his fall - ye only, only ye, could atone for man. "God forbid that I should glory save in the cross of our Lord Jesus Christ by whom the world is crucified unto me and I unto the world." No, my dear, for it is never pleasant to the sinner to have his true condition told him.

And he who is faithful and speaks plainly is sure to incur his displeasure -- And, my dear, for in looking back on my own life and conduct what unfaithfulness do I see, how often have I been prevented by some man-fearing spirit from reproving the sinner and telling him his errors, pointing out his sins, and the awful consequences of them. And when I look back upon it with shame I am forced into the resolution that however long or short God may spare me to spend the spent in your service, I shall endeavor to deal more faithfully with you, altho the more faithful I be to you the less I may be loved. Yes, if you sin, you may be expected to be told of it; if you are disorderly, you may expect your disorders to be disclosed. If you forget God, you must be reminded of your duty -- Thus shall I endeavor to wash my hands of the blood of your guilt; and, whether you love me or not, if you can be prevailed upon to love Christ, my highest wishes shall be attained. For my heart's desire and prayer to God, is that you may all be spared.

And now, in view of the situation which we occupy; in view of this day, the first Sabbath of the new year; in view of death and eternity; and in solemn view of the judgement sent of Christ, what should the resolutions be? Mine should be and shall be to be more faithful to your souls, your fellow Christians and every professor of religion here; to be more faithful to God, to mark with tears and prayers the advancement of his kingdom and the glory.

Oh, think how little you are doing for the savior who loved you with an everlasting love and gave himself so freely for you. One might doubt whether these Christians here were Christians at all -- Simon son of Jonas, lovest thou me? And you, my unconverted, for who have had a savior so long offered to you, and have just as long rejected him, what should your resolution be? That this year you will give yourself to Christ; That you will not shout to God to spare you to spend another year in rebellion and forgetfulness of God. If you resolve thus, delay it not but come now and prostrate yourselves at the feet of the throne. If that Jesus, whom you have insulted, and who, in spite of all the insults you have offered him, still calls and still invites you to repent, -- let each one of you say to him as the convicted Paul said on the road to Damascus, "Lord, what wilt thou have me do?". God answered this question plainly when he assured you that Jesus is the way, the truth and the life, and that Jesus Christ alone presents to you the true remedy against the wrath of God; Tis a sure remedy; Tis a glorious remedy; and in the plentitude of his compassion, and with bonds of the tenderest love he entreats you to escape saying, "O that my people would harken to me -- Be instructed O Jerusalem, lest my soul depart from thee -- why, why will I die, oh house of Israel?"

1841

CHAPTER III

HENRY CLAY
(1777-1852)

One biographer has observed that even at four, Henry Clay "was not afraid of anything or anybody. But he was insensitive."[1] These qualities of fearlessness and susceptibility were to continue throughout Clay's life and contribute to his greatest glories and his greatest defeats. Persistency of purpose, coupled with a delicacy of feeling, may produce a personality difficult to balance and, indeed, Clay's career is spotted with the marks of his disparate nature. Throughout his life, he seemed guided by a self-confidence sure to culminate in success, yet he never attained his one great goal. Remembered first and foremost as an extraordinary orator-statesman, Clay's four-time assault on the office of President is almost forgotten.

From the beginning, Clay seemed destined to enter politics by way of his interest in oratory, so it is perhaps not so surprising that as an orator he should linger in the memories of his admirers. Clay himself credited the art of oratory with the shaping of his life: "I am indebted for the primary and leading impulses that stimulated my progress and have shaped and moulded my entire destiny ... this practice of the art of all arts."[2]

As a boy of nine, his hero was Patrick Henry, considered by some historians to be the greatest orator in America's history. Little Henry Clay asked his mother to teach him to read so that he might memorize Patrick Henry's speeches. Clay had somehow found a pamphlet which contained Henry's famous "Treason" speech, with its memorable line, "If this be treason, make the most of it", and, standing on a stump near the banks of Machump's Creek, he delivered the speech to an audience of one, a little slave boy named Jim who was his constant companion.[3]

Although in later life Clay liked to refer to his poor beginnings, according to biographers, he was in fact descended from a prosperous line of Virginia farmers, and his maternal ancestors were planters. Henry's father, John, a Baptist clergyman, was imprisoned at one time for his vigorous attempts at "soul saving", but he also owned 500 acres of land and 20 slaves.[4]

John Clay died when Henry was four years old, and shortly thereafter his mother married Captain Henry Watkins, a brother-in-law of her sister. For reasons lost to time, the rest of the family eventually moved to Versailles, Kentucky, leaving Henry, then fourteen, behind in Virginia. Through Captain Watkins' influence, Henry obtained a job in Richard Denning's store in Richmond until, about a year later, an opening in a clerk's office occurred.[5]

Henry had developed his fine handwriting by practicing "Learning is necessary to success" over and over again, and his excellent penmanship soon brought him to the attention of George Wythe, Chief Justice of the High Court of Chancery, and the first professor of law in the United States. Suffering from a hand disability, Judge Wythe needed an amanuensis, and Henry acquired the position. Wythe assisted Henry in his thirst for knowledge and lent him books -- Plutarch, Homer, some grammars and histories -- which further intensified his interest in the humanities, and led him to the reading of law under Robert Brooke, attorney general of Virginia. In less than a year after he began his studies, he passed the Virginia bar exam.

Kentucky, where his family ties now were, was the burgeoning frontier of the "West", a place where a young man of talent and ambition might quickly establish himself, and Henry decided to settle in Lexington, "the largest town west of the mountains". At the age of twenty, he arrived with letters of introduction to the most prominent legal practitioners in the area. John Breckinridge, James Brown and George Nicholas all assisted the energetic grey-eyed lad in gaining a foothold in his newly-adopted state.

His rise to oratorical eminence got off to a shaky start, however, when James Brown took him to the local debating society's meeting at Captain Postelwait's Tavern (later the Phoenix Hotel) on Main Street. The subject for discussion was the French Revolution, and, without advance warning, Brown asked Clay to speak on the topic. Henry stood up and began: "Gentlemen of the Jury!" Howls of laughter erupted, but the faux pas was courteously turned to fellowship and Clay had made his entree into public speaking. Always a quick learner, Clay passed the Kentucky bar exam a month before he reached twenty-one, and thus completed his formal prerequisite for a life in politics.

High on Lexington's social ladder stood Thomas Hart, James Brown's father-in-law and one of the richest men in the West. It was perhaps inevitable that Clay should meet this man, who was also born in Hanover County, Virginia, and marry his daughter, Lucretia. With this union came the management of Hart's legal affairs, and a promising future was almost certainly insured. Clay's boyhood dream of becoming another Patrick Henry was near at hand.

Politically Clay allied himself with the Jeffersonian Republicans, and his speaking out against the Alien and Sedition Acts of 1798 made him a favorite with Republican voters. He was elected to the State Legislature in 1803. As Council for Aaron Burr, who was under investigation for his schemes in the Southwest, Clay enhanced his career through association with the then popular figure. By the time Burr's popularity took its drastic turn downward, Clay's public status was secured through his impressive personal record, and what might have proved a disastrous connection faded in the public memory.

Meanwhile, Clay had filled an unexpired term in the United States Senate. There he argued for a reading of the Constitution broad enough to permit federal funding of internal improvements, a position which would lead him to embrace what he called "The American System", whereby protective tariffs for manufacturers would be established, and a home market and better transportation for the farmers would materialize.

Clay returned to the Kentucky legislature in 1807, and in 1809 was again sent to serve in the U.S. Senate. He strongly argued the need for expanding home manufactures, and his powers of persuasion were also turned to a defense of Madison's seizure of Florida. His greatest effort, however, came in his successful opposition to rechartering the National Bank, which he thought unconstitutional.

In the next Congress, Clay transferred from the Senate to the House of Representatives, for it was then considered the defender of the people's interests. Clay had found his most suitable arena and rose to the position of Speaker on November 4, 1811. His sympathy for the West guided his economic and expansion policies, and he became known, in a strange juxtaposition of allusions, as both "The Western Hotspur" and "Gallant Harry." Clay headed the "War Hawks" who encouraged war with Great Britain in 1812, but, by 1814, this remarkable politician was active as a negotiator on the U.S. Peace Commission at Ghent, where his influence on the war settlement was keenly felt.

Bolstered by his previous accomplishments, Clay could claim to speak for Kentucky and rose ever nearer to national distinction. He spoke for internal improvements by the federal government, for measures to insure national preparedness, and for the protective tariff of 1816. He also urged that the U.S. aid Latin America, and maneuvered to enhance his position as a spokesman on foreign affairs, probably with an eye cast on becoming Monroe's Secretary of State. When the post went to John Quincy Adams, Clay edged into a constant confrontation with Monroe's policies.

Working parliamentary mastery in Congress, Clay successfully promoted the 1820 Missouri Compromise. His astute manipulation and careful tact led to his acclamation as "The Great Compromiser." Though he left Congress in 1821, he returned to serve in 1823-25. Again, as Speaker he pursued an intensely "nationalistic" program. A rare interruption of his antipathy to the Monroe Administration came with his support of the Monroe Doctrine.

In 1824 Clay made his first bid for the Presidency. One of his friends said that Clay, as a Presidential candidate, "had one serious fault; he was too outspoken." He ran fourth and last. However, when no single candidate received a majority of the electoral votes, the election was decided by the House of Representatives. Though instructed by the Kentucky Legislature to support Andrew Jackson, Clay helped elect John Quincy Adams instead, who then appointed him Secretary of State. Jackson was outraged and thereafter attacked what he called Clay's "bargain and sale" tactics.

Senator John Randolph of Virginia called the alliance between Adams and Clay "like a marriage between Old Massachusetts and Young Kentucky; between the frost of January and the young, blithe, buxom, blooming May...not so young, however, as not to make a prudent match and sell her charms for their full value." Clay was angrily aroused and challenged Randolph to a duel. Though neither was hurt (one report stated that Randolph fired in the air), this and many other less dramatic incidents betokened a lasting public impression that was to frustrate continually Clay's presidential hopes.

Years later at a banquet honoring his retirement into private life, Clay was to speak of his support of Adams in doleful terms:

I will take this occasion now to say, that I am, and have been long satisfied, that it would have been wiser and more politic in me, to have declined accepting the office of Secretary of State in 1825. Not that my motives were not as pure and as patriotic as ever carried any man into public office. Not that the calumny which was applied to the fact was not as gross and as unfounded as any that was ever propagated. Not that valued friends, and highly esteemed opponents did not unite in urging

> *my acceptance of the office. Not that the administra-*
> *tion of Mr. Adams will not, I sincerely believe, advan-*
> *tageously compare with any of his predecessors, in*
> *economy, purity, prudence, and wisdom... But my*
> *error in accepting the office, arose out of my under-*
> *rating the power of detraction and the force of ig-*
> *norance, and abiding with too sure a confidence in*
> *the conscious integrity and uprightness of my own*
> *motives.* [6]

This statement, delivered in his old age, perhaps more than any other of his public utterances suggests the wistfulness and anguish of possessing a nature of contrary strengths. He was right, but he was deeply hurt.

Jackson, Calhoun and William H. Crawford of Georgia joined forces in opposition to the Adams Administration and the National Republican Party, and in 1828 the Jacksonian Democratic Party won a convincing victory. Clay retired to his Ashland estate, known by then as "the Monticello of the West," but continued to attack Jackson over such issues as the spoils system, the use of veto power, and the Indian policies.

Clay's interest in his house and farm went back to his early association with Thomas Hart when he openly wished to have such a house as his one day. He raised Hereford cattle which he imported from England, bred horses, and even sold eggs, chickens, butter and vegetables to the Phoenix Hotel. Content for the moment with his wife and eleven children, he relaxed by playing poker with his friends. Lucretia's personality is partially revealed by her response to an inquisitive lady who said to her one day, "Isn't it a pity your husband gambles so much!" "Oh, I don't know," Mrs. Clay retorted, "he usually wins." [7]

Clay re-entered the Senate in 1831 to lead the opposition to Jackson. In December of that year he was nominated for President by the National Republican Convention but was defeated in the campaign of 1832 by Jackson's use of the Bank issue.

In 1833 Clay formulated the compromise tariff which ended the nullification crisis. He declined to seek the Whig presidential nomination in 1836, and returned, rather reluctantly, to the Senate in 1837. The Panic of that year put the Whigs in an almost "can't lose" position for the elections of 1840. As a candidate, Clay came out strongly against slavery, but was urged by his colleagues and supporters not to announce publicly his position. To this advice, he replied "I'd rather be right than be President," and, indeed, he had to settle for principle as he lost the nomination to William Henry Harrison.

When President Harrison died after only one month in office, Clay found himself in opposition to Tyler's policies, and he resigned from the Senate in 1842. Two years later, however, he was again nominated to run against James K. Polk, to whom he lost over the annexation issue. Clay was against the annexation of Texas because he felt certain it would lead to war with Mexico. The accuracy of his prediction was painfully clear when he lost his favorite son, Henry, Jr., in the ensuing war.

Clay was snubbed for the Whig nomination in 1848. At seventy-one he was thought too old to be President, a predicament Alben Barkley would face in the next century. Modern historians have written that Clay "deserved to be President more than any other who rose to political prominence between the War of 1812 and the Civil War,"[8] but Zachary Taylor rode his military achievements to victory.

In 1849 Clay again returned to the Senate. There he constructed the Compromise of 1850. In a series of proposals artfully supported in his stands on the Senate floor, Clay coaxed through a policy widely credited with postponing the Civil War for ten years.

Lincoln called Clay "my beau ideal of a statesman, the man for whom I fought all my humble life," and he campaigned for Clay's election. At the memorial service for Clay in Springfield, following Clay's death on June 29, 1852, Lincoln said:

> *Our country is prosperous and powerful; but could it have been quite all it has been, and is to be, without Henry Clay? Such a man the times have demanded, and such in the providence of God was given us.*[9]

Clay is regularly ranked with Calhoun and Webster as the foremost orator to grace the halls of Congress in the nineteenth century. Numerous analysts have probed and compared their rhetorical styles and historical impacts. The focus of such analyses is rightly on Clay's major parliamentary addresses. Offered in support of proposals pending before the U.S. Senate or House of Representatives, these speeches are aimed at a special audience in a particular setting. But because such speeches are so well-known, we have chosen to highlight Clay's oratory from a different point of view.

The speech following was delivered in the Senate on April 30, 1834. Its prompting occasion was the debate on the Poindexter Resolution, but its wider subject is "Dictators in American Politics." Clay's main purpose is the denunciation of his arch-foe, Andrew Jackson. His audience is clearly not only the Senators assembled to hear him speak, but his constituency in Kentucky and even the wider constituency in the nation.

Noted for his magnetic personal presence and his adept use of all the tools of the orator's trade, Clay was undoubtedly an imposing figure in Congress. His gaze is said to have pierced many a man. On this day in 1834, a smoldering and righteous anger rendered his tongue sharper than usual, his tone more biting, his command of the audience more keen.

Picture Clay, as one observer has done, gesticulating "all over, using his hands, his feet, his body, even his glasses and his snuffbox to express his emotions and thoughts,"[10] and return to "The Golden Age of Oratory" with all its grandiloquence.

Dictators in American Politics

Delivered in the United States Senate on the Poindexter Resolution, April 30, 1834 -- Denouncing Andrew Jackson.

Never, Mr. President, have I known or read of an administration which expires with so much agony, and so little composure and resignation, as that which now, unfortunately, has the control of public affairs in the country. It exhibits a state of mind feverish, fretful and fidgety, bounding recklessly from one desperate expedient to another, without any sober or settled purpose. Ever since the dog days of last summer, it has been making a succession of the most extravagant plunges, of which the extraordinary Cabinet paper, a sort of appeal from dissenting Cabinet to the people, was the first, and the protest a direct appeal from the Senate to the people, is the last and the worst.

A new philosophy has sprung up within a few years past called phrenology. There is, I believe, something in it, but not quite as much as its ardent followers proclaim. According to its doctrines, the leading passion, propensity and characteristics of every man are developed in his physical conformation, chiefly in the structure of his head. Gall and Spurzheim, its founders, or most eminent propagators, being dead, I regret that neither of them can examine the head of our illustrious Chief Magistrate. But if it could be surveyed by Dr. Caldwell, of Transylvania University, I am persuaded that he would find the organ of destructiveness prominently developed. Except an enormous fabric of executive power for himself, the President has built up nothing, constructed nothing, and will leave no enduring monument for his administration. He goes for destruction, universal destruction, and it seems to be his greatest ambition to efface and obliterate every trace of the wisdom of his predecessors.

He has displayed this remarkable trait throughout his whole life, whether in private walks or in the public service. He signally and gloriously exhibited that peculiar organ when contending against the enemies of his country in the battle of New Orleans. For that brilliant exploit no one has ever been more ready than myself to award him all due honor. At the head of our armies was his appropriate position, and most unfortunate for his fame was the day when he entered on the career or administration as the chief executive officer. He lives by excitement, perpetual, agitating excitement, and would die in a state of perfect repose and tranquility. He has never been without some subject of attack, either in individuals, or in masses, or in institutions. I myself have been one of his favorites, and I do not know but that I have recently recommended myself to his special regard. During his administration this has been his constant course. The Indians and Indian policy, internal improvements, the colonial trade, the Supreme Court, Congress, the bank, have successively experienced the attack of his haughty and imperious spirit. And if he tramples the bank in the dust, my word for it, we shall see him quickly in chase of some new subject of his vengeance.

This is the genuine spirit of conquerors and of conquest. It is said by the biographer of Alexander the Great that, after he had completed his Asiatic conquests, he seemed to sigh because there were no more worlds for him to subdue; and, finding himself without further employment for his valor or arms, he turned within himself to search the means to gratify his insatiable thirst for glory. What sort of conquest he achieved of himself the same biographer tragically records.

Already has the President singled out and designated, in the Senate of the United States, the new object of his hostile pursuit; and the protest which I am to consider is his declaration of war. What has provoked it? The Senate, a component part of Congress of the United States, at its last adjournment, left the Treasury of the United States in the safe custody of the persons and places assigned by law to keep it. Upon reassembling, it found the treasure removed; some of its guardians displaced; all remaining, brought under the immediate control of the President's sole will; and the President having free and unobstructed access to the public money. The Senate believes that the purse of the nation, by the Constitution and laws, is entrusted to the exclusive legislative care of Congress. It has dared to avow and express the opinion in a resolution adopted on the 28th of March last. That resolution was preceded by a debate of three months' duration, in the progress of which the able and zealous supporters of the executive in the Senate were attentively heard. Every argument which their ample resources, or those of the members of the executive, could supply was listened to with respect and duly weighed. After full deliberation, the Senate expressed its conviction that the executive had violated the Constitution and laws. It cautiously refrained, in the resolution, from all examination into the motives or intention of the executive; it ascribed no bad ones to him; it restricted itself to a simple declaration of its solemn belief that the Constitution and laws had been violated. This is the extent of the offense of the Senate. This is what it has done to excite the executive indignation and to bring upon it the infliction of a denunciatory protest.

The President professes to consider himself as charged by the resolution with "the high crime of violating the laws and Constitution of my country." He declares that "one of the most important branches of the Government, in its official capacity, in a public manner, and by its recorded sentence, but without precedent, competent authority, or just cause, declares him guilty of a breach of the laws and Constitution." The protest further alleges that such an act as the Constitution describes "constitutes a high crime -- one of the highest, indeed, which the President can commit -- a crime which justly exposes to an impeachment by the House of Representatives, and, upon due conviction, to removal from office, and to complete and immutable disfranchisement prescribed by the Constitution." It also asserts: "The resolution, then, was an impeachment of the President, and in its passage amounts to a declaration by a majority of the Senate that he is guilty of an impeachable offense." The President is also of the opinion that, to say the resolution does not expressly allege that the assumption of power and authority which it condemns was intentional and corrupt, is no answer to the preceding view of its character and effect. The act thus condemned necessarily implies volition and design in the individual to whom it is imputed, and, being lawful in its character, the legal conclusion is that it was prompted by improper motives and committed with an unlawful intent..."The President of the United States, therefore, has been, by a majority of his constitutional triers, accused and found guilty of an impeachable offense."

But, I would ask, in what tone, temper and spirit does the President come to the Senate? As a great State culprit who has been arraigned at the bar of justice or sentenced as guilty? Does he manifest any of those compunctious visitings of conscience which a guilty violator of the Constitution and laws of the land ought to feel? Does he address himself to a high court with the respect, to say nothing of humility, which a person accused or convicted would naturally feel? No, No. He comes as if the Senate were guilty, as if he were in the judgment seat and the Senate stood accused before him. He arraigns the Senate; puts it upon trial; condemns it; he comes as if he felt himself elevated far above the Senate, and beyond all reach of the law, surrounded by an unapproachable impunity. He who professes to be an innocent and injured man gravely accuses the Senate and modestly asks it to put upon its own record his sentence on condemnation! When before did the arraigned or convicted party demand of the court which was to try, or had condemned him, to enter upon their records a severe denunciation of their own conduct? The President presents himself before the Senate, not in the garb of suffering innocence, but in the imperial and royal costume, as a dictator, to rebuke a refractory Senate; to command it to record his solemn protest; to chastise it for disobedience.

> The hearts of princes kiss obedience
> So much they love it; but to stubborn spirits
> They swell, and grow as terrible as storms.

The President thinks "the resolution of the Senate is wholly unauthorized by the Constitution and derogative of its entire spirit." He proclaims that the passage recording promulgation of the resolution affixes guilt and disgrace to the President "in a manner unauthorized by the Constitution." "But, " says the President, "if the Senate has just cause to entertain the belief that the House of Representatives would not impeach him, that can not justify the assumption by the Senate of powers not conferred by the Constitution." The protest continues: "It is only necessary to look at the condition in which the Senate and the President have been placed by this proceeding to perceive its utter incompatibility with the provisions and the spirit of the Constitution and with the plainest dictates of humanity and justice. A majority of the Senate assume the function which belongs to the House of Representatives and convert themselves into accusers, witnesses, counsel and judges and prejudge the whole case." If the House of Representatives shall consider that there is no cause of impeachment, and prefer none, "then will the violation of privilege as it respects that house, of justice as it regards the President, and of the Constitution as it relates to both, be more conspicuous and impressive." The Senate is charged with the "unconstitutional power of arraigning and censuring the official conduct of the executive." The people, says the protest, will be compelled to adopt the conclusion "either that the Chief Magistrate was unworthy of their respect, or that the Senate was chargeable with calumny and injustice." There can be no doubt which branch of this alternative was intended to apply. The President throughout the protest labors to prove himself worthy of all respect from the people.

That the President did not intend to make the journal of the Senate a medium of conveying his sentiments to the people is manifest. He knows perfectly well how to address them his appeals. And the remarkable fact is established by his private secretary that, simultaneously with the transmission to the Senate of his protest, a duplicate was transmitted to the *Globe*, his official paper, for publication, and it was forthwith published accordingly. For what purpose, then, was it sent there? It is painful to avow the belief, but one is compelled to think that it was only sent in a spirit of insult and defiance.

The President is not content with vindicating his own rights. He steps forward to maintain the privileges of the House of Representatives also. Why? Was it to make the House his ally and to excite its indignation against the offending Senate? Is not the House perfectly competent to sustain its own privileges against every assault? I should like to see, sir, a resolution introduced into the House alleging a breach of its privileges by a resolution of the Senate, which was intended to maintain unviolated the constitutional rights of both Houses in regard to the public purse, and to be present at its discussion.

Is the President scrupulously careful of the memory of the deed or the feelings of the living in respect to the violations of the Constitution? If a violation by him implies criminal guilt, a violation by them can not be innocent and guiltless. And how has the President treated the memory of the immortal Father of his Country, that great man who, for purity of purpose and character, wisdom and moderation, unsullied virtue and unsurpassed patriotism, is without competition in past history or among living men and whose equal we scarcely dare hope will ever be again presented as a blessing to mankind? How has he been treated by the President? Has he not again and again pronounced that, by approving the bill chartering the first Bank of the United States, Washington violated the Constitution of his country? That violation, according to the President, included volition and design, was prompted by improper motives and was committed with an unlawful intent. It was the more excusable in Washington because he assisted and presided in the convention which formed the Constitution. If it be unjust to arraign, try unheard, and condemn as guilty, a living man filling an exalted office, with all the splendor, power and influence which the office possesses, how much more cruel is it to disturb the sacred and venerable ashes of the illustrious dead, who can raise no voice and make no protests against the imputation of high crime!

What has been the treatment of the President toward that

other illustrious man, yet spared to us, but who is lingering upon the verge of eternity? Has he abstained from charging the Father of the Constitution with criminal intent in violating the Constitution? Mr. Madison, like Washington, assisted in the formation of the Constitution, was one of its ablest expounders and advocates and was opposed, on constitutional ground, to the first Bank of the United States. But, yielding to the force of circumstances, and especially to that great principle that the peace and stability of human society require that a controverted question, which has been finally settled by all the departments of Government by long acquiescence and by the people themselves, should not be opened to perpetual dispute and disturbance, he approved the bill chartering the present Bank of the United States. Even the name of James Madison, which is but another for purity, patriotism, profound learning and enlightened experience, can not escape the imputations of his present successor.

And, lastly, how often has he charged Congress itself with open violations of the Constitution? Times almost without number. During the present session he has sent in a message, in regard to the land bill, in which he has charged it with an undisguised violation -- a violation so palpable that it is not even disguised and must, therefore, necessarily imply a criminal intent. Sir, the advisers of the President, whoever they are, deceive him and themselves. They have vainly supposed that, by an appeal to the people and an exhibition of the wounds of the President, they could enlist the sympathies and the commiseration of the people -- that the name of Andrew Jackson would bear down the Senate and all opposition. They have yet to learn, what they will soon learn, that even a good and responsible name may be used frequently, as an indorser, that its credit and the public confidence in its solidity have been seriously impaired. They mistake the intelligence of the people, who are not prepared to see and sanction the President putting forth indiscriminate charges of a violation of the Constitution against whomsoever he pleases, and exhibits unmeasured rage and indignation when his own infallibility is dared to be questioned.

CHAPTER IV

BEN HARDIN
(1784-1852)

In the early nineteenth century, Kentuckians usually obtained their ideas from each other rather than from books or mass media. Good speakers were in demand and could usually find a good audience. Persuasive speech was a gift of leadership which was at a premium among the pioneers. And Ben Hardin was one of those who realized that "oratory ranked among the absolute necessities of life."[1]

As a member of the House of Representatives for ten years, the State Legislature for three years, and the State Senate for four years, Hardin had many opportunities to exercise his "necessity," and demonstrated a particularly cutting sarcasm. As an active campaigner for Henry Clay's candidacy in 1832, he illustrated this gift, described as follows:

> *He depicted the President occupying an easy chair in one of the private rooms of the White House, a weak, ill-educated, vain, old man, in the hands of the wily-fox, Van Buren. There was more truth than poetry in the picture. The particular flattery being administered at the time was the repetition of the number of high sounding names his admiring following had bestowed upon him. "General Jackson," says Van Buren, "You are the Old Roman." "Yes," responds the General. "I am the old Roman; if I ain't I would like to know who is." "General Jackson," says Van Buren again,*

"You are the second Father of your country." "Oh, yes," answers Jackson (who was childless), "I am the Father of my country, if I am the Father of nothing else." [2]

Another instance which exemplifies Hardin's ironic mode of speaking took place in Grayson County where Hardin was presenting a case involving a small sum of money. One of the witnesses was a county schoolmaster, a profession for which Hardin had an antipathy:

Speaking of the schoolmaster, Hardin reported: "He gave his testimony, and every now and then he would throw in a word of four, five or six syllables, utterly inappropriate to the sense ... and I saw at once he was a county schoolmaster. He had proved the making of the settlement, and, said I, "When did it take place?" "On the 39th of October, "said he. "Oh! The 39th of October, you say?" "Yes, Sir." "Are you not mistaken: Was it not the 29th?" "No, Sir, I know the use of words as well as you do, Mr. Hardin, and say it was the 39th." [3]

Hardin's own sporadic education may have accounted for his stubborn opinion. His formal schooling was acquired in various locations around Nelson County, where his family had moved from Westmoreland County, Pennsylvania, when he was four years old. He attended schools taught by Daniel Barry and Ichabod Radley, Mr. Knott and Dr. James Priestly,[4] and one can only surmise his views of the quality of education he was exposed to. In 1804, Hardin read law in the office of his cousin, Martin D. Hardin, in Richmond, and later read under Felix Grundy, a well-known lawyer and politician in Bardstown.

In 1806, Ben Hardin opened a law office in Elizabethtown where he practiced for two years. One day he asked a man a fee of three hundred dollars to defend him for murder. When the prospective client remarked that he could get a Bardstown lawyer for that price, Hardin went home and told his wife to pack for a move to Bardstown.[5]

In addition to being a good speaker, Hardin was also a very successful attorney. He first held public office in March, 1810, when he was appointed the Commonwealth's Attorney for the district. This appointment put him in company with the best lawyers of the day and brought him a good income. In August, 1810, he was elected to represent Nelson County in the State Legislature, and his political career began.

During his first session of Congress, in 1815, Hardin was appointed to two committees: Soldiers, Widows and Orphans; and Changing the Western Line of the Indian Territory. He engaged in frequent debates, especially with Henry Clay, who was elected speaker of the House, and with whom Hardin would later share a close friendship.

On one occasion Hardin made a speech on the repeal of the direct tax and criticized the administration and its manner of operation. Typical of his direct style, he closed with a statement of his philosophy of government spending:

> *Whenever a farmer in the country purchases more than he can pay for, we suspect he is going to ruin, and that a commission of bankruptcy will soon issue against him. Whenever a government lavishly disburses money, more than her income, it equally proves that the Government is going to ruin ....How can we pay off the National debt, if we give in to these projects of invalid crops, military academics, turnpike roads, canals, etc., which are to consume so much money?* [6]

The most important legislation introduced at this session of Congress was John C. Calhoun's bill to charter a national bank. Clay supported the measure, and Hardin's fervent speech in opposition to the bill earned him a nickname which he kept for the rest of his life. After the speech, John Randolph characterized Hardin as a "vigorous but unpolished speaker," and said that "Hardin is like a kitchen-knife when whetted on a brick; he cuts roughly, but cuts deep." [7]   From then on, Hardin was called "Old Kitchen-Knife."

In 1844, Hardin made his last major effort on behalf of the Whig party, campaigning throughout Kentucky for Henry Clay's attempt at the presidency.   One of Hardin's speeches supporting Clay's candidacy, given at Elizabethtown, was reported by a member of the audience.   Hardin compared the merits of the two candidates by saying that Polk had no ambitions in life which could not be realized on the banks of the Duck River.   On the other hand, "Henry Clay had walked the mountain tops for half a century -- like a giant ... leaving his footprints in the living rock."[8]

After Clay's defeat, Hardin never again took part in national politics, although he was involved in State affairs, and served as Secretary of State under Governor Owsley from 1844 to 1847.[9]

As a lawyer, however, Hardin was active for over fifty years.   His courtroom behavior is described as follows:

> During the progress of any important cause in which he had been retained, he might be seen pacing the body of the court-house -- without the bar, but within hearing of the proceedings -- his hands clasped behind his back and muttering to himself all the while -- and thus even prepared many of his most elaborate arguments.   His voice was sharp and piercing, and he was strongly energetic, both in action and delivery.   Wit -- drollery -- sarcasm -- invective -- these were his chief forensic weapons, and terrible weapons they generally proved in his hands.[10]

To provide variety in the speeches included, the editors have chosen to present Hardin's summary in one of the most famous murder trials in Kentucky history -- The Wilkinson - Murdaugh Case.

Edward Wilkinson was a lawyer from Mississippi who was engaged to be married to Mary Eliza Crozier of Bardstown in December, 1838. Wilkinson, his brother, and an attorney friend, Mr. Murdaugh, arrived in Louisville on their way to the wedding when they participated in an altercation at the Galt House. A tailor by the name of Redding had been retained to make a suit for Wilkinson. When it was finished it apparently did not fit as Wilkinson wished, so he proceeded to make some insulting remarks about Redding's skill. Redding and two of his friends then attacked the Wilkinson party as they entered the barroom, and in the ensuing fights Redding's friends were killed.

The Wilkinsons and Murdaugh were arrested and jailed to await an examining trial. Excitement ran high, and there were fears of lynchings. Emotions were particularly amplified because of a remark Wilkinson made to Redding about his "class."

When the trial came, general feeling strongly favored the defense. Ben Hardin and Edward Bullock were the prosecuting attorneys, and John Rowan, S.S. Prentiss, Colonel Robertson, Samuel David, John B. Thompson, Charles M. Cunningham, James Taylor, and C.M. Wickliffe all represented the defense. The main action, however, centered around Hardin and Prentiss.

Prentiss, who was well-known as an outstanding speaker, referred to the thousand dollars Redding had paid Hardin to prosecute:

> One of the ablest lawyers of your county has been employed to conduct the private part of this prosecution; employed, not by the Commonwealth, but by the real murderers; him whose forehead I intend, before I am done, to brand with the mark of Cain, that in after life all may know and shun him.[11]

Hardin's summary speech lasted the better part of two days and was typical of his forthright style. He began his closing arguments:

*I little expected when I engaged in this cause in Louis-
ville last winter that I should ever have to address you
on the subject. Although I have been fifty years practicing in the Kentucky bar, this is the first time I ever
had to address a jury in this place, and I cannot help
feeling that I am as much a stranger here as any gentleman who has addressed you.*[12]

In spite of Hardin's brilliant oratory, the Wilkinsons and
Murdaugh were acquitted.

As an orator, Hardin's manner was simple and natural. He
was an exceedingly earnest speaker, with a voice which could
project into large crowds. He had the ability to attract and hold
crowds by using language not so much for its beauty as for its
utility, frequently inserting Bible verses, lines from familiar
hymns, or quotations from Burns or Homer.

In his later years, Hardin gained a reputation for talking
to himself. On one occasion he was walking down a street in
Bardstown, muttering to himself and gesticulating wildly, when
he was stopped by a man who said, "Mr. Hardin, people say
that you are losing your mind, and it seems to me to be true."
Hardin nonchalantly answered, "The people say I am losing
my mind do they? Do you know, sir, what people say of you
sir? Well, I'll tell you, sir, they all agree that you are a d---d
little fool."[13]

Throughout his life, Hardin was temperamental in his
relationships, as shown by his changeable attitude towards
Henry Clay. Another example is cited in his friendship with
John Rowan, after whom Hardin named one of his sons. However, an estrangement took place between them, and Hardin
thereafter referred to his son as Ben Rowan Hardin. But because the name Rowan was so firmly fixed, Hardin was the only
one to refer to his son by his new name.[14]

Hardin and Joseph Rogers Underwood of Warren County

were long-standing friends. Underwood was a lawyer, journalist and statesman and was generally critical of any proposition he didn't write. On one occasion when the members of the House had grown tired of Underwood's constant interruptions to improve the phraseology of a proposition, Hardin rose and said:

Mr. Speaker, I consider it one of God's mercies that the gentleman from Warren was not upon the earth in the days of our Saviour. If he had been, he would, infallibly, have moved an amendment to the Lord's Prayer, which, if adopted might have led to the damnation of the world.[15]

In the summer of 1852, Hardin was badly crippled when he fell from his horse and was confined to his home. During this last illness he made a profession of faith, which counteracted his earlier statement that "My wife is a member, and I am an outside pillar of the Methodist Church."[16] On September 24th, realizing the end was near, he summoned all his family to his bedside and requested a certain reading from the Bible. He then asked that he be buried in a spot next to his parents in Washington County, and his request was granted.

A wrought iron fence encloses the grave and an eight-foot marble shaft contains the following words:

"Ben Hardin of Bardstown"

Hardin lived in a time and place with a galaxy of great men. He, with six others, Felix Grundy, John Rowan, William P. Duval, Ben Chapeze, John Hays, and Charles A. Wickliffe, were called "The Bardstown Pleiades." He was not necessarily the greatest of these or his other contemporaries, but he did possess a genius which was representative of his age and his surroundings. He was, throughout his life, an intellectual force and "he had the good fortune to impress himself and his characteristics on his day and generation as few have done."[17]

Benjamin Hardin

The Wilkinson and Murdaugh Case

A speech made to the jury in the court house at Harrods-burg, Kentucky, March 15, 1839, for the prosecution in the trial of Judge and Dr. Wilkinson and Mr. Murdaugh of Mississippi, for murder of citizens of Louisville, Kentucky.

I shall, gentlemen, very humbly and very cordially congratulate you upon having this case brought so near a close. It has already been protracted beyond the usual limits of criminal trials by the extraordinary ingenuity and uncommon array of talent enlisted on the occasion. The gentlemen on the opposite side have felicitated you upon the politeness of your patience, and among others, I, too, return you my thanks for your attention.

I little expected, when I engaged in this case in Louisville last winter, that I should ever have to address you on the subject. Although I have been fifty years practicing at the Kentucky bar, this is the first time I have ever had to address a jury in this place, and I can not help feeling that I am as much a stranger here as any gentleman who has addressed you. I shall, however, in speaking to you, apply myself to an exposition of the facts and of the law bearing upon them, and, whatever may be your feelings, you will, I am sure, keep in mind that you are bound to exercise your reason, and that you owe a duty of no ordinary responsibility to yourselves, your characters and your country. That duty is a sacred trust reposed in you which you can not weigh lightly without injury to yourselves as well as wrong to others. Nor must you surrender up your reason to your passions and allow yourselves to be carried away by the shouts of applause from fashionable audience as if you were in a theater where a Julius Brutus Booth and a Miss Ellen Tree exhibit the practiced arts of controlling feelings and successfully eliciting the noisy plaudits of excitement. This is not a theater, this trial is not a farce, nor are you seated on those benches for amusement. This, gentlemen, is a solemn court of justice, a solemn tribunal in which your judge, presiding with becoming dignity, represents the majesty of the law, and in which you are expected to deliberate with becoming gravity upon circumstances of awful import. The appalling death of two fellow creatures is the occasion of your being assembled here, and the guilt or innocence of those at whose hands they fell is the object of your solemn investigation.

By law, and in conformity with the original institutions upon which all law is founded, this trial was to have taken place where the occasion of it occurred -- in the county of Jefferson. The Legislature, in its wisdom, has seen fit to change the venue from Jefferson to Mercer County, but why, I am unable to say. For even Colonel Robertson, the very able counsel for the defense, has admitted that, although for a time great excitement existed in Louisville, yet, after the investigation at the examining court, that excitement was altogether allayed.

In this country experience has always taught us that, when a change of venue is sought, the object is not to obtain justice, but to evade it. The object is to thwart and embarrass the prosecution and multiply the chances of eluding the responsibility of the law. How is this effected? Is it not by a removal to some place esteemed favorable to the accused, by a removal so distant from the scene of action that the expense and inconvenience render it probable but few of the witnesses can attend? By a removal to where witnesses of a character dubious, if not infamous, where known, may find credit because they are unknown? Here we are some seventy or eighty miles from the stage on which this tragedy was acted, yet we are asked why we did not bring the stick and the cowhide and Bill Holmes, the pilot, as if we were afraid to produce them were they within our reach. I would ask the opposite side in my turn, why the gentlemen have brought us eighty miles from the scene where we could have elicited the truth in every particular?

Mr. Prentiss (for the defense) really astonished me with one proposition he laid down with respect to the common law of this county, that every man is to judge for himself where the point of danger lies that entitles him to disable another, or to kill him, lest he might, in turn, by possibility, become the killed; so that, in fact, if it were so, the point of danger never could be defined by law, because what a brave man would consider no danger at all, a timid man would consider the point of danger bristling with a thousand deaths. Was there ever such a monstrous doctrine recognized by the laws of any community?

No, gentlemen, the law recognized no such absurdities. The law was laid down yesterday correctly by the district attorney, that when the killing of a man has taken place, it is murder, till the contrary is shown. What then becomes of this new doctrine, unknown to the law, that the slayer, and not the law, is to judge and presume the justification? The law itself says, all killing of one man by another is murder. The slayer, according to Mr. Prentiss, says: "Oh, no, I killed my man because I fancied he would kill me - it is not murder, it is justifiable homicide!" Yet the law again says if a sheriff who hangs a man by lawful authority and, in doing so, commits only a justifiable homicide, should, even, for the best motives, instead of hanging the man, as bound to do, chop his head off with a sword, though death must necessarily follow either way, yet is he guilty of murder, and liable to the punishment, for the killing contrary to the prescribed mode of his duty.

There are certain maxims of law laid down in the books which are never disputed, because they are founded upon reason and just principles; such, for instance, as these: If A kill B from necessity, to save his own life, the danger being undeniable, it is excusable homicide. If A kills B in a sudden heat of quarrel, it is manslaughter. If A kills B without what in law is called competent provocation, it is murder. If a man fires a pistol-ball into that crowd and kills a man, though it were his bosom friend against whom, personally, he could have no previous malice, it is murder, though he did not intend that death. It is murder in the eye of the law, because the recklessness of human life implied in the act shows that general malice to mankind, which is equally dangerous to the community as any private malice could be. All killing is murder, unless an excuse is shown, but words are no excuse, because they never bring a killing below the crime of murder; neither are indecent and contemptuous action justification, according to Raymond and Blackstone. Here is a maxim in point: If there is a previous quarrel between A and B and, some time after, in consequence of the previous quarrel, they fight, then nothing connected with the previous quarrel justifies a killing, and it can not be excused unless it clearly appear that B in killing A had to do so to save his own life.

Mr. Prentiss labored a position, and labored it ably, I admit, but Mr. Bullock had previously combatted its application successfully. The position is advanced upon the well-known quotation from Lord Hale: "If A, B and C be walking in company together, and C assaults B who flees, and is in no danger of being killed from C's pursuit, unless present help be afforded, and A thereupon kills C in defense of the life of B, it seems that in this case of such inevitable danger of the life of B, the killing of C by A is in the nature of self-defense; but it must plainly appear by the circumstances of the case as the manner of assault, the weapons with which it was made etc., that B's life was in imminent danger."

A man seeing another kill a third person may kill the man about to commit the felony, but then it is at his peril he does it, and he is responsible to the law for his interference. Upon this text, if you are to acquit Judge Wilkinson, it must appear that, when the stabbing took place, there must have been manifest danger to his brother's life; there must have been an apparent, an absolute necessity. To show that there was no such necessity, and to place before you in a clear view the leading features of the facts, I will now claim your attention to the review I shall make of them.

(At this point, Hardin gave the particulars surrounding the murder. He explained how the Wilkinsons and Murdaugh happened to be in Louisville and their relationship with Redding. He told of Redding making the coat for Wilkinson and of Wilkinson's subsequent displeasure with the fashion of the coat collar.)

We have our bankers, lawyers and doctors arrogating one rank in our society; the statesmen, heads of departments and officials another. Our mechanics and those who toil by the sweat of their brow to produce our riches are cast in the shade, and, knowing as they do that such an attempt, however noiselessly it is made, still exists palpably, is it any wonder they should become sensitive to every whisper that breathed to mark the invidious distinctions? Call a man a knave, and he may forget it, but call him a fool and he will never forgive you. Call a young lady a coquette, and she may pardon you, but tell her she is ugly and she will never abide you the longest day she lives. Tell a tailor he is a botch and he may not even get angry with you, but sneer at him about his goose and his profession and you insult him, though the words themselves are harmless. It is the allusion to prejudices that have existed which carries the poison of insult in its barb. Sir, we must not disguise the fact that there is a line of demarcation drawn by the proud and arrogant between themselves and those who live by the sweat of their brow.

Gentlemen, I have endeavored to trace facts as far as I have gone with minuteness and, having presented these facts to you, it is for you to determine whether they do not establish these conclusions. When the fight occurred in the barroom, it was brought on by Judge and Dr. Wilkinson and Murdaugh intentionally. If they brought it on, did they fight in their own defense, or because they had drawn the conflict on themselves? Could Meeks have inflicted death with a cow-hide, or Rothwell with a walking stick, so as to render the killing of them necessary or justifiable according to the true spirit of the law?

But here there is a proposition of law advanced by Mr. Prentiss which I must combat. He says that the law recognized that the point of resistance unto death begins where a man himself believes the point of danger ought to be fixed. Then we have no law at all -- we may burn up our law books, this revokes all they contain on the subject of homicide. Is it possible you, an intelligent jury, can be imposed upon by such sophistry? Is there so low an estimate of your understanding as to suppose it?

A is tried and acquitted because he is a base coward and apprehends danger at a point where there is no danger at all. B is tried for precisely a similar homicide in every particular, and because he is not quite as big a coward as A, but apprehends some danger, is found guilty and sent to the penitentiary for a term of years proportionate in duration to his lack of cowardice as contrasted with A. C, for precisely a similar homicide, because he is incapable of fear, is to be convicted of murder and straightway hanged!

Sir, the principle of self-defense does not warrant a man killing under the name of self-defense, if he is himself in fault by being the aggressor.

Are we not relaxing the laws -- which leads to anarchy, and from personal violence to popular usurpation? Are we not relaxing our financial vigilance -- which leads to corruption at the fountain head, and from private peculation to public defalcation? I tell you again and again, when you can lay your hands on great delinquents, make them an example; when you can grasp great defaulters, punish them; then will you more easily check pernicious discords and restore to its proper tension and tone the harmonizing power of your laws and your government. Whenever you see men wearing bowie-knives and daggers, hunt them down as you would bears and their cubs, from whom you can expect nothing but injury. The whole State of Kentucky looks to you this day for justice, for this is an awful investigation concerning the loss of two of her citizens. Two of our fellow citizens have been murdered and these gentlemen are here to answer for it. Some of the best blood of the country has been spilled as if the pen of slaughtered hogs, but because relatives of one of these butchered men employ counsel to aid the prosecution in developing the truth and guarding against the delusions of sophistry from the greatest array of talent the country can boast, or that wealth unbounded can produce, to elude the punishment due to the offended laws, you are told to take but a one-sided view of the evidence and to decide at any rate against the paid advocate. I have not asked these gentlemen what they are to be paid for eluding justice, because I did not consider that a sort of evidence which ought to influence your verdict.

Gentlemen, one question is, are we to tolerate this bowie-knife system under the false pretense of self-defense? I say, let your verdict act like the axe laid to the root of the tree and many a prayer will bless you for your timely check of its growth. Many a woman is made a mourning widow, many a child made a pitiable orphan and many a father childless by the use of the accursed weapon. You have it in your power to prevent the recurrence of such scenes.

Gentlemen, I beg of you in the name of Him who sits upon the cloud and rides upon the storm, mete out the measure of justice to these men and vindicate the honor of Mercer county. But do not stigmatize your county by doing, as Mr. Prentiss would have you do, by shouting: "Glory! Glory! Go, ye righteous, go to your homes in honor and innocence." Whatever you may do, I shall content myself with the conviction that, in my professional capacity, I at least, have done my duty.

I have been deputed by the widowed mother of the murdered Rothwell, and at the instance of the mourning sisters, to implore your justice. I have closed my mission. Between you and your country, between you and your God, I leave their cause.

CHAPTER V

JOHN J. CRITTENDEN
(1786-1863)

Biographers disagree as to the year of John Jordon Crittenden's birth; some record 1787,[1] while others cite 1786 as the actual date.[2] There is general agreement that he was born on September 10, in Woodford County, to Major John Crittenden and his wife, Judith Harris.

Crittenden received a good education for a man of his day, beginning at Pisgah Academy, a boarding school in Jessamine County. After completing his studies at the Academy, he went to Lexington to study law with George M. Bibb, followed by two years in Lexington, Virginia, at Washington Academy (now Washington and Lee). From 1805 to 1807 Crittenden attended William and Mary College, where the study of Hugh Blair's *Lectures on Rhetoric*, may have influenced his later speech-making. Literary societies were active at William and Mary and it is likely Crittenden participated in their programs. During the time Crittenden was there, attendance averaged fifty students per year and he made friends with men who later would be his close associates.[3]

The death of his father shortened Crittenden's studies, and he returned to Versailles where he opened a law office and practiced for a brief period. In 1807 he moved to Russellville, the business center of Southwestern Kentucky.

Crittenden soon became active in community affairs, and local politics. In 1809, Ninian Edwards, a leading citizen of Russellville, was appointed governor of the Illinois Territory. Edwards had taken a liking to Crittenden and had the young man appointed his aide and attorney-general. Crittenden's stay in

Illinois lasted until 1811, when he returned to Russellville, where he was married to Sallie Lee on May 25. [4]

In the summer of 1811, Crittenden ran his first political race and was elected to represent Logan County in the State Legislature. [5]   Records indicate that he spoke on only one issue during his first session in the legislature. At this time, United States Senators were appointed by the state legislature and some felt that the legislature had no right to instruct the senators on issues in Congress. In his first speech before the legislature, Crittenden argued that the legislature did have the right to instruct its senators since a senator represented his state in the national government. [6]

Following the legislative session of 1811, Crittenden fought in the Thames River Campaign of the War of 1812, along with several other well-known Kentuckians, including Isaac Shelby, John Adair and William T. Barry. [7]

After the Thames River Campaign, Crittenden returned to Russellville and, in 1814, was back in the state legislature. That same year, Governor Shelby entertained thoughts of appointing him to the United States Senate until he learned that Crittenden was only twenty-seven, thus too young to serve. He was elected Speaker of the House in 1815, over John Rowan of Nelson County.

In December, 1816, Crittenden was elected to the United States Senate from Kentucky. During this session of Congress, he had the distinction of being the youngest senator. He was appointed to several committees, including a special one on Indian Affairs, the Committee on the Judiciary and the Committee on Naval Affairs. His first opportunity to speak was on the Revolutionary Soldiers Pension Bill. There is no record of his speech; however, one member of his audience recorded that he was quite nervous at the start of his speech but gained confidence as the speech progressed, and the total effect "electrified a listening Senate with an eloquence which no first effort had ever before effected."[8]   He remained in the Senate until 1819 when he resigned to return to Kentucky for financial reasons.

Crittenden moved to Frankfort where he felt he would have a better chance to attract clients, and would also be in the center of the state's political activity.   He was employed frequently by Henry Clay, and also served as attorney for Robert J. Breckinridge, Robert P. Letcher, James Morehead, Joseph Underwood, James Madison and James Monroe.   Within two years he appeared in 428 cases.[9]

Crittenden early gained a reputation as a successful attorney. On one occasion he was defending a Mr. Gillespie, who was charged with the murder of a friend while both were drunk. The defendant admitted his guilt and related all the circumstances. Crittenden's speech in defense of Gillespie was called a masterpiece of oratory; after an emotional appeal he closed his speech with:

> Can any man in his senses, with a throbbing heart in his bosom, doubt this man's testimony? No, gentlemen of the jury, the truth gushes from his burdened heart in that hour of agony as pure as the water from the rock when smitten by the hand of the prophet.[10]

Gillespie was acquitted.   On another occasion Crittenden, defending a man who was accused of committing a capital offense, used the following allegory in his speech to the jury:

> When God in his eternal counsel conceived the thought of man's creation, He called to Him the three ministers who wait constantly upon the throne, - Justice, Truth, and Mercy - and thus addressed them: "Shall I create man?" "O God, make him not, " said Justice, "for he will trample upon thy laws." Truth said, "Create him not, O God, for he will pollute thy sanctuary." But Mercy, falling upon her knees, and looking up through her tears, exclaimed, "O God, create him, I

will watch over him in all the dark paths which he may be forced to tread." So God created man, and said to him, "O man, thou art the child of mercy: go and deal mercifully with thy brother."[11]

When Crittenden closed his speech, the members of the jury were in tears and brought a verdict of "not guilty."

Another well-known case in which Crittenden was involved for the defense was that of a student from Transylvania College accused of killing one of his fellow students in a brawl. Although the young man had no previous records of misconduct, feelings against him ran high in Lexington, and a change of venue was granted and the trial moved to Versailles. The prosecuting attorney had made a strong case for making an example of the student. Crittenden countered the argument by saying:

I agree with my stern and learned friend, we should make examples from time to time, even among the young and thoughtless, to check the heat of youthful blood and the violence of ungoverned passion; but, my countrymen, let us take that example from among our own people, and not seize upon the youthful stranger who came confidingly among us to profit by the advantages of our literary institutions, to learn to be a man in the best sense, honest, capable and cultivated. We have, I am grieved to say, frequent opportunities to make examples of our own sons, in our own borders. Let us do this then, when the occasion offers, but let us send this broken-hearted, trembling mother and her dear, loved son back to her home in peace. He has been overtaken in a great crime, but an acquittal, in consideration of his youth and other extenuating circumstances will be honorable to our great State and do no damage to the laws.[12]

The jury was out only a few minutes before deciding upon an acquittal.

Crittenden was elected to the state legislature repeatedly from 1819 until 1835, when he returned to the United States Senate. He expressed opposition to John C. Calhoun's bill authorizing anti-slavery documents to be taken from the Southern mail. He was in favor of a United States Bank, but against the sub-treasury system and the remission of fines against General Jackson for contempt of court in declaring martial law in New Orleans.[13] He generally supported Henry Clay and the other Whigs in Congress.

Crittenden's first opportunity to give a major speech came in February, 1836, when a proposal was made to distribute proceeds from the sale of public lands to the states. His reputation as a speaker had preceded him to Washington, and a large audience thronged the galleries to hear him. He spoke more than an hour without benefit of notes, after which a reporter described him as "easy, polished, elegant and dignified." He began in a very low, almost inaudible voice, but as the speech progressed, he became more vigorous and clear. His style was compared to that of Clay and Calhoun:

> *If I had not known he was speaking and heard him, I would have risked any wager that Calhoun was upon the floor, so exactly were his voice, enunciation and intonation like the great and remarkable man. At another time ... by the sound of the orator's voice, I should have said at once it was Clay, for his voice had all the expansion and music in it which characterized that of his great colleague's above that of any other man who speaks the English language.*[14]

In 1836, Crittenden was visited at his home in Frankfort by Daniel Webster. Crittenden used this occasion to show Webster around Kentucky and to take him to a local barbecue, the standard gathering place for politicians. During this period mass meetings served as political schools for uneducated men to hear the great speakers of the day. Webster was invited to address the crowd, but being unaccustomed to the stump-speaking situation he did not make his usually good impression on his listeners.

Webster was taken by surprise when the crowds shouted for Crittenden. Crittenden in turn, was amused by the proceedings and appealed to his friends "not to force him to hold up his little lights while greater lights were shining."[15]

During the next two years Crittenden spoke throughout the country on behalf of various Whig politicians. He was often on the platform with Clay, Webster, Millard Fillmore and Tom Corwin, speaking before audiences as large as ten thousand. After his efforts outside the state were completed, he returned to Kentucky and campaigned in Elkton, Hopkinsville and Russellville.[16]

In August, 1840, Crittenden went to Nashville, Tennessee, and addressed a crowd estimated at thirty thousand. In his speech he avoided specific issues, but he did attack Van Buren for being politically amoral and for standing on every side of every question. He closed by urging Tennessee to march beside Kentucky "in this great struggle for liberty."[17]

The Whigs were successful in the national election of 1840, and in March, 1841, President William Henry Harrison appointed Crittenden Attorney-General. Harrison convened the Twenty-Seventh Congress for May, 1841, to consider matters of national importance. Unfortunately, the President did not live to see it meet. He died on April 4 and was succeeded by his Vice-President, John Tyler. Crittenden remained in Tyler's cabinet until September when he, along with the rest of the cabinet, except Secretary of State Daniel Webster, resigned. He returned to Frankfort following his resignation and resumed his law practice.

Crittenden was not to remain a private citizen long. In January, 1842, Henry Clay resigned his seat in the Senate and Crittenden was the unanimous choice of the legislature to fill his unexpired term. During this time, the prospect of war appeared more and more likely. One issue related to the boundary line of Oregon. On April 16, 1846, Crittenden represented the conservative element of the Senate as their spokesman on the issue.

He closed his speech:

> When war becomes necessary for the vindication of our
> rights of honor, we will make it and meet it like men,
> and through all its horrors we can then look to the
> glory that is beyond. In such a war as that you may
> rely with confidence upon the patriotism and courage
> of our countrymen. With the generous ardor of their
> age, the whole youth of the country will, at your
> summons, rally around the standard of their country.
> I can answer for those I particularly represent -- the
> youth of Kentucky. They will take the field at the
> first signal. But I do not want to see their brave young
> blood that ought to be as dear to me as my own, wasted
> and poured out in idle, foolish or unnecessary war ...

As usual, Crittenden's speech was classed a success. One critic
noted that his black eyes, which were ordinarily lacking in radi-
ance, "sparkled like diamonds" during his address. Another
wrote, "I feel proud that I am a Kentuckian."[18]

Not all of Crittenden's orations in the Senate were of a
political nature. His sensitivity to the suffering in the world was
evidenced by a speech made on February 26, 1847. At this time
Crittenden introduced a bill for the Relief of the Suffering Poor
of Ireland. By way of introduction, Crittenden said, "I do not
rise with an empty parade of words to impress the picture of a
famished people upon the minds of this honorable body. I wish
only to discharge what I consider a solemn duty."[19]

Crittenden remained in the Senate until 1848, when he
resigned to become a candidate for governor of Kentucky, heading
the Whig ticket against the Democratic candidate, Lazarus Powell.
He campaigned throughout Kentucky, sometimes speaking three
times in one day. The major issue in the campaign was the relationship between Crittenden and Henry Clay and whether
Crittenden's support of Zachary Taylor, rather than Clay, in the

presidential election, was honorable. Crittenden defeated Powell 65,860 to 57,397 votes. [20]

Crittenden was inaugurated Governor on September 6, 1848, after which he turned his attention to directing Zachary Taylor's campaign for President. His management of Taylor's campaign resulted in a Whig victory in Kentucky as well as in the other states. It had been assumed by many that Crittenden would become Secretary of State in Taylor's Cabinet and Taylor offered him the position shortly after the election, but Crittenden declined the appointment and remained as Governor of the State. His decision was a serious blow to the General's administration. Crittenden had widespread support and there was strong feeling that he should have a central place in the Taylor administration. [21]

Crittenden's tenure as Governor allowed him little opportunity to influence the future course of the state. In his message to the legislature on December 30, 1848, he gave a preview of some of his ideas which would surface later:

> *Kentucky, situated in the heart of the Union, must and will exercise a powerful influence on its destiny. The dissolution of the Union can never be regarded -- ought never to be regarded -- as a remedy, but as the consummation of the greatest evil that can befall us.* [22]

Crittenden had long been interested in public education and during his term as governor he promoted the common schools. In his message to the legislature in 1849, he made a forceful plea for public education in the state, stressing that a strong educational program in Kentucky would result in the state's youth becoming more useful citizens.

In another address before the legislature in December, 1849, he again spoke on his theme of Kentucky's role in the Union:

Dear as Kentucky is to us, she is not our whole country; and, proud as we justly are of the name of Kentuckian, we have a loftier and more far-famed title -- that of American Citizen, a name known and respected throughout the world, and which, wherever we may be, has power to protect us from the despotism of emperor, of king ... Kentucky will stand by the, abide by the, Union to the last, and she will hope that the same kind Providence that enabled our fathers to make it will enable us to preserve it. [23]

Following Taylor's death, Crittenden resigned the governorship to accept President Fillmore's appointment as Attorney General. He was eager to return to Washington, for he missed being in the center of national affairs and he found himself spending more money than he made in running the governor's office. Many people were pleased to have Crittenden in the Cabinet for he was well-liked by people from both North and South. During his two and a half years as Attorney General, he wrote 132 opinions, most of a routine nature. He was also instrumental in assisting Fillmore in fostering good relations between Northern and Southern congressmen. Crittenden owned slaves but he opposed slavery as an institution and looked ultimately toward its extinction. [24]

Crittenden was invited to give an address to honor the late Henry Clay on September 29, 1852, in Louisville before a large audience. Clay and Crittenden had been close friends during most of their lives, although they had had their political differences. In his tribute to Clay, he said:

It was most fortunate for Kentucky to have such a representative, and most fortunate for him to have such a constituency as Kentucky, fortunate for him to have been thrown, in the early and susceptible period of his life, into the primitive society of her bold and free people. As one of her children, I am pleased to think that from that source he derived

some of that magnanimity and energy which his af-
ter-life so signally displayed. I am pleased to think
that, mingling with all his great qualities, there was
a sort of Kentuckyism (I shall not undertake to define
it) which, though it may not have been polished or
refined, gave to them additional point and power,
and free people of action. [25]

Crittenden remained Attorney General until 1853, when his term expired. He returned to Kentucky, involving himself in personal and legislative affairs. It was during this period that he defended a young man for murder in a case which was almost political suicide for him. Matt Ward, son of a long-time friend of Crittenden, was accused of the unprovoked murder of Male High School Principal, H. A. Butler. Public sentiment being strongly against Ward, the trial was moved to Elizabethtown. The elder Ward had wanted Crittenden to represent his son but had not asked him because he felt it might hurt Crittenden's reputation. Knowing the wishes of his friend, Crittenden volunteered to defend the youth. In the trial he presented a skillful defense and, in his statement to the jury, emphasized the discrepancies he had found among the witnesses. He made an eloquent plea to the merciful instinct of the jury and told them they must find for the defendant in order to insure their peace of mind. He asked them to keep on the side of humanity if they erred. He closed his summation with an explanation of his involvement in the case:

... it has been announced that I am a volunteer in this
case. It is true. Has the spirit of persecution gone so
far against this man as to drive from his side all counsel
and deprive him of the right to defend himself? I
have known him from boyhood; I have known his
family from my boyhood and have a friendship for
them. Under these feelings I have volunteered, and,
with feebleness, have assisted in this case. [26]

The Ward trial received much publicity throughout the state and many people were indignant when Matt Ward was acquitted, feeling that Crittenden had imposed false testimony upon the jury. Protest meetings were held in several towns and Crittenden's recently-won Senate seat was demanded. One Northern newspaper wrote that Crittenden would never outlive the memory of the trial and that he had lost his influence with his constituents because of it. [27]

Crittenden was astonished at the public reaction to the verdict. He admitted that in criminal law he always sympathized with the accused, as he explained, "not because I favor or approve the guilty, but because I hope they may be innocent, or not so guilty as charged to be." [28] In all the years he practiced law, Crittenden never served as prosecuting attorney.

The 1853-1854 legislature elected Crittenden for his final and most important term in the Senate, the years 1855-1861. In the summer of 1856, Congress adjourned and Crittenden returned to Kentucky to assist in Fillmore's Presidential campaign. Despite Crittenden's efforts, Kentucky went Democratic for the first time since 1828, when Jackson was elected. The Democratic candidate, James Buchanan, was successful at the national level and the Democrats won a majority in the Senate.

Crittenden was very much his own man in the Thirty-fourth Congress. He could not completely side with either Democratic or Republican factions. He was now the oldest member of the Senate, with his experience spanning forty years. He was described as being a fluent speaker with a "calm gentlemanly ease, which is evidently the result of habitual intercourse with the most cultivated society." [29]

During his final term in the Senate, Crittenden worked hard to save the Union. In 1856 he said, "I will compromise to the last syllable of recorded time to preserve the Union." [30] Two years later, the famous Kansas-Lecompton debate occurred, concerning the admission of Kansas to the Union. Crittenden had kept himself well-informed on conditions in Kansas through

Kentuckians who had settled there. He was well-equipped to debate Senator James Green of Missouri, who had called for the admission of Kansas. Word had been given out that Crittenden was to speak and the Senate galleries were filled. He began his speech:

> I feel how inadequate I am, Mr. President, to add any-thing to the various arguments that have been employed on this subject during the long discussion through which we have passed; and yet wish to express my sentiments and feelings on the subject before the Senate. I do not intend to occupy your time with exordiums, Sir. The right of the people to govern themselves is the great principle upon which our government and our insti-tutions all depend. It seems to me that this great principle is the present subject.

Crittenden spoke forcefully for two and a half hours before closing:

> I am a true son of the South: May prosperity fill all her borders and sunshine rest forever upon her head. But for all this, I do not love the Union less. I am a true citizen of the United States. I claim the whole of it as my great country; and for the preservation of the Union which makes it so, I will always be ready to say and to do whatever in me lies. It is in this spirit, Sir, that I have endeavored to humbly do my duty -- my duty to the South and to the whole country.[31]

When Crittenden finished speaking, he was greeted with spon-taneous applause which did not subside until John Breckinridge threatened to clear the galleries. The address was considered one of the weightiest statements of the problems of the period in U.S. history preceding the Civil War, and caused Crittenden to be mentioned as possible presidential material.

During the late 1850's, Crittenden spoke frequently throughout the country with one idea in mind: to preserve the

Union. Typical of his speeches was one given in Chicago at the National Agricultural Fair, September 13, 1859. He spoke of his respect for the Constitution and his love for the Union. "I am at home here," he said, "though I came with few acquaintances and friends in this part of the country; yet the whole land is my country. The Union makes us one people; May God preserve the Union." [32]

It was largely through Crittenden's efforts and inspiration that the Constitutional Union Party was formed in 1860, and many people were disappointed when he refused to have his name submitted as the presidential nominee. Although he was over seventy years of age, he remained "erudite, polished, friendly and eloquent." [33]

During the early part of 1860, Crittenden spoke often in Kentucky urging Kentuckians to take no part in the sectional strife but to stand as mediators between the North and South. On August 2, 1860, he spoke before a large audience in Louisville at Mozart Hall:

> Every one of you, I trust, remembers the farewell address of George Washington. Upon the first dawning of anything like an attempt to alienate one portion of the country from another, he tells us to frown indignantly upon it, upon the man who shall attempt even to impair the ties which bind us together as one people, and to be zealous and watchful of the Union as the great palladium of our rights ... Old Kentucky has ever been the strongest supporter of this Union, and under no circumstances, I trust, will she ever be seduced from that high character ... [34]

The work for which John Crittenden was to be best known was proposed in December, 1860, when he presented his famous compromise in a solicitous oration before his colleagues. He had formulated a series of resolutions which he hoped would reconcile the sections of the country and settle for all time the main questions of slavery. The Crittenden Compromise consisted of six unamendable amendments to the Constitution:

68

*(1) divide present and future territories at latitude 36°
30' and recognize slavery to the south but prohibit it
north of that line; (2) prevent Congress from legis-
lating against slavery in federal reservations within
slave states; (3) deny Congress the power to abolish
slavery in the District of Columbia so long as Virginia
or Maryland permitted slavery, or to prevent federal
officers from bringing their slaves into the district;
(4) guarantee protection for interstate slave trade
and transportation; (5) provide federal compensation
for claimants whose slaves escaped seizure through
popular aid, and empower the government to collect
such funds from counties in which the escapees were
aided; and (6) declare unalterable these and other
constitutional provisions respecting slavery.*

*The legislative actions aimed at (1) tightening and
reaffirming the Fugitive Slave Law, (2) urging states
to repeat questionable personal liberty laws and the
like, (3) modifying the system of fee collection under
the Fugitive Slave Law and limiting the responsibility
of citizens to "hunt up" fugitive slaves, and (4) strengthening enforcement of laws against importation of
slaves.*

During the speech every person listened attentively to his calm,
resonant delivery. The audience seemed fearful of missing a
single word spoken by the aged Senator. One congressman
wrote that Crittenden spoke "as if the muse of history were
listening to him."[35] The Associated Press described the speech
as "eloquent and sublime."[36]

It is generally agreed by historians that if the Republicans
had not defeated the Crittenden plan there would have been no
Civil War.[37]

Putting disappointment aside, Crittenden continued his
efforts on behalf of the Union. The Kentucky legislature met in
a called session on January 17, 1861, to decide the future attitude

of the state toward the Federal Government. On this occasion Crittenden was invited to address the assembly. He made a strong appeal for the Union by urging the members of the legislature "never to consider the question of dissolution." [38]

Crittenden's final gesture in the United States Senate came March 2, 1861, when he gave his farewell address. Although he was disappointed about the failure of his compromise, he gave a message of hope for the Union. Like his other speeches, this one was delivered without notes. He began the speech before a hushed audience:

> *I have not risen with any vain ambition or purpose to play orator. I have no set speech to make. The subject upon which I am to address the Senate is altogether too solemn and too interesting to the country to be made the occasion for declamation. I do not aim at it. I am a plain man and wish to speak plainly what I think and believe on this great subject.* [39]

Crittenden rebuked his colleagues for failing to act on his proposal. He went on to defend the Constitution and the stand Kentucky had taken. When he finished "the Senate was hushed," as one congressman wrote, "by the glorious beauty of his last earnest ... appeal for conciliation." [40]

Following the close of his Senate tenure, Crittenden returned to Kentucky where he was kept busy. He spoke at various places in the state advocating Kentucky's neutrality. In a speech at Lexington on April 23, 1861, he mentioned some ideas which he had been developing for some time. Kentucky, he felt, had no part in bringing on the war and had exerted every effort to prevent it. To be consistent, Kentucky should refuse to help either side and should stand as a mediator between the North and the South. [41]

Crittenden was persuaded to run as a Union Party nominee to the House of Representatives in the 1861 election. He was elected by an overwhelming majority and was returned to Congress as a seventy-five year old freshman in the House. He completed his term in the House and was a candidate for re-election at the time of his death on July 26, 1863.

As a Kentucky orator and statesman, Crittenden had few peers. As a statesman, he is credited with keeping Kentucky in the Union. As an orator, he drew crowds whether on the stump or in the halls of the Senate.

Henry Watterson wrote of him in the *Courier Journal*:

During fifty years John Jordan Crittenden stood peerless. He was not only the preux-chevalier of the politics of his time; not merely the captivating orator holding his audiences, at will, and the charming gentleman adored by women and men, but he was nearer right than any of his contemporaries; in every situation courageous, disinterested and farseeing. [42]

Speech of Honorable J.J. Crittenden, of Kentucky,

On His Resolutions

Delivered in the Senate of the United States, January 7, 1861.

Upon so momentous a question, where the public councils themselves are so divided and so distracted as not to be able to adopt, for the want of the requisite majority, those means that are supposed to be necessary for the safety of the country and the people, it has seemed to me not improper that we should resort to the great source of all political authority -- the people themselves. This is their government; this is their Union; we are but their representatives. I speak in no feeling of flattery to the people. No. I call upon them to pronounce their judgment, and do their duty to their country. If we cannot save the country, and they will not save the country, the country is gone. I wish to preserve it by all the means, ordinary and extraordinary, that are within our possible reach. That is the whole feeling, and that is the entire principle upon which I have acted in making this proposition. I see nothing improper in it.

It may be objected to as not a mode recognized by the Constitution. Well, sir, it is not forbidden by the Constitution, nor does it conflict with any principle of the Constitution, and it aims at nothing but what is entitled to influence here. That influence will be weighed by the Senate properly and justly. It is simply an appeal to the people to aid us, their representatives, by giving us their judgment and their opinion upon the subject. That judgment and opinion will not be humiliating to us. If they should condescend to pronounce their judgment and give their opinion, there is no humiliation in obeying the voice of a great nation, whose representatives we are, and whose servants we are proud to call ourselves. Their sentiments and their opinions will be our safest guide upon this question, surrounded as it is by so many difficulties, and disabled as we are by our own distractions and divisions in Congress from acting upon it without some power to control and to govern individual opinion.

Then, sir, as to the constitutional amendments which are proposed for the sanction of the people, and upon which they are to give their opinion, I had occasion some time ago to make a few remarks, and I intend now to add only a few more. I do not intend to go very much at large into this question. I do not know that I shall at any time -- certainly not now, when I am not fully apprised perhaps, of the various objections that may be made to them. The first remedy proposed consists in a new article to be added to the Constitution, and which proposed for its object to settle the question of territory, and the question of slavery in respect to territory and to settle that -- how? Simply to provide that all the territory north of 36° 30' shall be free from slavery; that on the South, slavery shall be recognized and protected as it now exists by the laws existing there for its protection, and to continue so until that territory, or any suitable proportion of it, shall be formed into a State and admitted into the Union. Then they are to be admitted with such provisions as they may choose to make in their constitution in respect to slavery -- excluding it or admitting it. This is all. To the North all is given; to the South it is only provided that things shall remain as they are until the territory becomes a State, and then it is to adopt this institution of slavery or not, according to the wish of the people that are interested in the new State. It seems to me there is something very just and very fair on the face of this proposition.

We are a great nation, composed now of thirty-three States. Fifteen of these have this peculiar institution of slavery; the others have excluded it, each acting according to its own free choice under the Constitution. Slavery existed in these and more States when the Constitution was formed. The Constitution took things as they were, recognized them as they were, and left them as they were, to the exclusive jurisdiction of the several

States. Those who had the institution of slavery were left to the sole dominion over it; those who were without it were left to the free and full course of their own will and of their own wisdom upon the subject, on the one side to continue to exclude it, or on the other side to continue to retain it. This was the broad, general, reciprocal justice which the Constitution did to all sections of the country.

Now sir, I ask the same standard and the same measure of justice. Let us take things as they are; that is the object. To the north of 36° 30′ slavery has been excluded. I say, therefore, slavery is excluded. To the south, slavery exists as a matter of fact. I ask you to recognize it. That was the principle upon which the framers of our Constitution went, recognizing the *status* existing at the time, adopting that, accepting that as a basis. This is what I understand in respect to all the States. This is all now that I ask; all this proposition is. There are, south of that line, the Indian Territory, and the Territory of New Mexico; that is all. Of the Indian Territory I need say nothing; that is appropriated to others, and upon the terms of that appropriation it rests. By those terms, however, slavery may be recognized as existing there; for the fact is it does exist potentially in New Mexico in virtue of the decision of the Supreme Court of the United States in the so-often quoted case of Dred Scott. They say that all the people of the United States have the right equally to go into the common territory of the United States, and carry with them any species or description of property recognized as such in the States from which they emigrate. Potentially, then, slavery does exist there; but more than that: by the great compromise measure of 1850, a territorial government was formed for New Mexico, and one of the compromises, one of the adjustments on that great occasion, was to give this Territory, which was a subject of dispute in respect to the question of slavery, power to "legislate on all rightful subjects of legislation." It was intended to cover this case; it did cover the case of slavery by the broad and distinct terms in which the power was given to the Territorial Legislature. That was the agreement between the North and the South: "We will say nothing about slavery ourselves, but we will constitute a territorial government, and we will give to that territorial government, representing the local interests, representing the local population, the power to dispose of this subject according to the wishes and according to the interests of the people of the Territory." In the exercise of that power, the people of the Territory did pass an act authorizing and regulating slavery in every particular; and that act now exists. Slavery only to a very limited extent exists there; but it exists by law actually.

Now, what does this amendment of mine propose? Not that gentlemen shall agree that slavery may exist there; not that they shall concede any principle; not that they shall concede any policy; but simply that they may recognize a fact, a fact that they cannot dispute -- the fact of the actual existence of slavery under actual law, emanating from that Territory under the power granted in the compromise of 1850, which was intended to settle the affairs of the country, and to relieve us from the troubles which have now returned. It was hailed by the whole people, accepted as a peace offering on all sides, and has been continued from that day. Under the power given by that act of Congress of 1850, slavery has been admitted into that Territory, and all that is proposed by my amendment is, as I said, simply to recognize that, and furthermore, the fact being recognized, that it shall be recognized that that state of things, that fact, shall continue as it is, until the Territory shall have acquired a sufficient population, according to the ratio of representation for Representatives, to entitle it to one member in Congress, and then to be admitted into the Union on an equal footing with the rest of the States, and with a constitution adopting or excluding slavery, according to the judgment of the people themselves.

This is the whole proposition in that respect. Well, I confess, sir, it seems to me that it is very little to grant. Some gentlemen are adverse to compromise. Well, gentlemen, you may call this a compromise. May it not with equal propriety be called an honest adjustment of rights? But if it were a compromise, is it not a fair compromise, and upon what principle are we opposed to compromise? All human life is but a compromise. From the cradle to the grave, if every step of it is a compromise, it has been usually blessed. A man, it is said, in respect to the compromise of a lawsuit, must be allowed to purchase his peace, even in private transactions. How is it in relation to divisions between great communities, different countries, or great sections of the same country? Are they not more necessary there? Are they not more demanded by the interests of society, more demanded by humanity itself, than in any condition of life? Just as much more demanded as the consequences are granted and more momentous, and more destructive ordinarily. If there were no compromise, parties would have to settle by force or by war these questions.

What gentleman, as a statesman, can stand upon that ground? Say that we are here, as I believe we are, upon the brink of intestine and civil war, that that war can be prevented by recognizing the fact of the existence of slavery, and agreeing that it shall continue for ten or fifteen years, until the territory shall become prepared to enter the Union as a state, and that Senators had rather encounter civil war, had rather encounter the destruction of this Union, and of this Government, than to agree to these terms -- upon what grounds? Upon any grounds of public welfare? Upon any avowed grounds of policy or of patriotism? Can any Senator stand upon that ground? What is his ground, then? The Republican party sees that by possibility, under this adjustment, that State, if it chooses slavery, may come into the Union hereafter as a slave State. Are their pledges against that under all circumstances? Are their general rules rules that admit of no exceptions? The old maxim is that the exception proves the rule. If the rule be reasonable, there are exceptions; and civil war, pestilence, famine, and everything else, are to be encountered, rather than to recede one single hair's breadth from a particular, prescribed doctrine. I cannot conceive it possible.

But suppose, Mr. President, that the ultimate result of it may be, if the people of the Territory choose, that it may hereafter be entitled, under this amendment of the Constitution, to come in as a slave State. What do gentlemen say to that? Is it a dogma that no slave State ever shall hereafter be admitted into this Union; and will they, for the maintenance and preservation of that dogma, sacrifice the country? Will they encounter civil war and disunion and all its fearful consequences, rather than yield up in a single instance this dogma of no more slave States? Surely if that dogma were to be pressed with every such heartfelt conviction, and such heartfelt zeal, it could not be but that, in the hearts that had so adopted and embraced it, such an exception might be made as this. When the fate of my country is on the one side and my dogma on the other, let the dogma go rather than the country be prostrated. Is any member of the Senate prepared to say, in the face of this country and of the world, that rather than yield up his dogma in a single instance, he will see the country go to ruin, or he will attempt to enforce his opinion by the sword? Is there any man who will do such a thing as that, so contrary to the law and teachings of the Almighty, and contrary to all humanity?

I do not recur to these things for reproach upon any section of our country. No, sir; I live it all too well. It is all my country. I am not the man to degrade any portion of it by any language I have to use.

This territory then, plainly and clearly, was acquired by us all. It is but the work of yesterday. Now, a portion attempt to take it. They have scruples about allowing us our full and unrestricted and unreserved equal right in the territory. Can this be proper? We are but one community, with diverse institutions in relation to domestic slavery, as well as in relation to many other subjects. We have grown up in, and cultivated habits suitable to, all the circumstances surrounding us, just as every people on earth have. The institution of slavery has given a variety to the form of society in which it exists. The absence of it has given form to a somewhat different condition of society, but equally adapted to its people. So it will be everywhere. You say, for instance, by way of mitigating the wrong done, that you only exclude slaveholders; you only exclude three hundred thousand -- not a section of the country; not States; not fifteen States; but three hundred thousand slaveholders in those States. Whether that is a correct computation of them I do not know: nor is it of the least importance to this argument. No; the wrong does not stop there. All the millions that have been reared in the society formed, and receiving its character, and receiving its complexion from that institution, though they may not be the owners of slaves, have been brought up and habituated to the habit and form of society which that institution has given birth to. That makes a difference in the habits of a people not to be worn off in a day or a minute -- transient, I admit; but they are, for the present, their habits. Their feelings and their habits go along together; and neither would you Northern men prefer to go into the society of these people under circumstances equal; nor would the Southern man, with his habits and feelings, prefer to go into Northern society, simply because of changes in the custom and habits; that is all. By restraining the slaveholders from going into any Territory, then you restrain the formation of any such habits as this other man, who is not a slaveholder in the Southern States, has formed. You do not expel him, but you erect a barrier; not an insuperable one; you create a new difficulty in his way in going there, where he is to meet with strangers, and strangers of somewhat different habits from himself.

This question of slavery has been, to no small extent, connected with the question of religion. The pulpit has taken it in hand; the pulpit has become the minister of politicians, and politicians have ministered to ministers of the Gospel, neither to the benefit nor profit of the Gospel; and now, as scruples about slavery -- are pleaded on one side. You do not plead it so nomine as a religious preference that you are entitled to, or as a religious distinction. You plead it, to be sure, as a distinct opinion of your own upon the subject of slavery; but you have been able to force that question of slavery into a great political position before the country, by the aid of the pulpit. It has become with some a religious feeling. I am not one of those who feel a disposition to speak, or allow myself to speak, disrespectfully of religion; but I point you to these things as facts that we see and know, that there has been a combination, a mixing up, of these questions with religion and with politics; and we are taught from the pulpit daily, not of the political improvidence, not of the po-litical impolicy of slavery; but we are taught that it is a great sin, and that we are to put it far away from us.

It is through a long train of events, of party controversies, that the country has been brought to its present deplorable condition. It would be idle to say that in the course of that long controversy all the blame has been on one side, and all the right on the other. Right and wrong have never been so exclusively divided in any human controversy. We have all contributed to excite those passions and those feelings which now bring our country into the most imminent peril. I shall not attempt to balance this account, and show clearly which has been in the wrong. That would be an idle attempt, and would do no good, if successful. It is not to the past so much that I would allude as to the present and the future. No matter whether I have been the wrong doer or whether I have received the wrong, when the question comes as to the safety of the country, as to the safety of the Constitution, I should act with a reference to that object, and not to any past or present controversies that I may have with parties or with individuals.

Mr. President, I am not here as the advocate of slavery. I am here as the advocate of the Union, honestly, sincerely, zealously. I am pleading for that; and I am pleading with the Senate to do that which I believe will preserve the Union and stop the course of revolution and of war, and which alone I believe will do it. If I plead for this solution of territorial difficulties, it is because I believe it is necessary to save the Union. Is it possible that any Senator could believe, with respect to this arid and sterile Territory, it could be an object with any gentleman to desire the extension of slavery? I do not believe myself that slavery can ever be invited there. Climate, soil, its remoteness from all the great avenues of commerce, all tend, in my opinion, to interpose natural barriers against it. That, however, is not so much the question as our right to go there at all. You have no more right to take away poor land than you have rich land, from our settlement. Upon the principles of the Constitution, you have no more right to take away one than the other; and it is not so much the violation of territorial authority as it is the violation of that principle of equality, that principle of equal right upon which every section stands.

I want it to be known -- and, as far as my poor voice can go, it shall go -- that this Constitution, so far from its being liable to be broken by anybody that chooses to secede, as they call it, is a grand and inviolable instrument, upon which no man should lay his unhallowed hand, or attempt to withdraw himself. If he is oppressed, let him take the responsibilites of revolution; let him defy the war; let him proclaim himself a revolutionist, and not attempt to hide his revolution in the little subtleties of law, and the little subtleties with which he surrounds secession, as it is called, I do not believe in it. It is no justification. My honorable friend from Louisiana (Mr. Benjamin) quotes Mr. Madison and Mr. Webster as authority for this doctrine. Why, sir, if the gentleman had extended his inquiry a little further, he would have seen that no doctrine was ever repudiated more precisely, exactly, and sternly, than this doctrine of secession was by Mr. Madison; and Mr. Webster's name and fame are identified with the argument by which he was supposed to have destroyed every pretext on which such a doctrine could stand. If it is intended merely as another name for revolution, be it so. I do not know that gentlemen have not a right to do so denominate their actions if they please; but a constitutional right to break the Constitution -- a constitutional right to destroy the Union -- would be indeed a strange form of government.

I am for the Union; but, my friends, I must be also for the equal rights of my State under this great Constitution and in this great Union. You say you do. I believe it. I do. But we must preserve it on the proper terms of equal respect and equal regard. The dogma of my State is, that she has as much right to go into the Territories with her slaves as you, who do not choose to hold such property, have to go without them. That is their dogma. Would it not be best for both of us to renounce the pretension to go on its own dogma at the expense of the other, and let us make that odious thing, if it must be called so -- a compromise -- again to restore our brotherhood? Balance the consequences of a civil war and the consequences of your now agreeing to the stipulated terms of peace here, and see how they compare on with another. I will not repeat again what is asked of you. It is but a trifle in point of territory, a trifle in point of any material value that can be assigned to it, and there is no breach of any principle. It is an exception, and a fair exception upon exceptional grounds, to the principle you avow. On the other side, you have civil war ---

CHAPTER VI

RICHARD HICKMAN MENEFEE
(1809-1841)

While her husband was out of town attending a meeting of the Kentucky State Legislature, Mary Lonsdale Menefee decided to name the new baby Henry Clay Menefee. When her husband returned, the baby was christened Richard Hickman Menefee. Nevertheless, Mrs. Menefee may have had prescience since contemporaries of her son ranked him, along with Clay and Crittenden, as one of the finest orators ever boasted by Kentucky.[1]

Although Richard Menefee lived only thirty-one years, his reputation as a public speaker was imposing enough for an early state history text to refer to him as "the young Patrick Henry of the West." And, while it is impossible to know what laurels he might have won had he lived longer, he earned, even in so short a season, at least a *note bene* in the annals of international relations. The particular speech included in this volume marks the first statement of Anglo-American brotherhood ever uttered in public by a U.S. statesman.

A county now commemorates the Menefee name, but Owingsville might have been Menefeeville if Richard's dynamic father had built the finest house in the area. Instead, on a bet with Colonel Thomas Dye Owings, he built the second finest house and the town took the Colonel's name. Richard was born there on December 4, 1809. His father died when Richard was six years old, and his mother later married Colonel George Landsdowne.

Richard's early education was home tutoring by his

mother, but at the age of twelve he entered Walter Dourne's preparatory school. The school curriculum was founded upon three books -- Thomas Dilworth's *Arithmetic* and *Speller* and The King James Version of *The Bible*. After two years of rigidly confined intellectual restraint, it is perhaps no wonder that Richard made an interesting, if not compensatory, breakthrough -- he became a barkeeper, selling peach or apple brandy at twelve-and-a-half cents a pint at a tavern in town. According to his biographer, John Wilson Townsend, Menefee and Patrick Henry are the only two Americans who ever developed from barkeeps to orators.

Within a year, however, Richard had returned to academe, this time as a teacher. He was fifteen years old. Perhaps sensing his need for more education himself, the young man went to live with his father's old friend, Edward Stockton, in Mt. Sterling and attended the local school for two years.

In spite of his obviously erratic scholastic preparation, at the age of seventeen Richard was accepted at Transylvania College, where he remained until the end of his junior year. While there he joined the Union Philosophic Literary Society, but there is no evidence he belonged to a debating group.

Without taking a degree from the college, he returned to Mt. Sterling and again taught in the local school for two years. One of his students, Sarah Bell Jouett, caught his eye, and three years later they were married. As the daughter of the well-known painter, Matthew Harris Jouett, Sarah Bell introduced him to new social worlds, and, perhaps through contacts he made in that circle, his interest in law was born.

He studied law under Judge James Trimble, a Commonwealth Attorney for the eleventh judicial district, and entered the Transylvania Law School at the age of twenty-two. In that same year Governor Thomas Metcalfe nominated him to succeed Judge Trimble as Commonwealth Attorney and the appointment was confirmed.

As both lawyer and Commonwealth Attorney, his speeches attracted attention. He reportedly dazzled listeners, not only with his erudition, but with his sparkling delivery and personal magnetism. An unverified report, noted by his biographer, claims that, on one of his visits to Kentucky, Daniel Webster heard Menefee speak and was so delighted that he took him in "his arms and embraced him."

In 1832 Menefee launched his first state political campaign and was elected to the legislature, where he captivated constituents for the next five years. In 1837 he was elected to the United States House of Representatives. His ill health forced him to retire completely from public life at the end of his term, but he practiced law in Lexington until his death in 1841.

Richard Menefee was known by his peers as Dick, and he is described as "just six feet tall, dark blue eyes, heavy lashes, light brown hair, full lips, perfect teeth." His speech was not ornate or drowned in allusions. He spoke simply, directly, but nonetheless forcefully and persuasively. One can only regret that so attractive and capable a statesman and orator was quieted so soon.

Speech

of

Richard H. Menefee

On the reference of the President's message relating to the attack of the Caroline. Delivered in the House of Representatives, Monday, January 8th, 1838.

("Mr. Menefee, on rising, observed that any debate on the present proposition, which was merely to refer the message of the President to the appropriate committees, involving no consideration of merits of the subject to which it relates, would, in his opinion, be premature, and calculated to produce injury without the possibility of any corresponding good. It would, he was sure, have been impossible for the House to have listened to the debates which have thus arisen, unfortunately, he thought, without at least a portion of the surprise and regret with which they had inspired him.")

The attack on the *Caroline*, if made as described, may warrant much of the excitement represented as now prevailing amongst the people of New York, and even justify a deep and general sensation in that quarter. But the liability of transaction of this sort to be perverted and exaggerated on the one hand, whilst the possible circumstances of justification or palliation on the other are suppressed, must admonish us to the hazard of founding either direct legislation or public declarations of opinion by individuals so nearly connected with government as ourselves, upon facts which have so recently occurred, and are so imperfectly ascertained.

Confining ourselves to facts, upon the existence of which

there is no dispute, and upon which, of course, an opinion may be allowed, it is substantially acknowledged by our government, in the message of the President of the 5th inst., his letters to the executive of New York and Vermont, his proclamation, and in his instructions to the law officers of the United States, that our citizens of the Canada frontier are strongly disposed to violate their neutral obligations to Great Britain, as those obligations are recognized by this government, and the movements of a hostile character were already made by them; that the executive is incapable, under the existing laws, of enforcing these obligations, and therefore appeals to Congress to arm him with the requisite powers. In none of these documents, it will be perceived, was the slightest apprehension expressed of a violation by the subject of Great Britain of their neutral obligations to us. The elements of mischief were admitted to be confined exclusively to our people, and every measure of the executive was designed for their repression.

If citizens of the United States have thus violated their neutral obligations, that of itself constitutes, on every principle, an offense complete against Great Britain, for which this nation is responsible. It is of no avail, in ascertaining the existence of the offense on the one hand, or of our national responsibility on the other, that those violations occurred without the instigation or countenance of the government, and even in violation of the positive municipal laws of the United States. As between foreign nations and this, ours is answerable if it fails to enforce an observance by its citizens of our national obligations. Any other rule would render neutrality insecure, and the maintenance of peace between contiguous nations difficult, if not impracticable, left, as it thus would be, at the mercy of the irritation and collisions unavoidably incident to the frontier. It is national responsibility only, which, by exciting the vigilance of government over unauthorized acts of its citizens, can check and repress this spirit and thereby avert war. Such our position, and our responsibilities as already acknowledged by the government.

It must be recollected, Sir, that a resort to arms, on account of illegal acts of the citizen, cannot be considered until reparation by his government has been demanded and refused.

It is now represented that the subjects of Great Britain have, likewise, in the case of the *Caroline*, violated their neutral obligations to us, under circumstances of great atrocity. Still, so far as appears, it was, as in the case of our citizens, an illegal and unauthorized act of the subject of Great Britain. We have no more just right to presume, in the absence of the fullest proof to the contrary, that this proceeding of British subjects was instigated, or in the remotest manner countenanced, by the British authorities, than would their government, to presume, under like circumstances, that the officially acknowledged aggressions against them by our citizens were the deliberate acts of our government.

It is reasonable to conclude, from the present state of our information, that neutrality has been violated and wrong done by the people of both nations. For the honor of ours, I hope it may ultimately appear that the offense of our people has not been so flagrant as that of the opposite side. Yet the information already communicated by the executive leaves no room to hope that the first aggressions did not proceed from us, and serve as a pretext, though I can hardly suppose a justification of what succeeded. If we have been most wronged, it is certain that Great Britain has been first wronged.

Now in the midst of this popular ferment, before the governments on either side are implicated, does not every consideration recommend self-possession and wisdom here? The right of individuals, and even nations, to sympathize in the cause, real or imagined, of freedom, is not contested; but it must be exercised in subserviency to justice and law, not at their expense. In an exigency like this, the public have a right to look to Congress for a proper tone of opinion. It must be expected that the lead will be taken, to a great extent, by this cause, the proceeding of which (our debates forming a part) will necessarily be regarded with peculiar interest by both nations. It is therefore, I conceive, of the highest consequence that our views, as here publicly expressed, should rise to the magnitude as well as the dignity of the occasion; and that the subject should be placed at once beyond the influence, and, if possible, the suspicion of the influence of passion or precipitation. Not that I imagine there is danger of war with Great Britain; of that, gentlemen may dismiss all apprehensions; for, sir, there will be no war over these border collisions. To imagine such an event, is ridiculous and absurd. A course of intemperate discussion here, may, nevertheless, greatly embarrass the two governments, by inflaming still farther the public mind, already too highly excited. But it will merely embarrass; for war, I repeat, will not come.

It would be superfluous to enter at large, in the present state of the controversy, into the numerous reasons which pronounce such a war utterly out of the question. It is enough, almost, to remember that the spirit of the age, and the religious and moral as well as political illumination of the world, stand opposed to war, especially between highly civilized Christian nations. The advance of mankind could by nothing be more strikingly illustrated than the prevailing aversion and abhorrence with which war is now regarded, except in the last deplorable extremity, as the only means of securing repose in honorable peace. War is now viewed as but an instrument of peace. In this condition of the world, is it to be credited that, the two nations foremost, by universal acknowledgment, in the career of civilization, religion, liberty, and law can, except from absolute madness, engage in the barbarities of war? Why should they? Is it not to be adopted till every peaceful appeal for justice has failed? Has such failure actually occurred? Has either evinced an intention to deny to the other the fullest justice, be their mutual injuries what they may? Who can, without a blush, suppose the existence of such an intention on our part possible? Does not generosity, then, as well as justice, require us, at the same time, to presume that a similar desire for peace, whilst it demands justice, animates the government of Great Britain?

If any contested principle of international law or national rights were involved in the existing difficulties between the two powers, such as the right of search on the high seas, or of impressment of seamen, as claimed and exercised by Great Britain prior to the war of 1812, their repose, and probably their peace might be disturbed now, as then. These were the principles contested by us from the first; and presented a case where peace was neither secured nor honorable, so long as the pretensions of Great Britain under them were tolerated. The war, on our part, was, I never doubted, both justifiable and necessary. That justification and necessity, however, did not rest on a detached aggression on an acknowledged right, but on the assertion by Great Britain, I repeat, of principles, with the maintenance of which she deemed her existence almost to be identified, but which our honor and interests as strongly impelled us not to tolerate; principles which would have authorized her to follow up her aggressions indefinitely, as to repetition and duration. Granting, therefore, the late aggressions, on either side, to have been as atrocious as the ascertained facts will warrant, or as the imagination of the most belligerent there can paint, still there is no contested principle involved. Neither power claims, or ever has claimed, the right to violate, in this manner, the property, or lives, or territory, of the other. Both, on the contrary, now admit, as they always have done, that such violations are wrongs, for the reparation of which the respective powers are liable. All the principles which govern the present difficulty are simple and admitted. It is but a question about facts, which, when ascertained and reciprocally presented, are disposed of by uncontested principles common to both powers. Can either, then, I demand, without national reproach, for an instant, in such a case, tolerate the idea that a resort to arms is possible? They are holding themselves aloft among the nations of the earth as the patrons and champions of human civilization and liberty throughout the world. The liberal spirit which they have breathed, and are daily breathing, into the institutions of mankind, has placed them already far beyond all others -- and side by side -- in the noble work of advancing the high destinies of our race. Extinguish these lights; or turn them to glare on each other in barbarity and blood, instead of shining in cooperation, as heretofore, for the illumination of mankind; and can the vision of any be so confined and imperfect as not to foresee the disasters to which such an event would expose the world; or, at least, all it contains worth preserving -- its Christian civilized liberty.

But, Sir, I repeat, we shall have no war with Great Britain. Nations under such high responsibilities to mankind, dare not go to war on an occasion like this. They cannot, without a portion of dishonor and disgrace, encounter and breast, as they would be a war, the enlightened and liberal spirit of this age, which their own efforts and example have so largely contributed to produce, and now mainly impel.

Their characters and positions, in other respects, give the amplest assurance that a resort to force is not now to be expected. No two separate nations have, perhaps, ever existed, at any period of time, between whom has prevailed, of what is valuable, so much that is common to both. Language, laws, religion, ancestry, historical renown, and the most intimate relations of commerce and pervading interchange of capital in other forms -- all conspire to condemn war between them as peculiarly calamitous and unnatural. It is true, as I have stated, that, notwithstanding all this, war has, in fact, occurred between them. Yet this multitude of kindred principles soon triumphed over temporary hostility, and reunited them, as the necessities of their relative positions ever must, as the high priests of human civilization and freedom. They defy their destiny, when their arms are turned against each other. The cause of human nature suffers under every blow they strike.

Such being the relative positions of the two powers, for the reasons and for the high purposes which I have mentioned, the simple fact that difficulties like the present now exist must strike every observer as in a high degree extraordinary. Whence, then, these disturbances, whilst every enlightened motive is against them?

It was admitted by the President, almost in terms, before the affair of the *Caroline*, that our citizens, by the violation of their neutral obligations, were endangering the peace of the two nations; and, in effect, that retaliation by the other side might be provoked. The danger was alleged by him to proceed, in the first instance, from our citizens, and the enactment of laws recommended to restrain them; treating throughout as a domestic cause of difficulty to be removed by domestic measures. What,

I ask, produced this lawless spirit amongst our people? For in that, and not in the defenseless state of our frontier, or in the seizure of the *Caroline*, lies the true cause of this emergency. Pains, I know, have been taken in this debate, by the friends of the administration, to cast the whole blame upon the people, to the entire exoneration of the government; a course not without a late precedent, from the same quarter, on another subject. This condemnation of the people is scarcely less unjust than the acquittal of the government. These errors of the people, (for such I readily admit them to be) find their palliation, if not justification, in the antecedent and more flagrant wrongs by the government itself. When the head of a government like ours becomes lawless and unjust, upon whom, in the eye of· reason, rests the blame, if those who lived under the government, taking shelter under the example, are infected with a similar spirit? Is not the influence natural and unavoidable? Does not the moral condition, in many respects, of our people, mournfully attest that a lawless spirit has found its way into our national councils? To all those whose judgements, and affections, and imaginations are united as they ought to be, and as I hope mine are, in devotion to their country, it is a source of humiliation and pain to be compelled to arraign their government in a matter so delicate as the conduct of its relations towards a foreign nation. But, sir, there is a stage in the progress of international controversies when to condemn one's own government, if in the wrong, is not only becoming the citizen, but rises into a solemn duty of patriotism. Not to do so, would be blindly to sanction and follow whithersoever the caprice, ambition or injustice of weak or wicked rulers might lead. The voice of the citizen, exposing and denouncing pernicious and unjust measure towards other nations, should be raised with freedom and constancy, up to the period when the appeal to arms is actually made, or becomes clearly inevitable. Then the patriotic citizen adheres to, and maintains to the utmost, his country, right or wrong. Always a delicate ground, it is peculiarly so from the critical relations now existing between this government and Mexico. Considerations of national pride might even now restrain the expression of sentiments when I most firmly entertain, were not the contending nation, Mexico, whose weakness, from internal dissension, is so generally conceded that nothing I might say could be construed into undue concession to her power. And, in the recurrence which I shall make to the conduct of our government towards Mexico during the Texas revolt, nothing of unfriendliness or disrespect is intended towards the new republic which has emerged from the revolt. On the contrary, it is the profound wish of my heart that its political institutions may be speedily and firmly consolidated, and that its civil career may be as tranquil and prosperous as its military has been striking and glorious.

Why this prompt and energetic action when Great Britain is concerned, so directly opposite to that when Mexico was concerned? Is not peace as sweet, and are not treaties as sacred in the one case as in the other? Is our measure of justice graduated by the power of the nations to whom we administer it? Do you deny to the weakness of an infant and distracted republic, what you grant, with a haste almost indecent, to the power of a great monarchy? Do you reverse the principles which govern brave and magnanimous nations? True bravery, Sir, exalts itself into magnanimity in the intercourse of the powerful with the weak. In proportion to the weakness of Mexico, should have been the punctilious observance of every obligation we owed her. Did the administration avail itself of that very weakness to disregard all its obligations? On the other hand, brave nations are apt to poise themselves when in collision with their equals or superiors in power, and are prone, from fear of imputation of undue concession to power, to a slow and stately port. Such is our posture towards Great Britain, the power of whose arms and the glory of whose name place her in the front rank of the nations of the earth. She is our peer. With her, when the nations exact justice, they must also perform it.

In the late executive proceedings in regard to Great Britain, to which I have referred, I rejoice to recognize a disposition to enforce, in good faith, the national obligations. But how humiliating the contrast between the treatment which the two nations respectively received! What can save the national honor from the just supicion, both at home and abroad, of the government having done, in regard to Great Britain, from fear, what it perfidiously omitted to do, from principle, in regard to Mexico? Yet, sir, as no nation ought to be allowed to persist in a course of injustice, I perceive, in looking to the ultimate results of this emergency, the elements of remote advantage affecting the national character, more than compensating for any immediate mischief it may occasion. This last precedent of a faith and justice will, I trust, obviate, to some extent, the evils of the former precedent of perfidy and injustice. There is nothing dishonorable in doing justice to Great Britain -- nothing humiliating. The dishonor and humiliation consist in having withheld it from Mexico. It is better for our youthful nation of free institutions, that an occasion has arisen this early to reinstate its character by rectifying its policy, than after persisting in error for a series of years, to confess and correct it, perhaps after fruitless and exhausting contests.

If, Sir, the indignation of mankind could fasten exclusively on the administration, by whom this pernicious policy has been practiced, I should experience the less sensibility; it might sink into quiet infamy, without a tear of mine, and hardly a regret over its fall. But the national honor is implicated, and, unfortunately, tarnished by the process which has infamized the hands to which it was committed.

Sir, neither nations nor individuals can be too early or profoundly penetrated with the sentiment, that inflexible justice to others, under all conceivable circumstances, is their true glory as well as interest. An immediate and temporary advantage may be gained, as experience has shown, by its violation; but experience has equally shown that, sooner or later, in some form or other, through the wise though often inscrutable dispensation of a just Providence, retribution will come, as it ought to. The application of that sentiment to the present conjuncture is simple and easy. For the injuries which were admitted by the President to have been done Great Britain by our citizens, we must, in proper time and form, afford her justice. The attack on the *Caroline*, on the other hand, presents an occasion for the most scrupulous examination by the government into the facts of that transaction, which, if found as now represented, exhibits an aggression upon us, which Great Britain, in proper time and form, must redress. And that this reciprocal justice will be extended by both powers, who is authorized to entertain the slightest doubt?

I must be allowed, then, to express my utter dissent from any attempt which may be here made, either by the friends or the enemies of the administration, under a state of information admitted to be doubtful and imperfect, on grounds of acknowledged passion, to force the two nations into false positions. Let us display calmness, moderation, and dignity, which are not only consistent with a firm and inflexible purpose to exact the most scrupulous justice, but afford the best proof of a determination to do so. Yet if, after all, against human expectations, the government of Great Britain shall, on proper application, refuse to disavow the late aggression of her subjects, and seasonably redress it, and force the necessity of an appeal to arms, our present power and past history leave on my mind no apprehensions of any result inconsistent with the national glory, and the complete vindication of a just cause. And when that deplorable contingency shall arise, it will be seen who are foremost to vindicate by arms the violated rights and offended honor has been stained, by withholding justice from an infant republic, because weak, or those who will tolerate no denial of justice by others, because they deny justice to none.

CHAPTER VII

CASSIUS M. CLAY
(1810-1903)

Cassius Marcellus Clay: rebel, extremist, iconoclast, politician, orator, rabble-rouser. One biographer wrote of him:

> *In an era of striking personalities, Cassius M. Clay stands out as the most colorful, controversial figure Kentucky has yet produced. He was a politician, diplomat, anti-slavery leader, orator, journalist and patron of the arts. His long life spanned the periods of slavery, Civil War and Reconstruction, and into it he crammed more adventure and incidents than a dozen average men.* [1]

One such adventure concerned a controversy between Clay and Robert Wickliffe over the slave question. The struggle between the two involved debate, pamphlets, and even a duel on April 24, 1841, over Wickliffe's charges that Clay was an agent of the Yankee abolitionist movement. [2] Fortunately, each man missed his mark when firing at ten -paces. But the duel did not end the Wickliffe-Clay battle. At Russell Cave Springs in Fayette County, Kentucky on August 1, 1841, during a speech by Wickliffe, Clay interrupted to say: "That handbill has been proven untrue." Immediately, Samuel Brown, a "political bully," called him a liar and struck him with an umbrella. What ensued is described by Clay:

> *I at once drew my Bowie-Knife; but, before I would strike, I was seized from behind, and borne by force about fifteen feet from Brown, who, being now armed with a Colt's revolver, cried, "Clear the way and let me kill the damned rascal ... " he held his fire; and, taking deliberate aim, just as I was in arm's reach,*

he fired at my heart. I came down upon his head with a tremendous blow, which would have split an ordinary skull. [3]

The fight ended with Brown sustaining severe cuts on the head, losing one eye and having one ear cut off. As soon as this enemy was disposed of, Clay raised his bloody knife and cried: "I repeat that the handbill was proven a falsehood; and I stand ready to defend the truth." [4]

Clay was prosecuted for mayhem in the affair, and his defense was conducted by his cousin, Henry Clay, and his brother-in-law, John Speed Smith. Henry Clay closed his speech to the jury with these words: "And, if he had not (done this), he would not have been worthy of the name which he bears." [5] The jury promptly returned with a verdict of not guilty.

Clay had resolved "to give slavery a death struggle" after hearing William Lloyd Garrison, an abolitionist, speak several times at Yale University where Clay was doing undergraduate work in 1831. In Kentucky, he was "the Moses of the emancipationists." He continued to speak out in spite of threats of violence. According to one writer:

... he harangued hostile audiences from every stump, scorching invectives and pleading the cause of the slave with all the power of his audience at these gatherings. On one such occasion he was interrupted during a speech with a question, "What are you going to do with the whites?" The response was typically Clay: "I will free the blacks first and you afterwards." [6]

In 1849 a Constitutional Convention was held in Kentucky, in which the anti-slavery advocates fought to amend the Constitution in favor of emancipation. The issue created bitter fighting for delegates, and several men were killed. Clay was at the forefront and was told he would be killed if he appeared at Stanford. Nevertheless, he arrived at the crowded courthouse on time and began his speech:

"Now gentlemen, for those who have respect for the law of God, I have this argument," and he put the Bible on the lectern. "For those who believe in the laws of man, I have this argument," and he put a copy of the Constitution on the lectern. Then fixing his eyes on the most threatening group in the house, he said, "and for those who believe in neither the laws of God nor man I have this argument," and he reached down in his old gray gripsack and pulled out two long pistols and he crossed them right there. Then he laid his bowie knife across them. It is said that he had no trouble after that...[7]

Shortly after this incident, Clay was involved in a verbal altercation with his opponent, Squire Turner, in Foxtown, a settlement between Richmond and Lexington. Clay, in a fit of anger, stabbed to death Turner's oldest son and suffered, himself, severe cuts and chest wounds.

This penchant for violence marred his political career but did not dampen his enthusiasm for the emancipationist cause. After losing the 1851 gubernatorial race, in which he was the Whig candidate, to Democratic candidate L. W. Powell, Clay met with leaders of the Free-Soil Party at a national convention in Cleveland. The new party's motto was "Free Soil, Free Speech and Free Men." He adopted the platform of the party and, in order to promote his views against slavery and the repeal of the Missouri Compromise, scheduled a lecture tour of the Midwest and the North. He used bitter ridicule and sarcastic taunts to arouse his listeners to action, and felt his efforts were rewarded by overflowing and enthusiastic audiences.[8] One speech was to be given at Springfield, Illinois, in the rotunda of the State House. But, denied the rotunda, he held the meeting on July 10, 1854, in a wooded area near the city, where 1500 people gathered. He began by comparing himself with John the Baptist, who came preaching in the wilderness, and closed the speech with a plea for an organization of freemen which would:

... strike at the monster aggressor whenever it could be reached under the Constitution -- an organization of

men of whatever politics, of Free Soilers, Whigs and Democrats, who will bury past animosity and, repenting past errors which all have been guilty of, unite in hurling down the gigantic evil which threatens even our liberties. [9]

Clay's undaunted intensity, coupled with his talent for oratory, compelled him into politics throughout his life. When the Republican Party began to form in 1854 in Michigan and Wisconsin, Clay lost no time in affiliating with it. He felt the new party advocated principles for which he had been struggling for years, and found himself "in sympathy with the great-minds and heroic hearts of the Nation." In fact, Clay's opposition to slavery was credited with the organization of the party on a national level. A convention was held at Pittsburgh in 1856 for this purpose. Shortly after the national Republican Party was organized, Clay assisted in forming the Madison County Republican Association.

He first met Abraham Lincoln in 1856 during a large political rally in Springfield, Illinois, at which Clay was the main speaker. Lincoln, who had followed Clay's career through the Lexington papers which his wife, a native of that city, received, listened patiently to Clay's animated appeals. Following the speech, Lincoln made this statement: "Yes, I always thought, Mr. Clay, that the man who made the corn should eat the corn."

Throughout the 1856 campaign, Clay was recognized as an effective speaker, adjusting his oratory somewhat to suit his audience. Saving his most polished efforts for a New York City address, he declaimed upon the impending crisis of the South before the Young Men's Republican Central Committee:

In vain do men go to Nashville and Knoxville, and to Memphis, and to Charleston in their annual farce of southern commercial conventions to build up southern commerce, and to break down the abolition cities of Philadelphia, Boston and New York. The orator rises upon a Northern-made carpet; clothed cap-a-pie in Northern fabrics, and offers his resolutions written upon Northern paper with a Northern pen, and returns to his home on a Northern car; or being killed, is put into a Northern shroud, and buried in a Northern coffin, and his funeral preached from a text from a Northern hymn book, set to Northern music. And they resolve and resolve, and forthwith there's not another ton of shipping built, or added to the manufacturer of the South, and yet these men are not fools! They never invite such men as I to their conventions, because I would tell them that slavery was the cause of their poverty, and that it is free labor which they need.[10]

However, it was generally acknowledged that Clay's speaking efforts were aimed at gaining support for the presidential nomination in 1860. He not only dropped hints about his availability to represent the South, but he openly sought support from such men as influential Leslie Combs of Lexington. In spite of these efforts at the Chicago convention, he was unable to secure enough votes to receive the nomination. As a consolation prize, the delegates gave him three cheers.

Although disappointed by the defeat, Clay congratulated Lincoln and volunteered his services on behalf of the campaign and the party. He spoke mainly in Indiana, but also made appearances in Kentucky, Ohio, and Illinois. In July, 1860, he received the following note of thanks from Lincoln:

I see by the paper ... that you are filling a list of speaking appointments in Indiana -- I sincerely thank you for this, and I shall be further obliged if you will, at the close of the tour, drop me a line giving your impressions of our prospects in the state.

Still more you will oblige us if you will allow us to make a list of appointments in our state commencing, say, at Marshall in Clark County, and thence South and West along our Wabash and Ohio River border ...[11]

Delighted by the Republican victory, Clay expected, by way of reward, to be appointed Secretary of the War Department. Instead, he was offered an appointment as Minister Plenipotentiary to Spain, which he refused. However, he did accept a position as Minister to Russia.

His failure to get the cabinet position was attributed to the same reason which cost him the nomination: his program was too regional. Also, Lincoln's advisers felt Clay might harm the administration if he remained too close. They were apprehensive about Clay's tendency to rush into every controversy around him, and they also knew of the antagonism between Clay and William H. Seward, which began when Clay, in one of his speeches, referred to Seward as a drunkard.

Clay was confirmed as Minister to Russia by the Senate on March 28, 1861. The St. Petersburg post was unpopular with most office seekers. Several eminent men had held the position briefly and other appointees never even accepted the post; others accepted but returned on the next boat.[12] But Clay found this position to his liking and, except for one return trip between 1862 and 1863, he remained in Russia until relieved on September 25, 1869. During his tenure there, he was involved in several skirmishes with various individuals, including Secretary of State William Seward. The one major event which occurred during these years, however, was the purchase of Alaska. Although Clay wanted to take much credit for the deal, he actually had little influence on it. He discussed the annexation at Berea College in 1895:

> *I think that what I have done as liberator, what I have done for education, what I have done for freedom of the press and speech, what I have done as dictator in defense of Washington in 1861, ... are all forgotten, I shall be remembered as the author of the annexation of Alaska.*[13]

The Berea speech was considered by critics as the expressions of a man in his dotage.

In 1862, Clay returned to Russia to bring his family back because his wife disliked the climate. His visit extended into 1863, and he took advantage of every opportunity to criticize the war policies of the Lincoln administration. But he avoided an open break with the President and told Lincoln privately, "Although you may not always present my special views, you have always *my confidence and support* to carry out your own -- for you are the Chief of the Nation -- not I."

Anticipating the possibility of the Emancipation Proclamation, Lincoln sent Clay to Kentucky in August to assess the situation. Clay gave an address before a joint session of the Kentucky legislature in which he touched on foreign policy, national policy and state policy. In discussing national policy he was moderate and cautious, explaining that the Republicans had originally only intended to limit slavery. He recommended that Kentucky take advantage of Lincoln's offer of compensated emancipation. Above all, he said, "the state should adopt the policy of emancipating the slaves of all disloyal masters, not for the sake of the Negro, but for the purpose of weakening the masters."[14] The Kentucky lawmakers reacted favorably to the speech, and Clay happily reported to Lincoln that his Kentucky mission was successfully accomplished.

Clay's last speaking tour before returning to Russia was presumably on behalf of the 1862 Republican candidates, but his speeches were "pitifully hackneyed and appreciated only by partisan audiences." They were mainly autobiographical accounts of his efforts as agitator and had no effect upon the fall elections.

After returning from Russia in 1869, Clay continued to be active in public affairs, speaking frequently to all types of audiences. In 1871, he was invited to speak near Lexington at a Fourth of July meeting of the largest group of blacks ever gathered in Kentucky. In the address, "he advocated the Union, the Constitution, equal rights of all before the law. He claimed the interest of the blacks and old masters were the same." He also recommended education, not revolution, as a means of common understanding. The audience reacted with wild enthusiasm.

Clay also became involved with the Cuban Aid Society, of which he was elected president. Horace Greeley was vice-president, and Charles H. Dana, treasurer. The society's purpose, as announced by Clay, was to arouse the moral support of the people in the United States to recognize the independence of Cuba. In speeches on behalf of the Society, he criticized the Republican Party and became a pioneer among the Liberal Republicans.

Making another effort at political power in the 1870's, Clay became an ardent supporter of states' rights. He aimed at breaking the power of radicals and restoring the southern states to local control. Blaming radicals for the disorder in the South, he appealed to the southern Democrats to support the liberal movement. At Covington, Kentucky, in 1872 he told one audience:

> Let us save the States; let us save the South, and by saving the States and saving the South, we save the Union and the liberties of the ...Constitution... Do you owe an allegiance to the present administration? No, you owe it to those who fought your battles. You owe no gratitude to Ulysses S. Grant; he never voted for you in his life.[15]

Following the presidential election of 1872, in which Clay was defeated and Grant re-elected, Clay spent the next three years involved with reading, public affairs, and a large correspondence. He hoped to become vice-president in the 1876 election and, in order to help realize that goal, left the Republican Party and joined the Democrats in 1875. That year he gave many speeches for the Democratic candidates in Ohio and Mississippi. The major thrust in this campaign was in Mississippi where his audiences consisted mainly of blacks, and each engagement usually drew several thousand people. The routine for the Mississippi meetings called for a debate between the "Radical" representative and Clay, after a chairman and a secretary had been chosen. Frequently the meetings lasted most of the day, with Clay claiming that he defeated his opponent on every point of the debate.

Nevertheless, he was unable to win the second place on the Democratic ticket. Furthermore, the Democratic presidential nominee, Samuel J. Tilden, lost the election. Having made a serious effort for nomination in both major parties and failing each time, Cassius Clay, according to one biographer, deserved a place in the forefront of hard-luck candidates in U.S. politics.[16]

In addition to politics, Clay was interested in the advancement of education in Kentucky, and was also instrumental in promoting the Kentucky Historical Society. In February, 1878, invited to speak to the Society, he delivered an address typical of his autobiographical style:

> ... No man goes farther than I in devotion to one noble state. Have I not given proof on the battlefield; and in self-sacrifice with surroundings more terrible than bayonets and cannon balls? Yet my aspirations are not for the State or Nation only, but for all Nations. Knowledge is the basis of all civilization. As the common-law of our inheritance secures a person and property and freedom to ourselves, so let us do our part in building up a like community of nations. Let this be one aspiration, the highest that inspires humanity, that brings us in nearest approach to God.[17]

Among the many issues Clay concerned himself with were prohibition, labor and women's suffrage. In a discourse delivered in June, 1887, to the Yale class of 1832, he discussed all three issues. He started the speech on a note of nostalgia, as Yale was his alma mater:

> I began here my public career, and perhaps shall here end it. Temperance is well; in eating and temperance in drinking; temperance in all things.

Yes, labor has its grievances. The public lands should not be allowed to foreigners, nor to railroad corporations; nor to any combinations of capital, save for the plant necessary to combine industries and moral intellectual culture.

Women suffrage is the most serious question now pending .... Eighteen hundred years have not effaced the ruins of woman's fall. The Republican, Democratic, Labor and Prohibition parties may flourish and may fade, but woman suffrage gained, all is lost -- like the dead world it may be -- forever.[18]

Clay completed a manuscript on the subject of women's suffrage in 1894, which he called *Icarus*. He dedicated the work to women, "because they are threatened with new calamities by the attempt at equality with men in the exercise of suffrage."[19]

It is not surprising that a man of Clay's versatility should emerge from a background of culture, classical education and contact with famous, controversial figures of the day. Born at Clermont, in Madison County, to wealthy slave owners, Clay started an early education at Richmond Academy. Later he studied Latin under Joshua Fry at Fry's home on the Dix River, and French at the College of St. Joseph's in Bardstown. He also attended Transylvania College, where he heard some of Kentucky's leading speakers of the time, such as N.L. Rice, Henry Clay, Robert J. Breckinridge, Robert Wickliffe, and John Pope. Subsequently, Clay enrolled in the junior class at Yale in 1831, where he studied Latin, Greek, philosophy, history and rhetoric. He also joined one of the literary societies and became active in debate. At Yale he met Andrew Jackson, John C. Calhoun, John Quincy Adams, John Greenleaf Whittier, Daniel Webster, and Edward Everett. More influential than all of these, however, was William Lloyd Garrison, whose abolitionist speeches generated Clay's resolve to battle slavery. Here he also gave his first anti-slavery speech in an address commemorating the centennial of Washington's birth. He closed with a plea: "May not a blinded people rest secure in disbelief and derision till the birth-right left us by our Washington is lost, till we shall be aroused by the rushing ruins of a once glorious Union."

After graduation from Yale, Clay returned to Kentucky where he completed law studies at Transylvania in 1834. But, as a novice embarking upon a career in politics, he was not fully aware of the differences separating the planters and the white artisans. He attempted to remain a member of the wealthy class and serve the labor interests as well, advocating, throughout his career, a southern industrialism while defending the economic principles of the American system.

He showed, for the first time, public rebellion against the prejudices of his class when he campaigned successfully in the 1840 race for a seat in the General Assembly to represent Fayette County. Prior to this, he had represented Madison County two terms in the Kentucky House of Representatives, gaining a reputation as an able speaker. Ironically, this was the last election which Cassius Clay was to win.

Clay began to achieve national recognition while campaigning for Henry Clay in the presidential election of 1844. He was also beginning to gain a reputation as an effective stump speaker. One biographer described his skills:

> He had great skills as a speaker and debater. His speeches were logical and convincing. He commanded a large vocabulary and few surpassed him in the use of telling epithets. He had a sense of humor and he was quick at repartee. Frequently his enthusiasm for his cause carried him too far in ridicule and abuse of his adversaries; for that reason he rarely convinced them. His knowledge of history, literature, and science and his statistical information contributed to his effectiveness. In a word, oratory was his greatest talent.[20]

But even Clay's biographers could not describe him consistently.

He was, according to them, both unconvincing and effective, convincing and ineffective. As a result of these contradictory sides of Clay's nature, numerous problems resulted for Henry Clay because of Cassius' speaking on his behalf. Cassius' outspokenness on the slavery issue and the annexation of Texas, which he saw as an instrument of slave expansion, contributed, in the estimation of several biographers, to Henry Clay's loss of the presidency.

At the outbreak of the Mexican War in 1846, Clay, to the surprise of many, enlisted as a private. He felt that by entering the war he would gain influence which would benefit his future efforts against slavery. He was elected captain of his unit, the "Old Infantry Cavalry," which was composed of men from Lexington, and after a short period of drill, the unit departed for the war zone. Soon after arriving at Encarnacion, the unit was captured and held prisoner-of-war until release was negotiated several months later.

Following this war experience, Clay began to appear on the lecture circuit, speaking on slavery and related subjects in Philadelphia, Baltimore, and other cities, as well as in Kentucky. He even ran for governor on the Whig ticket against Democratic candidate L. W. Powell. But in spite of speaking throughout the state, he lost the election.

Because of his dynamic and persistent efforts in the cause of freedom, Clay became acquainted with such personalities as Julia Ward Howe, Lucy Stone Blackwell and Elizabeth Cady Stanton. On one occasion he was being entertained with a mixed group of blacks and whites at the home of Lucretia Mott in Cleveland. When wine was served at the gathering, one of the party proposed a toast to Cassius, saying, "Ladies and gentlemen, please fill your glasses; let us drink to the health of Cassius M. Clay -- Liberator. Though he has a white skin, he has a black heart." [21]

Cassius Clay did not win all his battles, certainly, but he rarely succumbed to defeat. His marriage to Mary Jane Warfield ended in divorce in 1878. However, true to character, Clay felt he must have the last word in the dispute and accused Mary Jane of making the first breach in the marriage. In November, 1894, at the age of eighty-four, Clay married fifteen-year-old Dora Richardson. Naturally, the marriage caused much discussion, but Clay defended his action in a letter to a Lexington newspaper:

In marrying a young girl and a peasant, I but exercise the privilege allowed the humblest citizen of the republic, and to spend my money as it pleases me and nothing more. The disparity of ages is our own business and nobody else's. [22]

Clay was hardly humble, and many thought him somewhat daft. But James Lane Allen, a Lexington newspaper correspondent, was present at the Clay-Richardson wedding and described the event for his readers:

Some think the old General is crazy, but I do not think so. His mind is as clear as a bell. I do not even think he is in his second childhood, but if he is, I shall hereafter have no fear of growing old. [23]

However, the marriage lasted only three years, and in 1897 Dora left Clay's home, White Hall, and sued for divorce, which was granted. Soon after, Clay advertised for another mate. His offer of marriage was widely circulated and brought him many responses, but none proved acceptable.

The last years were lonely for Cassius Clay. He sought companionship with the plants and animals and at night would open his shutters to allow the bats into the house so he could enjoy their flutterings. He imagined his enemies were out to get him, and turned his house into a fortress. Fearing his servants were trying to poison him, he kept four ferocious dogs which were unleashed only at night. Occasionally he would put on a black robe and cap, take his bowie knife and search the grounds around his house. During these years he became something of a legend and was known as the "Lion of White Hall." It is said he died in the midst of the worst storm on record in Central Kentucky on July 22, 1903, at the age of ninety-three.

Cassius Marcellus Clay never realized his political dreams but he did, indeed, leave a distinct mark on U. S. history. He has been called "a man of inconsistent extremes... of gentleness and violence, restraint and blinding passion." With the force of extremism he fought the injustice of extremism; with "blinding passion" he fought blind passion;[24] sometimes with gentleness, oratorical acuity and charm, he persuaded. Enigmatic, eccentric, influential, he will not be forgotten in the continuing struggle for justice.

The Man Died, But His Memory Lives

(An address delivered before the faculty and students of Yale College, February 22, 1832, the occasion being the celebration of the centennial birthday of George Washington.)

Gentlemen of Yale College:

Were a stranger to visit this land, in this time of peace and plenty, this mildness and tranquility of Nature, and hear, at a distance, the loud peals of cannon and the murmurs of assembled multitudes, behold crowds of both sexes and every age, moving in anxiety to the churches and places of public convocation, in amazement he would exclaim, "What means this hurried array! this mighty tumult! What threatened invasion; what great political commotion; what impending convulsion of Nature draws together thirteen millions of human beings?"

Illustrious, departed shade, whom we this day call to memory, this could not be! For from what land shall he come who knows not thy great and virtuous deeds? What language shall he speak who has not heard the name of Washington?

We are assembled to-day, a great and intelligent nation, to offer up our thanks to the Author of our being for the many and signal favors bestowed upon us as a people; to give to departed worth our highest approbation, the voluntary tribute of grateful remembrance; to manifest to mankind and our posterity the regard which we entertain for the blessings of religious and political freedom, which our gallant ancestors have bequeathed us; to make ourselves better men and better citizens. It is enough for one man that thirteen millions of human beings have assembled in his name. Any efforts which I might make to color his fame by indulging in panegyric would be trifling with the feelings of this assembly, for, from the throbbing bosom and brightening eye, I perceive that you have outstripped the slow pace of language and already given way to the grateful emotions of the soul. I shall therefore briefly touch upon a few incidents of his life and proceed to some other considerations which may not be inappropriate to the occasion. It was the good fortune of Washington to unite in one personage the far distant and almost incompatible talents of the politician and soldier. It would not, I presume, be considered disrespectful to say that this circumstance is the only one which made a material distinction between him and some others of his noble compatriots. Other men may have conceived as high designs and entertained as exalted patriotism, but it was for Washington to conceive and execute, and what he declared with the pen in the cabinet, to conclude with the sword in the field. Other men would have been proud of the honor of preeminence in either department, but Washington drank deep of the glory of each, and was not intoxicated with the draught, for he was subject to temptation on a most signal occasion, yet his virtue and patriotism failed not in the hour of trial.

Success has crowned his efforts against a foreign foe. His followers, stung with the ingratitude of a preserved country, who refused the poor tribute of soldier's wages, were united to him by the strongest ties -- the sense of common suffering and injustice. Inflammatory letters were industriously circulated throughout the army by an insidious enemy. The republic, in its very infancy, was about to pass the way of all democracies and on the eve of yielding up her dearly-bought liberties to her chieftain. Then do we see the grey-headed patriot coming forward in deep and sorrowful mood, and hear his faltering voice, entreating them to spare themselves -- to spare him -- what? An ignominious death? No! to spare him the titles, the honors, the arbitrary power for which others have deemed the risk of life not too dear a sacrifice. Raising the intercepted letters to his face while the gathering tear suffused his sight, he uttered those memorable words, "My eyes have grown dim in the service of my country." Where, in the long annals of the reputed sayings of departed sages, shall we find the equal of this more than eloquence -- this pouring forth of the soul? It was then that tyranny was rebuked, and liberty drew immortal inspiration. For selfishness and power were disrobed of their tinseled ornaments, ambition loosed his deadly grasp and liberty and virtue, in union, winged their heavenly flight!

What, then, remains for this occasion? Washington is gone and his virtues and his exploits are reserved for mention at other times. The effects, my countrymen, the effects! "The man died, but his memory lives." How many like the great Emmet have died and left only a name to attract our admiration for their virtues, and our regret for their untimely fall, to excite to deeds which they would but could not effect! But what has Washington left behind, save the glory of a name? The independent mind, the conscious pride, the ennobling principle of the soul -- a nation of freemen. What did he leave? He left us to ourselves. This is the sum of our liberties, the first principle of government, the power of public opinion -- public opinion, the only permanent power on earth. When did a people flourish like Americans? Yet where, in a time of peace, has more use been made with the pen or less with the sword of power? When did a religion flourish like the Christian, since they have done away with intolerance? Since men have come to believe and know that physical force can not affect the immortal part, and that religion is between the conscience and the Creator only. He of 622, who with the sword propagated his doctrines throughout Arabia and the greater part of the barbarian world, against the power of whose tenets the physical force of all Christendom was opposed in vain, under the effective operations of freedom of opinion, is fast passing the way of all error.

Napoleon, the contemporary of our Washington, is fast dying away from the lips of men. He who shook the whole civilized earth, who, in an age of knowledge and concert among nations, held the world at bay, at whose exploits the imagination becomes bewildered, who, on the eve of his glory, was honored with the pathetic appellation of "the last, lone captive of millions in war," even he is now known only in history. The vast empire was fast crumbling to ruins whilst he yet held the sword. He passed away and left "no successor" there. The unhallowed light which obscured is gone, but brightly beams yet the name of Washington!

This freedom of opinion which has done so much for the political and religious liberty of America has not been confined to this continent. People of other countries begin to inquire, to examine and to reason for themselves. Error has fled before it and the most inveterate prejudices are dissolved and gone. Such unlimited remedy has, in some cases, indeed apparently proved injurious, but the evil is to be attributed to the peculiarity of the attendant circumstances or the ill-timed application. Let us not force our tenets upon foreigners, for, if we subject opinion to coercion, who shall be our inquisitors? No, let us do as we have done, as we are now doing, and then call upon the nations to examine, to scrutinize and to condemn! No! they can not look upon America to-day and pity, for the gladdened heart disclaims all woe. They can not look upon her and deride, for genius and literature and science are soaring above the high places of birth and pageantry. They can not look upon us and defy, for the hearts of thirteen millions are warm in virtuous emulation; their arms steeled in the cause of their country. Her productions are wafted to every shore; her flag is seen waving in every sea. She has wrested the glorious motto from the once queen of the seas and high on our banner, by the stars and stripes, is seen:

> *Columbia needs no bulwark,*
> *No towers along the steep,*
> *Her march is o'er the mountain wave,*
> *Her home is on the deep.*

But on this day of freeman's rejoicings, and all this mutual congratulation, "this feast of the soul, this pure banquet of the heart," does no painful reflection rush across the unquiet conscience, no blush of insincerity suffuse the countenance, where joy and gratitude should hold undivided sway? When we come this day, as one great family, to lay our poor offering on the altar, to that God who holds the destinies of nations in his hand, are there none afar off, cast down and sorrowful, who dare not approach the common altar, who can not put their hands to their hearts and say: "Oh, Washington, what art thou to us? Are we not also freemen?"

Then what a mockery is here! Foolish man, lay down thy offering, go thy way, become reconciled to thy brother and then come and offer thy offering.

In the language of Thomas Jefferson: "Can the liberties of a nation be sure when we remove their only firm basis, a conviction in the minds of the people that these liberties are the gift of God? That they are not to be violated but with His wrath? Indeed, I tremble for my country when I reflect that God is just; that His justice can not sleep forever; that the revolution of the wheel of fortune, a change of situation, is among possible events; that it may become probable by supernatural interference! The Almighty has no tribute which can take sides with us in that event." And shall these things be? 'Tis fit that he should chide who bears the name.

But ye philanthropists, if ye so term yourselves -- whether real or feigned -- I care not -- leave to ourselves, give opinion full score, examine, scrutinize, condemn, but let us alone. Know ye not yet the human heart? It has its afflictions, but it has its jealousies and its revenge, too. But if you attempt to snatch justice from our arms -- our destined bride, lovely maid of every perfection -- we will plunge the assassin's dagger to her dagger, to be mourned by her followers as well as by her destroyers!

"Leave us to ourselves" should be the motto of our republic, the first principle of national legislation. Not license to lawlessness and crime; not that liberty which is so often shouted forth without meaning -- defiance of wholesome laws and their severe and rigid execution. But let us alone -- let us exercise reason and public opinion as regards our temporal interests as well as our immortal welfare.

If we come to honor Washington to-day, to sanction his

principles, which have been approved in times past, I can not forbear pressing upon the minds of my audience, from various parts of the Union, the necessity to concede something to public opinion in the construction of our Federal league; to be indulgent to one another. If you do not, my countrymen, I very much fear that this, the first centennial celebration of the birth of Washington, will be the last on which a mighty nation will have met.

It is a principle generally admitted among politicians that the most despotic government in peace is the most efficient in war, and the reverse. This principle applied to us admits of much limitation. If we war with foreigners, and all united, I venture to say we are the most powerful nation on earth, comparing our physical resources, for we war not for a change of masters, but for ourselves -- for freedom. But if we war with each other, which God forbid, we are the weakest nation in existence, because we are the farthest removed from executive influence; more subject to individual will. Our strength is in public opinion, in unanimity. We revolt on the most favorable circumstances. No ignominious death of traitors awaits us; defeat, at worst, is but an unwilling marriage with a haughty but yet loving lord. States come to the contest, armed, provided, unanimous, fighting ostensibly under the banner of the Constitution, if not in supposable cases, in the real spirit of our Federal league.

I would not speak lightly of the Constitution of America; long may it exist to the honor of its framers and the greater glory of those who support it well, but I should not deem it safe to appeal to the letter of any copy, in defiance of the great original, written in the breast of every American.

In the political arena the glove is already thrown down; the great Northern and Southern champions stand in sullen defiance; bristling crests are seen extending to the extreme verge of the lists; the mystery of intense feeling pervades the hosts; "non tumultus, non quies; quale magni metus, et magnae irae silentium est."

My countrymen, this must not be; the issues are too great to depend upon the fall of one man. 'Tis yours -- you, the people of the United States -- to look well to it!

The warning voice of Cassandra is abroad! May not a blinded people rest secure in disbelief and derision till the birth-right left us by our Washington is lost, till we shall be aroused by the rushing ruins of a once "glorious Union!"

CHAPTER VIII

JOHN CABELL BRECKINRIDGE
(1821-1875)

Of the several Kentucky families significantly involved in the political history of the state, perhaps none endures more tenaciously than the Breckinridge family. The roster of notable kinsmen includes John Breckinridge, Attorney-General under Thomas Jefferson; Robert J. Breckinridge, Moderator of the General Assembly of the Presbyterian Church, the highest national office of the denomination; William C.P. Breckinridge, educator, lawyer, Confederate Colonel; and, of course, the United States Representative from Kentucky's Sixth District, John B. Breckinridge. However, amid this cluster of Breckinridge luminaries, John Cabell Breckinridge shines conspicuously as one of the most colorful and controversial figures in the family. This playmate of Mary Todd became a presidential opponent of Abraham Lincoln; this member of the U.S. Senate was expelled by the very body which he served; and this Vice-President of the United States became the Secretary of War for the Confederacy.

The only son of Joseph Cabell and Mary Smith Breckinridge, John Cabell was born at the ancestral home, "Cabell's Dale," near Lexington, Kentucky on January 21, 1821.[1] His education included attendance at Pisgah Academy in Woodford County, Kentucky, and later, graduation from Centre College in Danville. In addition, he attended the College of New Jersey (now Princeton University) and Transylvania College, where he received his law degree in 1841.

No one seems to know why this man, whose heritage was so eminently Kentuckian, chose to practice law first in Iowa, instead of in his home state, especially since he had studied under

Governor William Owsley. In any event, Breckinridge opened his office in the town of Burlington, where he remained only a short time before moving first to Georgetown, Kentucky and then to Frankfort and to Lexington. He also acquired a bride, Mary Cyrene Burch, during this period.

In 1844 at the age of twenty-three, John Cabell canvassed the state for James Knox Polk, and, hence, against his fellow Kentuckian, Henry Clay. While campaigning he was observed by Henry's illustrious relative, Cassius Clay, as "tall, well-formed, with fair complexion, regular face, of great mental power, large blue eyes, and auburn hair, intellectual, composed, and full of conscious genius and future prowess."

Breckinridge's "prowess" was first demonstrated in the Kentucky Legislature which he served from 1840 to 1851, at which time he was elected to the United States House of Representatives. Charles Kerr, in his *History of Kentucky*, notes that "Perhaps the most significant feature of the democratic victory of 1851 was the rise of a new star in the Kentucky firmament. This was John C. Breckinridge, destined by his genius and magnetic personality to win an affectionate following hardly surpassed by Clay's." [2]

This "new star" had, indeed, ascended. In 1853 President Franklin Pierce offered him a diplomatic post in Madrid, but he refused. Instead he continued in Congress, where he proved an able and entertaining speaker, until 1856, when he was nominated as Vice-President on the Democratic ticket. With the slogan "Buck and Breck," the team of James Buchanan and John Breckinridge swept into power. The height of Breckinridge's personal popularity was demonstrated by his fellow Kentuckians who voted for a Democratic President for the first time in almost thirty years.

But difficult and dangerous times waited their turn. The issue of slavery was dividing the Democratic Party as it would later divide the country. As presiding officer of the Senate during the years preceding the Civil War, Breckinridge tried to steer a neutral course, and his prestige and principles were strong. He decided to run for the Democratic nomination for President. But the deeply-split convention nominated Stephen Douglas instead.

Douglas, an outspoken abolitionist, outraged the Southern pro-slavery wing of the party, and they met in a separate convention to nominate their candidate. John Cabell Breckinridge was their choice.

According to one historian, "The Breckinridge democrats were largely men of audacity and action, who would have what they considered to be Southern rights protected or stop with no remedy short of secession." But Breckinridge himself felt he was not a "disunionist"; he was merely a Constitutionalist.

The rift in the Democratic camp was further undermined by the candidacy of John Bell, who represented the Constitutional Union Party. The weight of Abraham Lincoln, standing alone at the Republican pole, was to prove too mighty for those who clung so desperately, but separately, on the opposing end.

One can only guess at the sense of defeat and despair Breckinridge felt when, as Vice-President, he opened the certificate of election and announced Lincoln's victory. But Breckinridge's loss was nothing to be ashamed of. He collected seventy-two electoral votes from the eleven states of the Deep South as well as from Delaware and Maryland. And, while Lincoln received 180 electoral votes, he still received only forty per cent of the popular vote. Whoever won, the country was almost lost. Breckinridge had predicted that Lincoln's victory would destroy the nation, and at that time, he seemed prophetic. South Carolina, Georgia and the Gulf States, North Carolina, Virginia, Tennessee and Missouri seceded from the Union.

The following year Breckinridge returned to Congress by succeeding John J. Crittenden in the Senate, but the course of events made his stay a brief one. In general, the political leaders of Kentucky had attempted to remain noncommittal in the conflict which severed the States, but a secessionist group in the southwest area of the state set up a government and joined the Confederacy, although the legitimate government remained with the Union. Breckinridge's firm belief that the rights of the states were being violated by federal supremacy caused him to resign from the Senate the very year he was elected.

On September 18, 1861, armies of both sides invaded Kentucky, and on November 16, Brigadier General John C. Breckinridge assumed command of the 1st Kentucky Brigade of the Confederate States Army. Ironically enough, just thirteen years earlier, United States Army Major John C. Breckinridge had collected a volunteer regiment to fight for the annexation of Texas.

Charges of treason were made against thirty-two prominent Kentuckians, among them Breckinridge, John Morgan and Humphrey Marshall. In December, the United States Senate voted unanimously on the following resolution:

Whereas John C. Breckinridge, a member of this body, has joined the enemies of his country, and is now in arms against the government he had sworn to support; therefore, Resolved that the traitor Breckinridge be expelled. 3

Breckinridge's career with the Confederacy was as distinguished as his earlier service for the Union. He commanded the reserve troops at the Battle of Shiloh and was promoted to Major-General, and subsequently fought with Lee's army in the wilderness and was second in command in the Shenandoah campaign. During the last months of the war, he was appointed Secretary of War for the Confederacy by his fellow Kentuckian, Jefferson Davis.

At the war's end, Breckinridge had little choice but to exile himself until such time as the tide changed and he could return to his country. He escaped to England via Florida and Cuba and remained abroad for three years, visiting the Continent and Asia as well. Sadly, there seems to be no record of these years.

The Kentucky Legislature sent a petition to Congress in February of 1866. Signed by seventy members, it asked for the pardon of General Breckinridge. Pardon was granted and the General came home, traveling from Toronto where he had been awaiting permission to re-enter. In 1878, three years after his death, the Legislature again acted on his behalf by appropriating $10,000 for the erection of a statue "as a work of our respect to the memory of the deceased hero." There is a certain melancholy in a state's tribute to a prodigal son, but there is a joy in justice, too. Whatever else he did, John Cabell Breckinridge lived as a leader steadfastly adhering to his beliefs and he died with the people of his state still affectionately following.

The following speech clearly and adamantly states Breckinridge's position in his campaign to defeat Lincoln, Douglas and Bell in the election of 1860. His desire is "to restore the harmony of the States" and he denounces his opponents as leaders of disunity and calumny. The oratory is marked by the preferred tastes of the day: sentimentality, historical allusion, enormous self-confidence and concern with regional issues. If it seems long to the modern reader, this excerpt suggests it was not to the contemporary listener:

Fellow citizens, if my strength will last, can you bear with me a little longer? (Voice: Yes, a week -- go on.)

Removal of the United States Senate

A speech delivered in 1858; the occasion was the last gathering of the United States Senate in the old Senate chamber.

On the sixth day of December, 1819, we assembled for the first time in this chamber, which has been the theater of their deliberations for more than thirty-nine years.

And now the strife and uncertainties of the past are finished. We see around us on every side the proofs of stability and improvement. The capitol is worthy of the republic. New public buildings meet the view on every hand. Treasures of science and the arts begin to accumulate. As this flourishing city enlarges, it testifies to the wisdom and forecast that dictated the plan of it. Future generations will not be disturbed with questions concerning the center of population, or of territory, since the steamboat, the railroad and the telegraph have made communication almost instantaneous. The spot is sacred by a thousand memories, which are so many pledges that the city of Washington, founded by him and bearing his revered name, with its beautiful site, bounded by picturesque eminences and the broad Potomac, and lying within view of his home and tomb, shall remain forever the political capital of the United States.

It would be interesting to note the gradual changes which have occurred in the practical working of the Government since the adoption of the Constitution, and it may be appropriate on this occasion to remark on one of the most striking of them.

At the origin of the Government, the Senate seemed to be regarded chiefly as an executive council. The President often visited the chamber and conferred personally with this body;

most of the business was transacted with closed doors and took comparatively little part in the legislative debates. The rising and vigorous intellects of the country sought the arena of the House of Representatives as the appropriate theater for the display of their powers. Mr. Madison observed, on some occasion, that being a young man and desiring to increase his reputation, he could not afford to enter the Senate; and it will be remembered that so late as 1812 the great debates which preceded the war and aroused the country to the assertion of its rights took place in the other branch of Congress. To such an extent was the idea of seclusion carried that when this chamber was completed, no seats were prepared for the accommodation of the public, and it was not until many years afterwards that the semi-circular gallery was erected which admits the people to be witnesses of your proceedings. But now the Senate, besides its peculiar relations to the executive department of the Government, assumes its full share of duty as a co-equal branch of the Legislature; indeed, from the limited number of its members and for other obvious reasons, the most important questions, especially of foreign policy, are apt to pass first under discussion in this body, and to be a member of it is justly regarded as one of the highest honors which can be conferred on an American statesman.

It is scarcely necessary to point out the causes of this change, or to say that it is a concession both to the importance and to the individuality of the States and to the free and open character of the Government.

In connection with this easy but thorough transition, it is worthy of remark that it has been effected without a charge from any quarter that the Senate has transcended its constitutional sphere -- a tribute at once to the moderation of the Senate and another proof to the thoughtful men of the comprehensive wisdom with which framers of the Constitution secured essential principles without inconveniently embarrassing the action of the Government.

The progress of this popular movement in one aspect of it has been steady and marked. At the origin of the Government, no arrangements in the Senate were made for spectators; in this chamber about one-third of the space is allotted to the public; and in the new apartment the galleries cover two-thirds of its area. In all free countries the admission of the people to witness legislative proceedings is an essential element of public confidence, and it is not to be anticipated that this wholesome principle will ever be abused by the substitution of partial and interested demonstrations for the expression of a matured and enlightened public opinion. Yet it should never be forgotten that not France, but the turbulent spectators within the hall, awed and controlled the French Assembly. With this lesson and its consequences before us, the time will never come when the deliberations of the Senate shall be swayed by the blandishments or the thunders of the galleries.

It is impossible to disconnect from an occasion like this a crowd of reflections on our past history and of speculations on the future. The most meager account of the Senate involves a summary of the progress of our country. From year to year you have seen your representation enlarge; again and again you have proudly welcomed a new sister into the Confederacy; and the occurrences of this day are a material and impressive proof of the growth and prosperity of the United States. Three periods in the history of the Senate are in striking contrast, three epochs in the history of the Union.

On the third of March, 1789, when the Government was organized under the Constitution, the Senate was composed of the representatives of eleven States, containing three millions of people.

On the sixth of December, 1819, when the Senate met for the first time in this room, it was composed of the representatives of twenty-one States, containing nine millions of people.

To-day it is composed of the representatives of thirty-two States, containing more than twenty-eight millions of people, prosperous, happy and still devoted to constitutional liberty. Let these great facts speak for themselves to all the world.

The career of the United States cannot be measured by that of any other people of whom history gives account, and the mind is almost appalled at the contemplation of the prodigious force which has marked their progress. Sixty-nine years ago, thirteen States, containing three millions of inhabitants, burdened with debt and exhausted by the long war of independence, established for their common good a free Constitution on principles new to mankind and began their experiment with the good wishes of a few doubtful friends and the derision of the world. Look at the result to-day: Twenty-eight millions of people in every way happier than an equal number in any other part of the globe, the center of population and political power, descending the western slopes of the Allegheny mountains, and the original thirteen States forming but the eastern margin on the map of our vast possessions.

See, besides, Christianity, civilization and the arts given to a continent; the despised colonies grown into a power of the first class, representing and protecting ideas that involve the progress of the human race; a commerce greater than that of any other nation; free interchange between States; every variety of climate, soil and production to make a people powerful and happy; in a word, behold present greatness and in the future an empire to which the ancient mistress of the world in the height of her glory could not be compared. Such is our country, aye, and more, far more than my mind could conceive or my tongue could utter. Is there an American who regrets the past? Is there one who will deride his country's laws, pervert her Constitution or alienate her people? If there be such a man, let his memory descend to posterity laden with the execrations of all mankind.

So happy is the political and social condition of the United States, and so accustomed are we to secure enjoyment of a freedom elsewhere unknown, that we are apt to undervalue the treasures we possess and to lose in some degree the sense of obligation to our forefathers. But when the strifes of faction shake the Government, and even threaten it, we may pause with advantage long enough to remember that we are reaping the reward of other men's labors. This liberty we inherit; this admirable Constitution, which has survived peace and war, prosperity and adversity; this double scheme of government, State and Federal, so peculiar and so little understood by other powers, yet which protects the earnings of industry and makes the largest freedom compatible with public order -- these great results were not achieved without wisdom and toil and blood; the heroic and touching record is before the world. But to all this we were born and, like heirs upon whom has been cast a great inheritance, have only the high duty to preserve, to extend and to adorn it. The grand productions of the era in which the foundations of this Government were laid reveal the deep sense its founders had of their obligations to the whole family of man. Let us never forget that the responsibilities imposed on this generation are by so much greater than those which rested on our Revolutionary ancestors as the population, extent and power of our country surpass the dawning promise of its origin.

It would be a pleasing task to pursue many trains of thought, not wholly foreign to this occasion, but the temptation to enter the wide field must be rigorously curbed; yet I may be pardoned, perhaps, for one or two additional reflections.

The Senate is assembled for the last time in this chamber. Henceforth it will be converted to other uses; yet it must remain forever connected with great events, and sacred to the memories of the departed orators and statesmen who here engaged in high debates and shaped the policy of their country. Hereafter the American and the stranger, as they wander through the capitol, will turn with instinctive reverence to view the spot on which so many and great materials have accumulated for history. They will recall the images of the great and good, whose renown is the common property of the Union; and chiefly, perhaps, they will linger around the seats once occupied by the mighty three whose names and fame, associated in life, death has not been able to sever; illustrious men who, in their generation, sometimes divided, sometimes led, and sometimes resisted public opinion, for they were of that higher class of statesmen who seek the right and follow their convictions.

There sat Calhoun, the senator, inflexible, austere, op-pressed, but not overwhelmed by his deep sense of the importance of his public functions, seeking the truth, then fearlessly following it -- a man whose unsparing intellect compelled all his notions to harmonize with deductions of his rigorous logic and whose noble countenance habitually wore the expression of one engaged in the performance of high public duties.

This was Webster's seat. He, too, was every inch a senator. Conscious of his own vast powers, he reposed with confidence on himself, and, scorning the contrivances of smaller men, he stood among his peers all the greater for the simple dignity of his sensa-tional demeanor. Type of his Northern home, he rises before the imagination, in the grand and granite outline of his form and intellect, like a great New England rock, repelling a New England wave. As a senatorial orator, his great efforts are historically associated with this chamber, whose very air seems to vibrate beneath the strokes of his deep tones and his weighty words.

On the outer circle sat Henry Clay, with his impetuous and ardent nature untamed by age and exhibiting in the Senate the same vehement patriotism and passionate eloquence that of yore electrified the House of Representatives and the country. His extraordinary personal endowments, his courage, all his noble qualities, invested him with an individuality and a charm of character which in any age would have made him a favorite of history. He loved his country above all earthly objects. He loved liberty in all countries. Illustrious man! Orator, patriot, philan-thropist, whose light, at its meridian, was seen and felt in the remotest parts of the civilized world, and whose declining sun, as it hastened down the west, threw back its level beams in hues of mellowed splendor to illuminate and to cheer the land he loved and served so well.

And now, senators, we leave this memorable chamber, bearing with us unimpaired the Constitution we received from our forefathers. Let us cherish it with grateful acknowledgments to the Divine power who controls the destinies of empires and whose goodness we adore. The structures reared by men yield to the corroding tooth of time. These marble walls must molder into ruin, but the principles of constitutional liberty, guarded by wisdom and virtue, unlike material elements, do not decay. Let us devoutly trust that another Senate, in another age, shall bear to a new and larger chamber this Constitution, vigorous and inviolate, and that the last generation of posterity shall witness the deliberations of the representatives of American States still united, prosperous and free.

CHAPTER IX

JAMES PROCTOR KNOTT
(1830-1911)

It is rare for a politician to be remembered for a single speech and scarcely anything else. Lincoln's "Gettysburg Address" is memorable, but then so is the man. Few forget the famous lines from John Kennedy's inaugural speech, and few forget his personality, his family, his death. Who remembers J. Proctor Knott besides Kentuckians who live in the county named after him or students of state history who might recall him as an early governor? Yet no work which contains examples of great Kentucky orators can exclude him because of one address to Congress, the "Duluth Speech."[1]

James Proctor Knott was a serious-minded, rather grave man, but his "Duluth Speech" has been called the "wittiest piece of satire that the political literature of the day has been able to produce." Knott was not a very famous man, but his speech was published by every important newspaper in the country, and "it was translated in four or five different languages as the best piece of humor or irony by any American." He was never able to transcend the title "great humorist" nor the expectations of his audiences, who wanted more of what he was either loathe or unable to give. He regretted he'd ever made the speech. It over-shadowed his identity and his dreams. Yet without it, there would be little of the man to remember.

With the introduction of J. Proctor Knott, then, a kind of reversal of historical approaches is necessary. Usually we are familiar with the man and so we read his speeches. In this instance, it is the speech which excites interest in the man, and, if research can be trusted, Knott appears to be right -- he is different from the tone and flavor of the speech, but perhaps no less interesting.

This dignified, scholarly, even sentimental man was born near Raywock, Marion County, Kentucky, on August 29, 1830. His ancestors were from the landed gentry and for generations had supplied clergymen to the Church of England. He was given a thorough and classical education by his father who was a school teacher in Washington County, and he later attended Columbia Seminary in Lebanon, Kentucky.

When his father opened a school in Shelbyville, Knott became its "professor of natural science." He later taught at Big Springs in Breckinridge County and in Lebanon. While there he became interested in law and studied under the Honorable Clement Hill.

Having decided to become a lawyer, Knott also chose to leave Kentucky, and he moved to Scotland County, Missouri. He wrote of his arrival that he came "with a Sunday suit, some law books and a five-franc piece." He was soon admitted to the Missouri bar and at the age of twenty-seven he represented Scotland County in the Missouri Legislature. He was appointed Chairman of the Judicial Committee and conducted the impeachment proceedings of one Judge Albert Jackson of Stoddard County, who was accused of high crimes and misdemeanors. Knott's prosecution speech of this occasion brought him immediate attention, and Jackson's subsequent conviction established the young lawyer as a strong force in the future of Missouri politics.

In 1858, Governor Robert M. Steward appointed Knott to fill the unexpired term of Attorney General Ephriam B. Ewing, and two years later he was elected to the same office. In the same year he was chosen as a delegate to the Democratic National Convention. But his speedy rise to prominence was soon abruptly halted.

Knott tried hard to keep Missouri from becoming involved

in the Civil War, although his feelings for the individual rights of the states were well-known. As a result of his convictions, he refused to take an oath of allegiance to the federal government. He felt that he took such an oath upon assuming his office and that was all the constitution should demand. He wrote to his mother his justification for his action:

> I denied the right of any minion of oppression to compel me to take an oath of any kind whatever without the sanction of law, and I would have suffered myself to be impaled upon the bayonets of his mercenaries before I would have succumbed to his unauthorized behests.

He was imprisoned for a short time as a result of his refusal, and his days in Missouri were obviously numbered. He also told his mother:

> Well, we have a brand new Executive department in Missouri made ostensibly to secure peace and quiet in the state, but designed really in my opinion to fasten us with links of steel to the hideous juggernaught that is crushing the vitals out of our Constitution and grinding into the dust every vestige of American liberty -- I think of Missouri not as being the great battle field for the settlement of our National disputes but the theatre of another "War of the Roses" with its literal fratricidal strifes, besides the attendant train of unnumbered, unimagined calamities.

There are shades of sarcasm evident in these words, but the heaviness of heart does not presage the Swiftian wit that was to erupt ten years later.

After his release from prison, Knott returned to Lebanon, Kentucky, and opened a law office there. He was obviously looking for a fresh beginning, and he would soon duplicate his Missouri-initiated pattern of political growth.

In 1867 Knott was elected to the House of Representatives and remained in that body for sixteen years. His first formal speech was in March, 1868, when he spoke in opposition to a bill "to Guarantee a Republican Form of Government to the States." As always he was on the side of individual states' rights.

The next year he made a speech which astounded his supporters and confused his opponents, but it was not for its humor; it was rather for its amazing delivery. In speaking on the universal suffrage question, Knott cited fifty-two verbatim long passages from legal sources without once using either notes or books. *The Courier-Journal* said of this address:

> *By this masterly argument if by nothing else, he established his position as one of the few able lawyers in the House. In Kentucky he is justly regarded as one of our foremost party leaders in sagacity, integrity, and discretion.*

On January 27, 1871, Knott sent off his oratorical skyrocket. A bill was introduced at the opening of the third session of the 41st Congress which asked for an extension of time for construction of a railroad from the St. Croix River to the West Coast of Lake Superior, with a branch to the town of Bayfield, Missouri. The title to the lands was to revert to the builders of the road when construction of the line was completed. Apparently the bill aroused little interest until Knott requested time to speak on it. He was against giving away of the public domain and began his speech in a serious, almost obsequious vein; but soon he dipped into satire by poking fun at the little settlement of Duluth, with its 2,000 inhabitants, the lake terminus of the railroad. He then proceeded, in a series of exaggerated rhetorical questions, to reduce the bill's consideration to inanity. As he continued speaking, the galleries convulsed in laughter, "applauding his witty sallies, the effect of which was heightened by his comic style of delivery."

What had possessed him? According to a biographer, "The speech came as a surprise even to the closest friend of the orator." Apparently, without precedent, Knott was the wittiest man in Congress, "the hero of Duluth," a very funny fellow. But he could never again make his peers take him seriously. He could never show that grave, solemn side that had driven him to political fame in two states without his listeners expecting an outburst of burlesque or bombast.

Knott became governor of Kentucky for one term from 1883-1887 and was afterward a delegate to the Kentucky Constitutional Convention of 1891 which drew the present constitution of the state. He organized and served as Dean of the Law School of Centre College, returning to those early preoccupations with scholarly, serious pursuits.

James Proctor Knott died in Lebanon, Kentucky, in 1911. The population of Lebanon at that time was 3,000; the population of Duluth was 80,000.

The following poem, in Knott's handwriting, may confirm what philosophers have long suspected about comics -- deep down, beneath that veneer of levity and whims, is a tender, soulful heart.

I

Be near me, darling, in my last, sad hour,
  And softly kneel my lowly couch beside,
When neither Love, nor Pity hath the power
  To stay the ebb of Life's fast failing tide —
When on my cold and pallid brow shall rest
  The clammy dew of Azrael's fatal breath,
And this fond heart — to thine so often pressed
  Grow still beneath the icy touch of Death.

II

Be near one that thy loving eyes may light
  My weary spirit on its lonely way
Amid the gloom of that long, starless night,
  For which there waits no dawn of coming day.
Enchain thine arms about my neck, and press
  Upon my parchèd lips thy farewell kiss
And with the rapture of thy last caress
  Inspire my parting soul with deathless bliss

III

But Oh! I know thou canst not come to me —
Between us now there yawns a gulf as wide
And dark, as that eternal, shoreless sea
Whose stagnant depths the buried millions hide.
To pass that bourne, I know thou hast no power —
Another fondly claims thee as his own
And thou must smile on _him_ in that sad hour
When I must go to Death's cold realm — _alone_,*

*Courtesy, Kentucky Library, Western Kentucky University

Hon. J. Proctor Knott

(This speech was delivered in the House of Representatives, January 27, 1871; and few well-read persons visit Congress, even at this late date, without seeking a glimpse of the author of "the speech on Duluth.")

The House having under consideration the joint resolution (S. R. No. 11) extending the time to construct a railroad from the St. Croix River or lake to the west end of Lake Superior and to Bayfield, Mr. Knott said:

Mr. Speaker: If I could be actuated by any conceivable inducement to betray the sacred trust reposed in me by those whose generous confidence I am indebted for the honor of a seat on this floor; if I could be influenced by any possible consideration to become instrumental in giving away, in violation of their known wishes, any portion of their interest in the public domain for the mere promotion of any railroad enterprise whatever, I should certainly feel a strong inclination to give this measure my most earnest and hearty support; for I am assured that its success would materially enhance the pecuniary prosperity of some of the most valued friends I have on earth; friends for whose accommodation I would be willing to make almost any sacrifice not involving my personal honor or my fidelity as the trustee of an express trust. And that fact of itself would be sufficient to countervail almost any objection I might entertain to the passage of this bill, not inspired by an imperative and inexorable sense of public duty.

But, independent of the seductive influences of private friendship, to which I admit I am, perhaps, as susceptible as any of the gentlemen I see around me, the intrinsic merits of the measure itself are of such extraordinary character as to commend it most strongly to the favorable consideration of every member of this House, myself not excepted, notwithstanding my constituents, in whose behalf alone I am acting here, would not be benefited by its passage one particle more than they would be by a project to cultivate an orange grove on the bleakest summit of Greenland's icy mountains.

Now sir, as to those great truck lines of railway, spanning the continent from ocean to ocean, I confess my mind has never been fully made up. It is true they may afford some trifling advantages to local traffic, and they may even in time become the channels of a more extended commerce. Yet I have never been thoroughly satisfied either of the necessity or expediency of projects promising such meager results to the great body of our people. But with regard to the transcendent merits of the gigantic enterprise contemplated in this bill I never entertained the shadow of a doubt.

Years ago, when I first heard that there was somewhere in the vast terra incognita, somewhere in the bleak regions of the great Northwest, a stream of water known to the nomadic inhabitants of the neighborhood as the river St. Croix, I became satisfied that the construction of a railroad from that raging torrent to some point in the civilized world was essential to the happiness and prosperity of the American people, if not absolutely indispensable to the perpetuity of republican institutions on this continent. I felt instinctively that the boundless resources of that prolific region of sand and pine shrubbery would never be fully developed without a railroad constructed and equipped at the expense of the Government, and perhaps not then. I had an abiding presentiment that, some day or other, the people of this whole country, irrespective of party affiliations, regardless of sectional prejudices, and without distinction of race, color or previous condition of servitude, would rise in their majesty and demand an outlet for the barrens, drained in the rainy season by the surging waters of the turbid St. Croix.

These impressions, derived simply and solely from the eternal fitness of things, were not only strengthened by the interesting and eloquent debate on this bill, to which I listened with so much pleasure the other day, but intensified, if possible, as I read over this morning the lively colloquy which took place on that occasion, as I find it reported in last Friday's *Globe*. I will ask the indulgence of the House while I read a few short passages, which are sufficient, in my judgement, to place the merits of the great enterprise contemplated in the measure now under discussion beyond all possible controversy.

The honorable gentleman from Minnesota (Mr. Wilson) who, I believe is managing this bill, in speaking of the character of the country through which this railroad is to pass, says this:

We want to have the timber brought to us as cheaply as possible. Now, if you tie up the lands in this way, so that no title can be obtained to them -- for no settler will go on these lands, for he cannot make a living -- you deprive us of the benefit of that timber.

Now, sir, I would not have it by any means inferred from this that the gentleman from Minnesota would insinuate that the people out in his section desire this timber merely for the purpose of fencing up their farms so that their stock may not wander off and die of starvation among the bleak hills of the St. Croix. I read it for no such purpose, sir, and make no such comment on it myself. In corroboration of this statement of the gentleman from Minnesota, I find this testimony given by the honorable gentleman from Wisconsin (Mr. Washburn). Speaking of these same lands, he says:

Under the bill, as amended by my friend from Minnesota, nine-tenths of the land is open to actual settlers at $2.50 per acre; the remaining one-tenth is pine-timbered land, that is not fit for settlement, and never will be settled upon; but the timber will be cut off. I admit that it is the most valuable portion of the grant, for most of the grant is not valuable. It is quite valueless; and if you put in this amendment of the gentleman from Indiana, you may as well just kill the bill, for no man and no company will take the grant and build the road.

I simply pause to ask some gentlemen better versed in the science of mathematics than I am to tell me, if the timbered lands are in fact the most valuable portion of that section of country, and they would be entirely valueless without the timber that is on them, what the remainder of the land is worth which has no timber on it at all.

But further on I find a most entertaining and instructive interchange of views between the gentleman from Arkansas (Mr. Rogers), and the gentleman from Wisconsin (Mr. Washburn), and the gentleman from Maine (Mr. Peters) upon the subject of pine lands generally, which I will tax the patience of the House to read:

Mr. Rogers -- Will the gentleman allow me to ask him a question?

Mr. Washburn, of Wisconsin -- Certainly.

Mr. Rogers -- Are these pine lands entirely worthless except for timber?

Mr. Washburn, of Wisconsin -- They are generally worthless for any other purpose. I am perfectly familiar with that subject. These lands are not valuable for purposes of settlement.

Mr. Farnsworth -- They will be after the timber is taken off.

Mr. Washburn, of Wisconsin -- No, sir.

Mr. Rogers -- I want to know the character of these pine lands.

Mr. Washburn, of Wisconsin -- They are generally sandy, barren lands. My friend from the Green Bay district (Mr. Sawyer) is himself perfectly familiar with this question, and he will bear me out in what I say, that these pine-timber lands are not adapted to settlement.

Right: Portrait of Barton W. Stone
Courtesy, Disciples of Christ Historical Society

BORN 1772 - DIED 1844

Below: Artist's sketch of Stone preaching at Cane Ridge, August 7-12, 1801
Courtesy, Disciples of Christ Historical Society

CANE RIDGE REVIVAL

an artist of an opening phase of the revival held at Cane Ridge, Bourbon County, tucky, August 7-12, 1801.

HENRY CLAY
Courtesy, Kentucky Library

BEN HARDIN
Courtesy, Jack Muir

JOHN J. CRITTENDEN
Courtesy, Kentucky Library

RICHARD MENEFEE
Courtesy, Kentucky Library

CASSIUS M. CLAY
Courtesy, Kentucky Department of Public Information

" July 8 – 1898.
For Genl. Green Clay" – Now
White Hall, Ky. – Colyer Meriwether
&c. I send you vol. 1. of my
Life &c. – vol. 2d – not yet out –
for the S. H. Association, in lieu
of subscription; as my means
are limited. My eyes are weak
from the criminal "Vendetta"
waged against me by my divorced
wife Mary Jane Warfield Clay,
– who cannot marry again during
my life.
          Truly C. M. Clay.

" Don't give up
the Ship" –

I send my views on the
Political situation.
          C. M. Clay.

Typical of Cassius Clay's curt notes

JOHN C. BRECKINRIDGE
Courtesy, Kentucky Library

J. PROCTER KNOTT
Courtesy, Kentucky Library

your Friend
Henry Watterson

HENRY WATTERSON
Courtesy, Kentucky Library

Carry A Nation
Your loving
Home Defender

CARRY NATION
From her autobiography

LAURA CLAY around 1880
Courtesy, Ester Bennett

AUGUSTUS O. STANLEY

ALBEN BARKLEY
Courtesy, Kentucky Department of Public Information

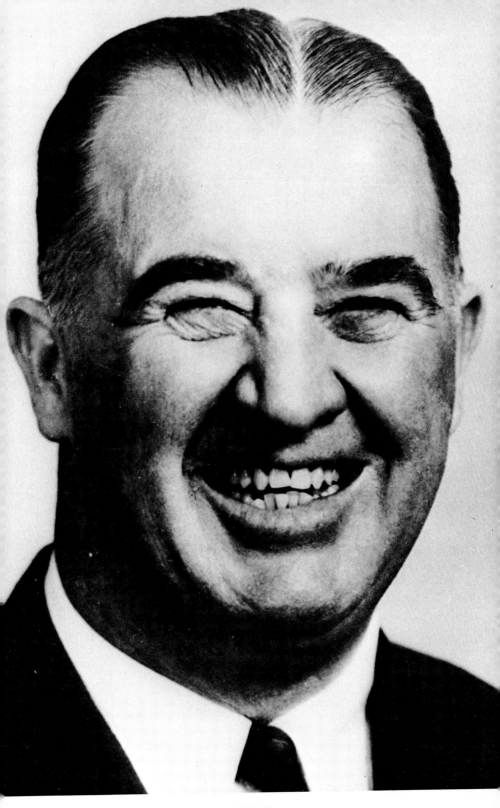

A.B. CHANDLER
Courtesy of Mr. Chandler

Mr. Rogers -- The pine lands to which I am accustomed are generally very good. What I want to know is, what is the difference between our pine lands and your pine lands.

Mr. Washburn, of Wisconsin -- The pine tree timber of Wisconsin generally grows upon barren, sandy land. The gentleman from Maine (Mr. Peters), who is familiar with pine lands, will I have no doubt, say that pine timber grows generally upon the most barren lands.

Mr. Peters -- As a general thing pine lands are not worth much for cultivation.

And further on I find this pregnant question, the joint production of the two gentlemen from Wisconsin:

Mr. Paine -- Does my friend from Indiana suppose that in any event settlers will occupy and cultivate these pine lands?

Mr. Washburn, of Wisconsin -- Particularly without a railroad.

Yes sir, 'particularly without a railroad.' It will be asked after awhile, I am afraid, if settlers will go anywhere unless the Government builds a railroad for them to go on. I desire to call attention to only one more statement, which I think sufficient to settle the question. It is one made by the gentleman from Wisconsin (Mr. Paine) who says:

These lands will be abandoned for the present. It may be that at some remote period there will spring up in that region a new kind of agriculture which will cause a demand for these particular lands; and they may then come into use and be valuable for agricultural purposes. But I know, and I cannot help thinking that my friend from Indiana understands, that for the present, and for many years to come, these pine lands can have no possible value other than that arising from the pine timber which stands on them.

Now, sir, who, after listening to this emphatic and un-equivocal testimony of these intelligent, competent, and able-bodied witnesses; who that is not as incredulous as St. Thomas himself will doubt for a moment that the Goshen of America is to be found in the sandy valleys and upon the pine-clad hills of the St. Croix? Who will have the hardihood to rise in his seat on this floor and assert that, excepting the pine bushes, the entire region would not produce vegetation enough in ten years to fatten a grasshopper? Where is the patriot who is willing that his country shall incur the peril of remaining another day without the amplest railroad connection with such an inexhaustible mine of agricultural wealth? Who will answer for the consequences of abandoning a great and warlike people, in possession of a country like that, to brood over the indifference and neglect of their Government? How long would it be before they would take to studying the Declaration of Independence and hatching out the damnable heresy of secession? How long before the grim demon of civil discord would rear again his horrid head in our midst, 'gnash loud his iron fangs and shake his crest of bristling bayonets'?

Then, sir, think of the long and painful process of reconstruction that must follow, with its concomitant amendments to the Constitution; the seventeenth, eighteenth, and nineteenth articles. The sixteenth, it is of course understood, is to be appropriated to those blushing damsels who are, day after day, beseeching us to let them vote, hold office, drink cocktails, ride astraddle, and do everything else the men do. But above all, sir, let me implore you to reflect for a single moment on the deplorable condition of our country in cause of a foreign war, with all our ports blocked, all our cities in a state of seige, the gaunt specter of famine brooding like a hungry vulture over our starving land; our commissary stores all exhausted, and our famishing armies withering away in the field, a helpless prey to the insatiate demon of hunger; our Navy rotting in the docks for want of provisions for our gallant seamen, and we without any railroad communication whatever with the prolific pine thickets of the St. Croix.

Ah, sir, I could very well understand why my amiable friends from Pennsylvania (Mr. Myers, Mr. Kelley, and Mr. O'Neill) should be so earnest in their support of this bill the other day, and if their honorable colleague, my friend, Mr. Randall, will pardon the remark, I will say I considered his criticism of their action on that occasion as not only unjust but ungenerous. I knew they were looking forward with the far-reaching ken of enlightened statesmanship to the pitiable condition in which Philadelphia will be left unless speedily supplied with railroad connection in some way or other with this garden spot of the universe. And besides, sir, this discussion has relieved my mind of a mystery that has weighed upon it like an incubus for years. I could never understand before why there was so much excitement during the last Congress over the acquisition of Alta Vela. I could never understand why it was that some of our ablest statesmen and most disinterested patriots should entertain such dark forebodings of the untold calamities that were to befall our beloved country unless we should take immediate possession of that desirable island. But I see now that they were laboring under the mistaken impression that the Government would need the guano to manure the public lands on the St. Croix.

Now sir, I repeat I have been satisfied for years that if there was any portion of the inhabited globe absolutely in a suffering condition for want of railroad it was these teeming pine barrens of the St. Croix. At what particular point on that noble stream such a road should be commenced I knew was immaterial, and so it seems to have been considered by the draftsman of this bill. It might be up at the spring or down at the foot-log, or the water-gate, or the fish-dam, or anywhere along the bank, no matter where. But in what direction should it run, or where should it terminate were always to my mind questions of the most painful perplexity. I could conceive of no place on 'God's green earth' in such straitened circumstances for railroad facilities as to be likely to desire or willing to accept such a connection. I knew that neither Bayfield nor Superior City would have it, for they both indignantly spurned the munificence of the Government when coupled with such ignominious conditions, and let this very same land grant die on their hands years and years ago, rather than submit to the degradation of a direct communication by railroad with the piney woods of the St. Croix; and I knew that what the enterprising inhabitants of those giant young cities would refuse to take would have few charms for others, whatever their necessities or cupidity might be.

Hence, as I have said, sir, I was utterly at a loss to determine where the terminus of this great and indispensable road should be until I accidentally overheard some gentlemen the other day mention the name of "Duluth!" Duluth! The word fell upon my ear with peculiar and indescribable charm, like the gentle murmur of a low fountain stealing forth in the midst of roses, or the soft, sweet accents of an angel's whisper in the bright, joyous dream of sleeping innocence. Duluth! 'Twas the name for which my soul had panted for years, as the hart panteth for the water-brooks. But where was Duluth? Never, in all my limited reading, had my vision been gladdened by seeing the celestial word in print. And I felt a profounder humiliation in my ignorance that its dulcet syllables had never before ravished my delighted ear. I was certain the draftsman of this bill had never heard of it, or it would have been designated as one of the termini of this road. I asked my friends about it, but they knew nothing of it. I rushed to the library and examined all the maps I could find. I discovered in one of them a delicate, hair-like line, diverging from the Mississippi near a place marked Prescott, which I supposed was intended to represent the river St. Croix, but I could nowhere find Duluth.

Nevertheless, I was confident it existed somewhere, and that its discovery would constitute the crowning glory of the present century, if not of all modern times. I knew it was bound to exist in the very nature of things; that the symmetry and perfection of our planetary system would be incomplete without it, that the elements of material nature would long since have resolved themselves back into original chaos if there had been such a hiatus in creation as would have resulted from leaving out Duluth. In fact sir, I was overwhelmed with the conviction that Duluth not only existed somewhere, but that wherever it was it was a great and glorious place. I was convinced that the greatest calamity that ever befell the benighted nations of the ancient world was in their having passed away without a knowledge of the actual existence of Duluth; that their fabled Atlantis, never seen save by the hallowed vision of inspired poesy, was, in fact, but another name for Duluth; that the golden orchard of the Hesperides was but a poetical synonym for the beer gardens in the vicinity of Duluth. I was certain that Herodotus had died a miserable death because in all his travels and with all his geo-graphical research he had never heard of Duluth. I knew that if the immortal spirit of Homer could look down, from another heaven than that created by his own celestial genius, upon the long likes of pilgrims from every nation of the earth to the gushing fountain of poesy opened by the touch of his magic wand, if he could be permitted to hold the vast assemblage of grand and glorious strains, he would weep tears of bitter anguish that, instead of lavishing all the stores of his mighty genius upon the fall of Ilion, it had not been his more blessed lot to crystallize in deathless song the rising glories of Duluth.

Yet, sir, had it not been for this map, kindly furnished me by the Legislature of Minnesota, I might have gone down to my obscure and humble grave in an agony of despair, because I could nowhere find Duluth. Had such been my melancholy fate, I have no doubt that, with the last feeble pulsation of my breaking heart, with the last faint exhalation of my fleeting breath, I should have whispered, "Where is Duluth?"

But, thanks to the beneficence of that band of min-istering angels who have their bright abodes in the far-off capital of Minnesota, just as the agony of my anxiety was about to culminate in the frenzy of despair, this blessed map was placed in my hands; and, as I unfolded it, a resplendent scene of in-effable glory opened before me, such as I imagine burst upon the enraptured vision of the wandering peri through the opening gates of paradise. There, for the first time, my enchanted eye rested upon the ravishing word "Duluth."

This map, sir, is intended, as it appears from its title, to illustrate the position of Duluth in the United States; but if gentlemen will examine it, I think they will concur with me in the opinion that it is far too modest in its pretensions. It not only illustrates the position of Duluth in the United States, but exhibits its relations with all created things. It even goes further than this. It lifts the shadowy veil of futurity and affords us a view of the golden prospects of Duluth far along the dim vista of ages yet to come.

If gentlemen will examine it, they will find Duluth not only in the center of the map, but represented in the center of a series of concentric circles one hundred miles apart, and some of them as much as four thousand miles in diameter, embracing alike in their tremendous sweep the fragrant savannas of the sun-lit South and the eternal solitudes of snow that mantle the ice-bound North. How these circles were produced is perhaps one of those primordial mysteries that the most skillful paleologist will never be able to explain. But the fact is, sir, Duluth is pre-eminently a central place, for I am told by gentlemen who have been so reckless of their own personal safety as to venture away into those awful regions where Duluth is supposed to be, that it is so exactly in the center of the visible universe that the sky comes down at precisely the same distance all around it.

I find, by reference to this map, that Duluth is situated somewhere near the western end of Lake Superior, but as there is not a dot or other mark indicating its exact location, I am unable to say whether it is actually confined to any particular spot, or whether "it is just lying around there loose." I really cannot tell whether it is one of those ethereal creations of intellectual frost-work, more intangible than the rose-tinted clouds of a summer sunset; one of those airy exhalations of the speculator's brain, which I am told are ever flitting in the form of towns and cities along those lines of railroad, built with Government subsidies, luring the unwary settler as the mirage of the desert lures the famishing traveler on, and ever on, until it fades away in the darkening horizon, or whether it is a real *bona fide*, substantial city, all "staked off," with the lots marked with their owner's names, like that proud commercial metropolis recently discovered on the desirable shores of San Domingo. But, however, that may be, I am satisfied Duluth is out there, or thereabout, for I see it stated here on this map that it is exactly thirty-nine hundred and ninety miles from Liverpool, though I have no doubt, for the sake of convenience, it will be moved back ten miles, so as to make the distance an even four thousand.

Then, sir, there is the climate of Duluth, unquestionably the most salubrious and delightful to be found anywhere on the Lord's earth. Now, I have always been under the impression, as I presume other gentlemen have, that in the region around Lake Superior it was cold enough for at least nine months in the year to freeze the smokestack off a locomotive. But I see it represented on this map that Duluth is situated exactly half way between the latitudes of Paris and Venice, so that gentlemen who have inhaled the exhilarating airs of the one, or basked in the golden sunlight of the other, may see at a glance that Duluth must be a place of untold delights, a terrestrial paradise, fanned by the balmy zephyrs of an eternal spring, clothed in the gorgeous sheen of ever-blooming flowers, and vocal with the silvery melody of nature's choicest songsters. In fact, sir, since I have seen this map I have no doubt that Byron was vainly endeavoring to convey some faint conception of the delicious charms of Duluth when his poetic soul gushed forth in the rippling strains of that beautiful rhapsody:

Know ye the land of the cedar and vine
Where the flowers ever blossom, the beams ever shine;
Where the light wings of Zephyr, oppressed with perfume,
Wax faint o'er the gardens of Gul in her bloom;
Where the citron and olive are fairest of fruit,
And the voice of the nightingale never is mute:
Where the tints of the earth and the hues of the sky,
In color though varied, in beauty may vie?

As to the commercial resources of Duluth, sir, they are simply illimitable and inexhaustible, as is shown by this map. I see it stated here that there is a vast scope of territory, embracing an area of over two million square miles, rich in every element of material wealth and commercial prosperity, all tributary to Duluth. Look at it, sir. Here are inexhaustible mines of gold, immeasurable veins of silver, impenetrable depths of boundless forest, vast coal-measures, wide, extended plains of richest pasturage, all, all embraced in this vast territory, which must, in the very nature of things, empty the untold treasures of its commerce into the lap of Duluth.

Look at it, sir! (pointing to the map) Do not you see from these broad, brown lines drawn around this immense territory that the enterprising inhabitants of Duluth intend some day to inclose it all in one vast corral, so that its commerce will be bound to go there whether it would or not? And here, sir, (still pointing to the map) I find within a convenient distance the Piegan Indians, which, of all the many accessories to the glory of Duluth, I consider by far the most inestimable. For, sir, I have been told that when the small-pox breaks out among the women and children of that famous tribe, as it sometimes does, they afford the finest subjects in the world for the strategical experiments of any enterprising military hero who desires to improve himself in the noble art of war; especially for any valiant lieutenant-general whose

> Trenchant blade, Toledo rusty,
> For want of fighting has grown rusty,
> And eats into itself for lack
> Of somebody to hew and hack.

Sir, the great conflict now raging in the old world has presented a phenomenon in military science unprecedented in the annals of mankind, a phenomenon that has reversed all the traditions of the past as it has disappointed all the expectations of the present. A great and warlike people, renowned alike for their skill and valor, have been swept away before the triumphant advance of an inferior foe, like autumn stubble before a hurricane of fire. For aught I know, the next flash of electric fire that shimmers along the ocean cable may tell us that Paris, with every fiber quivering with the agony of impotent despair, writhes beneath the conquering heel of her loathed invader. Ere another moon shall wax and wane, the brightest star in the galaxy of nations may fall from the zenith of her glory, never to rise again. Ere the modest violets of early spring shall ope their beauteous eyes, the genius of civilization may chant the wailing requiem of the proudest nationality the world has ever seen, as she scatters her withered and tear-moistened lilies o'er the bloody tomb of butchered France. But, sir, I wish to ask if you honestly and candidly believe that the Dutch would have ever overrun the French in that kind of style if General Sheridan had not gone over there and told King William and Von Moltke how he had managed to whip the Piegan Indians.

And here, sir, recurring to this map, I find in the immediate vicinity of the Pigeans "vast herds of buffalo" and "immense fields of rich wheat lands."

(Here the hammer fell. Many cries: "Go on!" "Go on!")

The Speaker. Is there objection to the gentleman from Kentucky continuing his remarks? The Chair hears none. The gentleman will proceed.

Mr. Knott. I was remarking, sir, upon these vast "wheat fields," represented on this map as in the immediate neighborhood of the buffaloes and the Piegans, and was about to say that the idea of there being these immense wheat fields in the very heart of a wilderness, hundreds and hundreds of miles beyond the utmost verge of civilization, may appear to some gentlemen as rather incongruous, as rather too great a strain on the "blankets" of veracity. But to my mind there is no difficulty in the matter whatever. The phenomenon is very easily accounted for. It is evident, sir, that the Piegans sowed that wheat there and plowed it with buffalo bulls. Now, sir, this fortunate combination of buffaloes and Piegans, considering their relative positions to each other and to Duluth, as they are arranged on this map, satisfies me that Duluth is destined to be the beef market of the world.

Here you will observe (pointing to the map) are the buffaloes, directly between the Piegans and Duluth, and here, right on the road to Duluth, are the Creeks. Now, sir, when the buffaloes are sufficiently fat from grazing on these immense wheat fields, you see it will be the easiest thing in the world for the Piegans to drive them on down, stay all night with their friends, the Creeks, and go into Duluth in the morning. I think I see them now, sir, a vast herd of buffaloes, with their heads down, their eyes glaring, their nostrils dilated, their tongues out, and their tails curled over their backs, tearing along towards Duluth, with about a thousand Piegans on their grass-bellied ponies, yelling at their heels! On they come! And as they sweep past the Creeks, they join in the chase, and away they all go, yelling, bellowing, ripping, and rearing along, amid clouds of dust, until the last buffalo is safely penned in the stockyards of Duluth!

Sir, I might stand here for hours and hours, and expatiate with rapture upon the gorgeous prospects of Duluth, as depicted upon this map. But human life is too short, and the time of this House far too valuable, to allow me to linger longer upon the delightful theme. I think every gentleman on this floor is as well satisfied as I am that Duluth is destined to become the commercial metropolis of the universe, and that this road should be built at once. I am fully persuaded that no patriotic representative of the American people, who has a proper appreciation of the associated glories of Duluth and the St. Croix, will hesitate a moment to say that every able-bodied female in the land between the ages of eighteen and forty-five, who is in favor of "women's rights" should be drafted and set to work upon this great work without delay. Nevertheless, sir, it grieves my very soul to be compelled to say that I cannot vote for the grant of lands provided for in this bill.

Ah, sir, you can have no conception of the poignancy of my anguish that I am deprived of that blessed privilege! There are two insuperable obstacles in the way. In the first place, my constituents, for whom I am acting here, have no more interest in this road than they have in the great question of culinary taste now perhaps agitating the public mind of Dominica, as to whether the illustrious commissioners who recently left this capital for that free and enlightened republic would be better fricasseed, boiled or roasted and, in the second place, these lands, which I am asked to give away, alas, are not mine to bestow! My relation to them is simply that of trustee to an express trust, and shall I ever betray that trust? Never, sir! Rather perish Duluth! Perish the paragon of cities! Rather than let the freezing cyclones of the bleak Northwest bury it forever beneath the eddying sands of the raging St. Croix!

CHAPTER X

HENRY WATTERSON
(1840-1921)

Throughout his long and illustrious life, Henry Watterson was passionately interested in people. His friendships ran the gamut from barbers and waiters to presidents and kings. He was equally at home as a journalist and an orator, a Pulitzer Prize winning editor, a president-maker. He lived from the *Ante Bellum* to the "Reconstruction" period and was both an astute observer of history and a participant in the direction it took.[1]

Although Watterson was not a native Kentuckian, he spent fifty-three of his eighty-one years as a citizen of the state. He was born in Washington, D. C., on February 16, 1840, where his father served as a representative of the Ninth Congressional District from Tennessee. The political arena was his playground, but his frail health, as well as a boyhood accident which caused the loss of his right eye, made him more introspective than extroverted, more thoughtful than ebullient, and he early turned to writing as his active force for changing and promoting his civic concerns. For over fifty years, he was editor of the Louisville *Courier-Journal*, shaping and strengthening its editorial policies, its high quality of journalism, molding its reputation as one of the outstanding newspapers in the United States, a position which it holds to this day.

And as a powerful editor, he was thrust into the public eye, where he gained an equally strong repute as an orator. His first appearance as a public speaker was in 1870, when he gave the memorial address for George Prentice, the former editor of the *Journal*, before the state legislature. The lyrical quality of the eulogy demonstrates Watterson's love of the English language:

Prentice rests in a quiet spot, where the violets which he loved to sing, and the meadow-grass, that grew greener in his song, shall presently come and grow above him; where the stars which he made into a thousand images shall shine by night; where the quiet skies that gave the kindliest joy to his old age shall bend over his grave. He is dead to a world of love and pity and homage .... The man is dead. But Prentice is not dead. [2]

This oratorical ability led him into the role of political spokesman for every presidential campaign from the Grant-Colfax election of 1872 to the Wilson-Marshall election of 1912.

The Republican Convention of 1872 was held in Cincinnati and was Watterson's first venture into "president making." The Liberal Republican Convention nominated Horace Greeley as its candidate, and Watterson supported him. As the editor of a Democratic paper, Watterson had the responsibility of convincing his readers to support the Republican nominee. He wrote:

He is an able man. He is an honest man. He is a good man. He may be cranky -- he may be curious, according to one preconception. Who knows? We do know that Grant is an iron-hearted, wooden-headed nutmeg, warranted to kill .... So, feeling toward Horace Greeley downright affection, not unmingled with the fear of the boy that didn't know what confounded notion the old man might take in his head, only he was sure the old man would neither lie nor steal; we take Horace Greeley. [3]

These remarks seem more like left-handed compliments than enthusiastic convictions, but, as a supporter of the South during the Civil War, it must have been impossible for Watterson to support Grant, although he was a life-long Democrat. Nonetheless, Greeley was defeated and, within a month of the election, dead.

Following this unsuccessful attempt to get his candidate elected, Watterson became interested in supporting New York Governor Samuel Tilden as the Democratic Presidential nominee in 1876. His affinity for Tilden is explained by the following biographer:

> *Idealogically ... they were very close, both were essentially conservative, both respected wealth and the established rules safeguarding property. Both believed in what they regarded as the Jeffersonian concept of limited government, and both stood sincerely for reform in the North and the conservative home-rule in the South.*[4]

At that convention, Tilden's friends had Watterson elected convention chairman. Watterson later recounted that he was reluctant to serve because of his poor eyesight and his lack of knowledge of parliamentary law. But upon promise of help in the recognition of delegates and the assistance of a parliamentarian, he agreed to accept. According to Watterson:

> *I had barely time to write the required keynote speech, but not enough to commit it to memory; nor sight to read it, even had I been willing to adopt that mode of delivery. It would not do to trust extemporization. A friend, Col. J. Stoddard Johnston, who was familiar with my penmanship came to the rescue. Concealing my manuscript behind his hat, he lined the words out to me between the cheering, I having mastered a few opening sentences.*

He further discussed the difficulties and the excitements he encountered as an initially unwilling political leader:

> *I lost my parliamentarian at once. I just made parliamentary law as we went. Never before or since did any deliberate body proceed under manual so startling and original. But I delivered each ruling with a resonance -- it were better called an impudence -- which had an air of authority ... I never had a better day's sport in my life.*[5]

Tilden received the Democratic nomination, and Watterson was shortly afterward elected to fill the unexpired term of Edward Y. Parsons, the Democratic representative from Louisville to Congress. Although he had conducted a hurried campaign, he nonetheless won 11,567 of the 12,244 votes cast.

In the Tilden-Hayes election of 1867, Tilden received the majority of the electoral votes. However, a Congressional decision named Hayes the winner. Following this event, Watterson advised the Democrats:

> *First -- Preserve the party organization intact, without flaw or doubt. Second -- Suppress violent thoughts and extreme ejaculation, for anger never mended any cause. Third -- Treat Hayes like a gentleman until he proves himself a usurper by his acts.* [6]

Again, Watterson's candidate had lost, but his belief in his party never faltered. He was much involved with William Jennings Bryan in all three of his presidential campaigns.

It was in connection with Bryan's first campaign that Watterson coined one of his most famous phrases: "No compromise with dishonor." This motto became the battle cry for Bryan's opponents, the Gold Democrats, and did much to increase Watterson's popularity with his fellow Democrats. One writer wrote of his first public speech to follow the appearance of the phrase:

> *There was breathless silence as he rose and made his way to the edge of the platform. He stood erect; his one eye gleamed; his white hair waved like the plume of Henry of Ravarie. Raising his right hand he said in a voice vibrant with emotion: "My fellow Democrats." He got no further. The great audience burst into a cheer that crashed out like the roar of a mighty cataract. It was fully ten minutes before he was able to proceed .... He swept the crowd to its feet ....* [7]

Watterson's last attempt at presidential making was successful. In 1910, George Harvey, spokesman for the conservative element of the Democratic party introduced Watterson to Woodrow Wilson at a dinner party. Wilson's version of the meeting is preserved in a letter he wrote to a friend on the following day:

Last evening I dined with Colonel Watterson of the Louisville Courier-Journal, *Colonel Harvey of* Harper's Weekly *and James Smith, the reputed democratic boss of New Jersey. Whatever one may think of Colonel Watterson, there can be no doubt of his immense political influence in his section of the country, and indeed throughout the whole South. He came on to make my acquaintance and before the evening was over said that, if New Jersey would make me Governor, he would take off his coat and work for my nomination in 1912.* [8]

Watterson did indeed fulfill his promise to work for Wilson's nomination, and in July, 1911, he was in Lexington to address the Kentucky Bar Association. He stated:

Woodrow Wilson stands before the people today as the rarest of phenomena, a public man who, elevated to office, faithfully keeps his pre-election promises .... Since he has put on the robes of office, he has displayed qualities that reveal his equipment for a part in the public affairs which no other man in the nation seems equally suited. [9]

No doubt Watterson's associations with politicians, actors (he personally knew such notables as Edwin Booth, John Drew, Otis Skinner and Mary Anderson), writers such as Mark Twain, whom he frequently saw, and others in the public eye gave him an immense appreciation for the visible audience, and he was launched on his career as a lecturer in an 1877 tour. This proved so profitable, financially and personally, that he later scheduled many more such tours. He stated that he was first impressed with the power of oratory as a small boy when he attended a camp-meeting and saw "dry theology translated into dramatic fervor."[10]

However, Watterson was not what would be called an effective speaker. He had a high-pitched voice and "his gestures too forced, abrupt, and repetitious." He also appeared to be ill at ease and very conscious of his audience during the first few minutes of his speeches. Despite such handicaps, he seemed always to achieve results. In discussing his oratory, one biographer remarked:

> His listeners within the first few minutes became accustomed to his voice, to the curiously erratic sawing motions of his arms, and the intense, piercing glance of his one good eye. They were impressed with his classical allusion, the sonorous rhythm of his sentences, and were deeply moved by the sentiments of patriotism he expressed. But mostly, they were caught by the charm of his personality which not even the still formality of the lectern could hide.[11]

And one member of the audience at a speech given in Louisville in 1877 wrote:

> The speech was characteristic, clear, candid, finished and graceful, breathing the same noble sentiments of heroism, evicting the same lofty spirit of liberal patriotism as when chronicling the death of Lee, the loved chieftain of the South ....[12]

By 1896, Watterson was almost as well known as an orator as a journalist. He was in demand as a speaker at all kinds of public gatherings: as an after-dinner speaker, a convention keynoter, a special occasion orator. He spoke, for instance, at the Indiana Press Association meeting in 1873, the Decoration Day commemoration at the National Cemetery in Nashville in 1877, and the Dedication of the World's Fair in Chicago in 1874. Devotion to his country and idealism permeated all his addresses. Exemplary of this constant theme is a speech delivered at Georgetown College on the occasion of the hundredth anniversary of the settlement of Kentucky:

I did not come here my friends to deliver what is called "an oration." I came to talk to you of Kentucky, as a Kentuckian; for though I was not born within the geographic lines which embrace what old Daniel Boone called " the country of Kentucke," it is the land of my forefathers, as of yours, made sacred to my heart by more green mounds than I have living kindred .... I go to sleep and dream .... I behold, in the gorgeous vision which comes to me in sleep, a Kentucky, realizing the ecstasy of Boone, "a second paradise" .... I say I dream of this; but I should add that I am a believer in dreams.[13]

Watterson died in 1921, at the age of eighty-one. *The New York Times* acknowledgement of his death was, in part:

That Watterson style, pungent, vivid, superlatively personal; those adhesive epithets, that storm of arrows, those 'razzers flying through the air, the ludicrous imagination, the swift sarcasm, the free frolic of ir- responsible manner, -- it was as if the page were not written but spoken and acted before you.[14]

The Compromises of Life

This speech was given on many occasions by Watterson. It was one of his "lecture circuit" addresses.

It is given out by those who have investigated the subject, and who think they have got at the facts, that the earth which we inhabit is round. I shall take this for granted, therefore, and observe that its movement is rotary. Hogarth's line of beauty and grace represents a simple, serpentine curve. The rainbow of hope and promise is semi-circular. The broad surface of the ocean, stretching away as far as eye can see in calm or storm -- a dream of peace or a nightmare of horrors -- is one vast oval of wave and sky. And life, which we are told is rounded by a sleep, must conform to nature's laws, or beat itself against the walls within whose rugged circumference nature dwells, for as nature abhors a vacuum, so she detests an angle, particularly in ideas, engineering, and women.

It is well to walk in a straight line, but the man who piques himself upon doing this, looking neither backward nor forward, nor to the right nor the left, is likely after a while to strike something, and, unless his heart is of stone, or iron, be sure it will not be the obstruction that yields the right of way.

Thackeray once wrote a queer little essay entitled "A Plea for Shams." It was merely a protest against brute literalism and an appeal for what certain cynics used to call French courtesy.

"Tell only the truth," exclaims the adage, "but do not always tell the truth," which means that we are not obliged to tell all we know merely because we know it and it is true. "Who gives this woman away?" says the clergyman in the half-empty, dim-lighted church. "I could," whispers a voice away down the darkling aisle. "I could, but I won't," a very sensible conclusion, as we must all allow.

I am to talk to you this evening about the Compromises of Life. That means that I am to talk to you about a great many things connected with the journey 'twixt Dan and Beersheba; for, as I have said, the world we live in is a compromise with warring elements and the Government we support is a compromise with conflicting interests, while life, itself, is but a compromise with death. If each man and each woman on our planet took the law into their hands, and stood for their individual, inalienable, abstract rights, resolved to have their will, or die, the result might vindicate the everlasting verities, but it would ultimately leave mankind and womankind in the position of the two feline controversialists who are supposed to have argued out their differences to a logical conclusion in the good County Kilkenny, some centuries ago. Happily, it is otherwise. Reasonable people take their cue from nature, whose law is live and let live, and, as a consequence, we have love and marriage, trade and barter, politics and parties, banks and babies, railroads and funerals, courts of equity and churches and jails, all regulated by a system of time-tables arranged somewhere beyond the stars and moving toward that shoreless ocean which we call eternity, and which will presently engulf us every one.

You will, I dare say, think me both paradoxical and heterodoxical when I declare to you that Truth is sometimes a great liar, that is to say that that may be true to the letter which is false to the spirit, and *vice versa*; Truth made by malice and cunning to serve the purpose of the basest wrong. On the other hand, there are certain lies, which we call white lies, because they are meant to do no ill, or mischief, but they rather are intended to spare sensibilities and to save trouble. Often they do neither; not infrequently they aggravate both. There is no one among us, I am sure, who has not had occasion to lament the miscarriage of some honest, amiable fiction, contrived, as we thought, most ingeniously to prevent White from knowing just what Black said, or did, and for putting everybody in a good humor. The angel who takes account of these things may sigh over them, though I fancy in the end, as was observed of Uncle Toby, he will blot them off his book with a tear, because, after all, they are only compromises between fact and fancy, whose roots, springing from love, or pity, have been watered by human kindness.

A quaint old friend of mine, whose copious draughts from the well of English picturesque were only equalled by his great integrity of character and goodness of heart, met a lady acquaintance at an evening party, and the conversation turned upon real estate, in which the two had considerable interest.

"Mrs. Grunty," says my friend, "you shorely didn't sell that lot o' your'n on Preston Street for five hundred dollars?"

The lady said she certainly had.

"Why, bless me," says my friend, "you could a' got six hundred for it!"

Next day the lady's agent called on my friend, offering an exact duplicate of the lot in question and demanding the advance price, according to the terms of the conversation of the previous evening.

"Why, bless me," exclaimed my friend, "did I tell her that? Dear, dear! Why, I was only a-entertainin' of her!"

This was the gentleman who, being asked on the witness-stand how he made his living, naively replied: "A-going of security and a-paying of the debt."

In neither of these instances was he strictly accurate; and yet, I venture to believe that, in that land where he long ago went to make his home forever, he has paid whatever penalty was fixed on the harmless compromises which his amiability sometimes made with the ruder things of this world.

In short, life, which is full enough of corners, every corner having its briers and brambles, would be unendurable if people always yielded to the impulse of the moment, and nothing to good sense and good feeling, blurting out the truth just as the humor seized them.

The truth to-day is not always the truth to-morrow. Each day is a kaleidoscope, changing its form and figures with every hour, from grave to gay, from lively to severe, from morn to noon, from noon to dewy eve, and he is the wisest who makes the most happiness, who inflicts least suffering, and, if now and then he has to throw a few flowers over a waste place here and there to lure some poor soul into the illusion that it is a garden, who shall speak the word that wakes the spell and spoils the conceit? Not I, indeed, for I firmly believe that

> *Where ignorance is bliss,*
> *'Tis folly to be wise.*

Since that unlucky misunderstanding between Adam and Eve in the Garden of Eden, which proved so disastrous to both of them and some of whose consequences you and I are still discharging through life's clearinghouse, there has been quite a rivalry between the man and the woman, each to get a little the better of the other. You will remember that, most ungallantly, most ungraciously, and, I must add, most imprudently, Adam sought to cast the entire burden of blame in the matter of the apple upon Eve. In point of fact, he turned state's evidence. Well, from that day to this, Eve has been making a play to square the account with Adam, and, as a result, Adam has had much the worst of it.

On a certain bleak winter night, when, quite numb with cold, he has left his boots in the hall below, and slipped off his outer garments at the bedroom door, he enters cautiously, gropes his way to the bedside, and, satisfying himself the wife is asleep, he begins to rock the cradle, first gently, then with greater energy. At last, when he is nearly frozen, and wholly nonplussed by the profoundness of the slumber of his better half, a sleepy voice, in which he fancies he detects a faint gurgle of irrelevant mirth, exclaims: "Oh, come to bed -- the baby isn't in that cradle!" On another occasion, an old friend of mine was going home at one of the "wee short hours ayont the twal," accompanied by a young journalist, who, of course, had to keep late hours -- all journalists do, you know -- and, when they had reached the point where their paths diverged, the elder said to the younger: What in the world shall I say when I get home?" And the younger, some three years married, replied, with ready resource and cheerfulness: "Be assured, my dear Isaac, it is much best to speak the truth. I shall go at once and waken my wife, and frankly tell her the press proke down!"

It is much best to speak the truth! Yes, but I think it would be best of all if Adam and Eve came to some understanding about these matters; if they reached some mutual agreement; if they compromised them, so to say.

"And these few precepts, son-in-law," observed an over-facetious paterfamilias at breakfast the day after the wedding, "when you get off with the boys and play the noble game, quit when you have lost what you can afford, go home and tell Maria, and it will be all right. If you drink and drip too much, realize it, go home to Maria, who will bathe your brow, and it will be all right. But on one point, dear son-in-law, let me admonish you. Where there is a woman, you lie." In order that in some moment of effusion, or inebriety, you may not by chance slip your trolley and tell the truth, "accustom yourself to lying!"

The woman is in perpetual fear of the man's nature; not his natural wickedness, or depravity; but his redundant vitality, exposed to the temptations that habitually assail it. And well she may be, well for him, well for her, well for us all. A world of wild beasts we should become, except for her restraining moral force, her exquisite sense of good and evil, her tenderness and life. We make jokes at her expense. We rally and tease her.

Ah, gentle dames, it ga's me greet,
To think how mony counsels sweet,
How mony lingthened, sage advices,
The husband fra the wife despises!

And, half amused, yet half afraid and half ashamed, we picture her

Gathering her brows like gathering storm,
Nursing her wrath to keep it warm.

But "for a' that and a' that, " too, know where to draw the line, and we do draw it -- every mother's son of us who is worth salt enough to pickle him -- at love and duty, at the home, the shrine where love and duty meet, to sing the song of the angels in Heaven.

But let us not grow sentimental. Having drawn the line, let us draw the curtain. Affection compromises all things. It is where there is not love, out, out upon the storm-laden ocean of life -- in the world of affairs, where men meet in furious contention, where the play of *The Rivals* is not a comedy, but a tragedy, where all is strife -- commercial, political -- avarice playing at hide-and-seek with honor, and expediency pouring lies into the pliant ear of ambition -- every man for himself, the devil to get the hindmost -- each tub to stand on its own bottom -- it is here where the shoe pinches, here that good men, great men, know the true need and meaning of tolerance, the God-like wisdom of the spirit of compromise.

Of what value were Jay Gould's millions -- of what value a single one of his dollars -- if over and beyond his wants a penny was gained at the cost of the blood and tears of one good man or woman? Of what value were Napoleon's victories? But, stay! Let me relate a parable, a fable with a moral, which might have happened any time these years of wondrous, romantic achievement upon the modern arena of battle -- our field of the cloth of gold -- the Stock Exchange.

A young man of four or five and twenty, poorly clad, much under the average height, eyes deep-sunken and of piercing blackness, thin, pale lips, wanders vacantly, restlessly, about this Stock Exchange. He roams in and out of its galleries like a caged lion. He gazes wistfully over the balconies into the seething pit below. He sees men pushing, hauling, howling, money-mad. Day in and day out the same; always the same; though not for him. But, why not? Why not? He knows no one who could secure him access there. He has not a dollar, even if he could obtain access. And yet he has evolved out of the darkness and isolation that surround him a secret, which, if he had the opportunity and the means of applying it, would yield him millions.

Accident throws this young man into the society of a young woman nearly as poor as himself, but beautiful and bright and noble. He loves her. She loves him. In the confidence of that love he discloses his secret to her. She listens, amazed, delighted. When he has finished his recital she exclaims:

"Why, with this astonishing knowledge, how comes it you are in a rage?"

"Alas," says he, "I have not a penny in the world. I have not a friend in the world. With a knowledge that has power to revolutionize the fiscal universe, I am as helpless, hopeless as a child!"

This woman is a woman of genius. She is a woman of action. She seizes the situation with the instinct of her nature.

"Why, " she exclaims, "I have very little money; but you need very little. Take it. I know the President of the Stock Exchange. I will introduce you to him. We will introduce you upon the floor. You, and this wondrous discovery of yours, will do the rest."

He falls upon his knees. He clasps her in his arms. He will go and get his millions. He will make her his wife -- nay, they will be married at once -- they will not delay a moment, because before tomorrow's day and night are over they will be rich, famous, and will live forever happy, loving one another and doing good all the rest of their days.

They are married. She is true to her word. He is true to his. He appears in the midst of that mad throng -- this strange little man with the miraculous secret. No one observes him; no one divines his secret; only the President of the Stock Exchange, to whom he has been presented and who has admitted him to the floor, has a friendly eye upon him. But his lines laid and his little all upon them, that awful secret begins to work like magic. A thousand dollars is quickly ten thousand, then ten thousand a hundred thousand, a hundred thousand a million, a million fifty million, and, amid the crash of fortunes and the fury of such a tempest as the world never knew before, the President comes down from his seat, and the young, the veritable young Napoleon of finance, is personally made known to the money kings and princes, some of whom he has ruined, others of whom he has crippled, and all of whom he has brought to his feet!

And the woman who has enabled him to do all this? Oh, she has been in the gallery up there. She has seen it all. First frightened, then delirious with joy, she has watched every turn of the wheel and known what turned it and who. The day is hardly half over. But the battle is fought and won. She bids him come -- come to the arms of a loving wife -- come to the rest of a happy home -- come, with riches, honors, all that fortune can give to man, e'en to that blessed peace that passeth understanding. Oh, no. He is not going to do anything of the kind. He has only ruined half the Stock Exchange. He is going back to ruin the other half. Oh, well -- what would you say of that man if, going back to ruin the other half, he lost all he had gained, including his original stake, and found himself at midnight, his mystery exploded and his fair young bride lying dead there before him, dead of grief and despair? What would you say if he found himself alone, abandoned and locked safely and forever in prison walls?

You know the story of Napoleon. It is related by Metternich, that famous interview at Dresden, that lasted, without food or interruption, from eight in the morning till eight at night; he, representing the Allied Powers, offered Napoleon peace with a larger France than he had found, and the confirmation of his dynasty, and that Napoleon refused it. He wanted all or nothing. He was going to ruin the other half. So he rushed upon Austria, and England, and Russia -- who were still able to stand against him -- and Waterloo -- and before the day was over he found himself a General without an army, an Emperor without a throne, flying for his life, to be caught and locked up like the ill-starred, unthinking, though brilliant, adventurer that he was. He had lost all, including his original stake --

He fought, and half the world was his,
*   He died without a rood his own;*
And borrowed of his enemies
*   Six foot of ground to lie upon.*

Do you not think he had better have compromised with the Powers before it was too late? I do, and, standing, as I have often stood, beneath that lofty dome in the Hospital of the Invalides in Paris, and looking down into that marble crypt upon the wondrous tomb below, and conceiving the glory meant to be there celebrated, it has seemed to me a kind of gilded hell, with a sleeping devil, planned by friends incarnate to lure men, and particularly French men, to perdition. And I never leave that place, with its dreary splendor, that somehow the words of a poor, ragged French poet do not come singing into my heart:

Oh, if I were Queen of France
*   Or still better Pope of Rome,*
I'd have no fighting men abroad,
*   No weeping maids at home;*
All the world should be at peace.
*   And if Kings must show their might,*
Let those who make the quarrels
*   Be the only ones to fight.*

I would compromise war. I would compromise glory. I would compromise everything at that point where hate comes in, where misery comes in, where love ceases to be love and life begins its descent in the shadow of the valley of death.

I would not compromise Truth. I would not compromise the Right. I would not compromise conscience and conviction in any matter of pith and moment involving real duty. There are times when one must stand and fight and die. But such times are exceptional; they are most exceptional; one cannot, without making himself ridiculous, be always wrapping the flag around him and marching down to the foot-lights, to display his extraordinary valor and virtue. And, in the long intervals, how often the best of us are mistaken as to what is Truth, as to what is Right, as to what is Duty. Too often, they are what we would have them to be. Too often, that which we want to do becomes that which we ought to do.

It will hardly be denied by those who know me that I have opinions and adhere to them with some steadiness. On occasions I am afraid that I have expressed them with too great plainness and positivity, and too little regard to the opinions of others. Well, there are moments when the thought comes to my mind that the other fellow, who doesn't agree with me or my opinions, may not be such a bad fellow after all; maybe both of us are right; maybe neither of us; for, in the end, how rarely things come round just as they were planned; yet, still the world goes jogging along, precisely as if you and I did not live in it.

Why should neighbors, who ought to be friends and brothers, quarrel about transactions that can never penetrate their roof-tree's shade? Why should differences about public affairs a thousand miles away make private enmities at home? I am sure I never loved any man less because he did not agree with me. I may think him a fool -- of course -- and tell him so -- if he isn't a bigger man than I am, or, better, if he is one of those big-hearted creatures who will only laugh at me -- but I shall not question either his motive or his sincerity. Those are his prerogatives, as they are mine, and, if I think him a fool, there is no law compelling me to keep his company; only I do keep it all the same, because, somehow, in spite of our occasional tiffs, we just naturally love one another; and, kneeling by the bedside of a sick child, or standing before the grave of a dead comrade, how mean and paltry seem the discussions we had about bimetallism and monometallism, and high tariff and low tariff, and the line! What is Lilly O'Killarney, the Hawaiian maiden from Blarney Castle, what is she to me, or I to her, that I should weep for her? What is it to you whether raw sugar be on the dutiable list, or free? To us in Kentucky now -- who always take sugar in our -- but that is a mere quibble of words, and I will not pursue the theme!

Thank God we live in a free land. It is every man's business to believe something, or to fancy that he does. It is every man's duty to vote, and he ought to vote according as he thinks, or as he thinks he is thinking. That makes what we call politics. That makes what we call parties. They are the glory of free institutions. And then, after we have finished voting as we thought, we disperse to our several homes, leaving a huddle of gentlemen, who pass as our representatives, to go to Washington. We call them politicians. They call themselves statesmen. We pay them -- though not very adequately -- to run the Government. Well, they go to Washington and they run it -- the Government -- and, if they don't suit -- and they generally don't -- we turn them out and send others to take their places, and so on *ad infinitum*. And thus we keep up free America, permeated by free institutions and free ideas, and a free, but sometimes a ribald press.

Now and then, we get a man at Washington who is clever enough to stay there a long, long time; and he becomes a leader, a great leader; a great Republican leader; but, in reality, he has lost his identity; for you just follow any two of these leaders, after they have fought that sham battle on the floor which has so edified their constituents in the gallery -- you just follow them downstairs or upstairs, and see how snugly they take their cold tea together; they have been there so long that they understand one another; they understand one another too well, perhaps; they actually love one another, they are obliged to; they know too much; they could not afford anything else. They, at least, have learned how to compromise everything except their seats in Congress ...

But if it be wise to agree to disagree one with another about the affairs of this world toward the determination of which no one of us has more than his single vote, why should we grow angry and dispute about the affairs of the world to come, toward the determination of which no one of us has any vote at all?

I cannot rid myself of the impression that there are many roads leading to Heaven. To be sure, I know nothing about it, actually, and, as a matter of fact, because I have never been there; though I have sometimes thought I might be, and have always nursed the hope that I was on the way. But what way? Well, I have had some advantages. I was born in the Presbyterian Church, baptized in the Catholic Church, educated in the Episcopal Church, and married into the Church of the Disciples. I came so near being made a Doctor of Divinity once that it took the interposition of two bishops and a school master to limit the investiture to that of Common Law. I do not think myself wanting in seriousness as to religion, or sincerity of allegiance to that sublime faith which has come to us from Calvary. But, for the life of me, I have never had it in my heart to hate any human being because he chose to worship God according to his conscience.

Perusing the story of the dark ages, when men were burnt at the stake for the heresy of refusing to bow to the will of the majority, it is not the voice of the Protestant or Catholic that issues from the flames and reaches my heart, but the cry of suffering man, my brother! To me a saint is a saint, whether he wears wooden shoes, or goes barefoot; whether he gets his baptism out of a font of holy water blessed by the Church of his adoration, or whether, dripping from head to heels, he comes up from the waters of Jordan shouting the hallelujah of his forefathers! From my very boyhood the persecution of man for opinion's sake -- no matter for what opinion's sake -- has aroused within me the only devil I have ever personally known.

Near the upper end of the Lake of Geneva, in Switzerland, there is a famous old castle. Seen from the lake, it is an incongruous white pile of towers and gables and bastions. But it will repay the tourist to go ashore and to cross the drawbridge which admits him to an inner and nearer view. Even in this practical and enlightened age, when dungeons no longer yawn to swallow the helpless, and racks are no more raised to torment the proscribed, and when they who are freest seem least to be jealous and proud of their freedom, it is impossible for any thoughtful man to come here and to stand within these walls, and to go away again without having his love of liberty refreshed and his detestation for oppression renewed, for it was here the patriot Bonnivard passed seventeen years, chained to one of the stone pillars of the castle keep, suggesting the motive for Byron's immortal poem, "The Prisoner of Chillon."

In this light, the Castle of Chillon becomes at once a fortress and a shrine, from which there is as little chance to escape for free and loving hearts to-day as during the long, dark night of its blood and terror there was for its victims.

You are shown the Star Chamber, which they called the Hall of Justice. You pass into the torture-room, and behold its cruel, horrible implements. You descend the narrow, winding stairway into the Vestibule of Executions. On the one hand is the stone bed on which the condemned spent their last night upon earth, and, on the other, the dungeon reserved for those who were not given the happiness to die. And there, just before you in the wall -- next to the lake -- is the casement through which they slid the bodies of the slain.

You enter the dungeon. It is just as Byron described it in his poem. The seven columns are there and the scant clefts in the rocks which admit a little sunlight. Upon three of the columns still hang the iron rings that held the chains that fastened the prisoners. Around the column to which Bonnivard was chained for seventeen years appear the marks worn by his footsteps, and, just above them -- carved by himself -- his name in rude letters, and close by it the names of Byron and Victor Hugo. They are all gone, now, the hero of the fourteenth century, the singers of the nineteenth, contemporaries at last before the eternal throne; but, from those letters that repeat their names, there rings out from the rocks a voice that seems to irradiate the gloom and to echo round the globe.

> *Chillon! Thy prison is a holy place!*
> *And thy sad floor an altar -- for 'twas trod*
> *Until the very steps have left a trace,*
> *Worn, as if thy cold pavement were a sod*
> *By Bonnivard! May none these marks efface,*
> *For thy appeal from tyranny to God!*

I have seen worse places, ranker, darker, fouler places, but never one more hideous in its suggestiveness, because, the story of Bonnivard and the poem of Byron apart, therein is concentrated and typified all that was brutal in feudalism, all that was cruel in bigotry, all that was heroic in resistance. They did not know anything about the compromises of life in those days. Might alone was right, and the axe, the gibbet, and the stake were the arguments which power relied on to carry forward its campaigns of education and reform.

I have said that the Government under which we live is a compromise between conflicting interests. It is less so now than it once was, but it must always rest upon the basis of compromises in the beginning, or it would never have existed at all.

I have lived through an epoch of sore travail. I was born in the national capital and grew to manhood there. I was brought into close, personal contact with the men who made disunion possible. I saw the struggle to save the Union; and the struggle to destroy it. I saw the good men of the North and the good men of the South bravely, nobly join heart and hand to maintain the compromises on which the Union rested. I saw those compromises one by one sink beneath the waves of sectional bitterness, artfully stimulated and partisan interest, craftily pointed. I knew the secret springs of personal ambition which were playing upon the popular credulity, and lashing it into a frenzy. As one of the day's reporters for the Associated Press, I stood by the side of Lincoln when he delivered his first inaugural address, and as I looked out over that vast throng of assembled Americans, wrought to fury by the passions of the time, I knew that it meant war; and I thought the heart within me, boy's that it was, would break, for I loved my country, its glorious traditions, and its glorious Union, its incalculable uses to liberty and humanity.

There was no sunshine in the heavens. There was no verdure on the hills. All seemed lost. Hate and strife ruled the hour; end, one side as resolute as the other, and the dove took her flight from earth, leaving the raven in her nest.

But all was not lost. God was with us even then, though we did not see Him, and He builded wiser than we knew, because are we not here this night, proud and happy, our Republic stronger than ever it was, all the old contentions settled, the monster of slavery gone forever, the monster of secession gone forever, our Government the marvel of the ages, rescued from every assault which has menaced and shattered feudal monarchies and dynasties; the flag flying at last as Webster would have had it fly, bearing upon its ample folds, as it floats over the land and the sea, those words, dear to every American heart, union and liberty, now and forever, one and inseparable! All was not lost, though perilously near it.

The generation which fought to finish the irrepressible antagonisms our fathers had compromised -- deciding for all time that the Government is a nation, and not a huddle of petty sovereignties, that the Constitution is the law, fixed and organic, and not a rope of sand -- is passing away. I can scarcely realize that I belong to that generation, that I, too, have borne a part in the consideration of problems toward the solution of which the best efforts of the best men have been but as the blind leading the blind. What mistakes we have made! What weaklings we have been! And how helpless, except for some saving grace in the American character and destiny! Happy it is that so many of us survive to tell the tale! Three hundred years ago there would have been fewer by half. In the good old days of the Inquisition and the Star Chamber we should have reached our ends, have compassed our designs, by torturing and killing those who got in our way. Let us give thanks to God that we have fallen upon gentler times; that we may do our love-making and our law-making as we do our ploughing, in a straight furrow; that it is the close of the nineteenth, not the opening of the sixteenth of the centuries. Even the tax-gatherer is to be preferred as a steady visiting acquaintance, to the headsman, and journalism, with all its imperfections, offers a fairer field for human investment than the battle-axe of the middle ages.

CHAPTER XI

CARRY A. NATION
(1846-1911)

Physically, she was a large woman of commanding presence. Almost six feet tall, she weighed 175 pounds and had extremely muscular arms. She did not hesitate to become involved in physical brawls with her opponents, who were frequently bartenders and sometimes policemen. She often used a hatchet to demolish bars, which she did in the name of God, by whom she felt called to ravage the demons of alcohol.[1] Her regular dress was a black and white deaconess uniform, and her verbal assaults equalled the violence of her hatchet-smashing escapades. Campaigning against alcohol, she traveled throughout the United States and went on a tour of Europe.

Carry Nation first became involved in saloon razing through her work in the Woman's Christian Temperance Union. Feeling the hand of God was involved in her early financial and marital problems, she was sure "that the Lord had chosen her to be a martyr to the cause of prohibitory enactments, not only against liquor and the saloon, but tobacco and fraternal orders as well."[2] She was also concerned about threats to the American home from sins abroad in the world and often signed herself, "your loving home defender."

After having gained some notoriety as a saloon smasher, she was engaged to go on the lecture circuit. Her first venture outside Kansas was into Iowa, where an estimated five thousand people turned out to welcome her at the Des Moines railroad station. However, fewer than five hundred actually paid to hear her lecture later that evening, and there were not more than three hundred present in Muscatine two nights later. Her manager called her first tour "an artistic success but a financial failure."[3]

In 1888, Carry Nation conducted a crusade in Lexington and other Central Kentucky communities. Having been warned against damaging the drinking establishments in Lexington, her activities there were limited to speeches. A member of the audience during one of her speeches at Midway wrote:

> *I recall with pleasure an interesting lecture on temperance she delivered some year during the 90's in Midway, her former home. She was not eloquent, but her talks were convincing and left a lasting impression.*[4]

In July, 1904, she had a speaking engagement in Elizabethtown, which she described as "one of those bad-rum-towns in Kentucky." On her way to the lecture hall she passed a saloon run by G. R. Neighbors. The following episode typifies numerous incidents during her tours throughout the country:

> *I passed this man and walking into his saloon, said, why are you in this business, drugging and robbing people? "Hush! You get out." I replied, "Yes, you want a respectable woman to get out, but you will make any woman's body a disgrace, you ought to be ashamed." After the lecture I passed his place again. He was sitting in a chair in front of the saloon and I said, "Are you the man that runs this business?" and in a moment and with an oath he picked up the chair and with all his strength, sent it down with a crash on my head. I came near falling, caught myself, and he lifted the chair a second time, striking me over the back, the blood began to cover my face and run down from a cut on my forehead. I cried out, "He has killed me," an officer caught the chair to prevent the third blow.*[5]

As a result of these divinely inspired activities, Carry had many brushes with the law. She was arrested often, and sometimes escaped a jail sentence by posting bond. Other times she was not so fortunate. By her own admission, she was jailed twenty-three times.[6] One of these arrests took place in 1902, during a speech she gave at Coney Island in Steeple Chase Park, when she became involved in an altercation with a man. Her graphic description of the incident shows her sense of correspondence with God in relation to her unstinting pursuits against the evils of alcohol.

> I was arrested, and stood my trial and was being sent to jail, when Mr. Tilyou, Manager of the Steeple Chase Park took me from the "Black Maria." The policemen who had the prisoners in charge was purple and bloated from beer drinking, he wanted me to go to a place in the front that was already crowded with women. I refused and he struck me on the hand that was holding up the iron bars of the little window and broke a bone, causing it to swell up. I said, "Never mind, you beer swilled, whiskey soaked saturn faced man, God will strike you." In six weeks from that time this man fell dead on the streets of Coney Island.[7]

During her stays in jail, Carry was sometimes approached by men who wished to exploit her notoriety by offering her large sums of money to tour the country with circuses and other entertainment enterprises. One proposal promised eight hundred dollars per week plus a police car and a maid. She resisted all such temptations until James E. Furlong, who was the head of a lyceum bureau in Rochester, New York, wrote suggesting she tour the Chautauqua circuits and give a series of speeches in New York and other eastern cities. This appealed to her missionary spirit, as she saw the stage as a possible vehicle to advance her calling. She accepted Furlong's offer.

Carry Nation's touring crusades in the cause of temperance continued vigorously after the turn of the century. She was not content with influencing the masses, and made an attempt to present her message to the chief executive. In 1904 she went to Washington to call on President Theodore Roosevelt, but was refused an audience. Then she appeared on the university circuit and was impressed with Harvard, where she said no saloons were allowed; but she condemned the universities of Michigan and Yale, feeling that Yale was the worst place she had ever seen. [8]

She valued her role as a watchdog in the temperance movement, as epitomized in a speech made in 1907 at the Women's Christian Temperance Union's national convention in Nashville:

I am called the watchdog of the nation. I am standing watch over the heads of the innocent women and children of this land who are fast asleep and propose to carry on the war until the last saloon is gone. [9]

In keeping with her words, she vacated the Tulane Hotel, where she had reservations in Nashville, upon learning the hotel had a bar.

From inauspicious beginnings, Carry Nation became one of the foremost exponents of prohibition in her era. She was born Carry Amelia Moore to a quite prosperous family living in a ten-room log house in Garrard County, Kentucky. Her father, poorly educated, wrote her name in the family Bible as "Carry" instead of "Carrie." This spelling was interpreted many years later by Carry as a mysterious omen from God. As a child, she was described as religious, stubborn, dictatorial, emotional and a natural leader.[10] These traits became more fully expressed as her missionary zeal developed.

After moving from Garrard County, when Carry was five, to Danville, and later to Woodford County between Versailles and Midway, the Moore family left Kentucky for Missouri in 1855. Carry attended Sunday School in Midway at the Orphans' Home where her father was one of the trustees. There she learned the Word of God. Much of her time there was also spent with family slaves, which may have intensified her natural emotionalism.

In Liberty, Missouri, Carry experienced the last of her spasmodic public education. It was during this last year of school, at the age of eighteen, that she first participated in public debate, which she was to enjoy so vigorously later in life. Attending a class in Smellie's natural philosophy, she was assigned the affirmative on the question: Resolved, "That animals have reasoning faculties." She represented her literary society, the Eunomiass, in an exhibition before the faculty and two other literary societies. She had not prepared sufficiently for the debate and went blank when her turn came. After one bad start, and some tearful blundering, she began again:

I know animals have the power to reason, for my brothers cured a dog from sucking eggs by having him take a hot one in his mouth, and it was the last egg we ever knew him to pick up. Why? Because he remembered the hot one and reasoned that he might get burned. Why is it that a horse will like one person more than another? Because he is capable of reasoning and knows who is best to him. [11]

Carry's anti-alcoholic inclinations began to develop after two unfortunate marriages with, ironically, two weak men. Her first husband, Charles Gloyd, had been a roomer in the household of her family in 1865, a temporary teacher and would-be doctor. His practice of medicine was not successful because of his chronic alcoholism, and the marriage was short-lived and unhappy. Carry felt that the Masons, to which her husband belonged, in addition to alcohol, were bad influences on her husband and mankind as well. When her father visited the couple in Holden, Missouri, a few months after the marriage, he found Carry pregnant and close to a nervous breakdown. He took her home with him, where she later gave birth to a daughter. Shortly thereafter, Charles Gloyd died, and Carry asked her mother-in-law to live with her. The responsibility of dependents prompted Carry to prepare herself to teach so she could support them. She earned a teaching certificate at the Normal Institute in Warrensburg and was given the primary room in the Public School in Holden. Her teaching career, however, ended after four years as the result of an argument with a member of the school board, Dr. Moore, over the pronunciation of the article *A*. The position subsequently went to Dr. Moore's niece, who no doubt pronounced it "correctly."

Her plans dissolved, Carry then set about to find another husband, deciding to accomplish this through prayer. She approached the Lord directly: "My Lord you see the situation ... I want you to help me ..."[12] In about ten days she met David Nation, a Civil War veteran, nineteen years Carry's senior. He had been unsuccessful as a minister and an attorney, and when Carry met him he was an editor of the *Warrensburg Journal*.[13] They were married in 1877, and this marriage proved as unsuccessful as the first. Carry was the breadwinner for the family which had mushroomed to six: her daughter, her mother-in-law, her mother, a step-daughter, her husband and herself. During the next few years, Carry purchased two hotels in order to feed the family: one in Columbia, Texas, the other in Richmond, Texas. The source of her money for the purchase is unknown. In Richmond, Carry turned again to religion, and after some experience with both Methodist and Episcopal churches, she opened her own nondenominational Sunday School, holding classes in her hotel dining room as well as the local cemetery.

When the hotel at Richmond burned in 1889, the Nations were on the move again. David worked intermittently as an itinerant journalist and later became a minister of the First Christian Church in Medicine Lodge, Kansas, after Carry acquired some property there. Carry was not only interested in her husband's sermons; she edited and re-wrote them two or three times. In addition, she aided him in delivery by seating herself conspicuously in the first row and prompting him loudly.[14]

It was in Kansas that Carry became actively involved

with the Women's Christian Temperance Union. She was appointed Jail Evangelist for her group, the Barber County WCTU. She was described as a great talker, temperamental and fierce at times, as she held meetings in the county jail and prayed with the prisoners.[15] There, too, in connection with her WCTU work, she became involved in her saloon-smashing career and the violent temperance evangelism which was to become her trademark. As one biographer depicted her evolvement:

> There was nothing obscure or mysterious about the development of Carry Nation's character and her transformation from a commonplace young woman of unusual meekness and self-effacement into the most industrious and bull-doggy that even the Middle West, hot bed of the bizarre and the fanatical, has ever produced. She followed the well beaten trail of mental instability and extravagant religious zeal, and she was urged onward, and from her point of view, upward, by a deeprooted persecution mania and a highly developed scapegoat complex.[16]

But Carry felt the word of God to be her power, sword, and shield. She felt the name, Carry A. Nation, signified her divine calling and destiny. Believing the hand of God was involved in her early financial and marital burdens, she became convinced she was God's advocate in the abolishment of sin, as she understood and interpreted it. Even the initials C.A.N. represented her destiny and success in executing it.[17]

As a speaker she may have been far from polished. She quoted frequently from the Bible and depended largely on emotional appeal to ignite her audiences. But her vitality and commitment to what she believed, her vigorous enactments, even her violent demonstrations, carved a unique place in history. Her favorite description of herself was as "a bulldog running along at the feet of Jesus, barking at what he doesn't like." Carry was convinced she had learned Jesus' likes and dislikes from his own lips.[18] She did more than bark. She smashed, argued and built her own life. Until her death, on June 2, 1911, she strove to clear the country, even the world, of sin, working out her own unalterable destiny.

Spiritual Authority For My Christian Work[19]

Carry Nation

Sometimes a rock; sometimes a hatchet; God told me to use these to smash that which has smashed and will smash hearts and souls. The sound of this loving deed will stir conscience and hearts, and while I can not finish the smashing, the voters of this nation will use their ballots that will, and this impulse will Carry A. Nation.

God sent an angel from heaven to tell Gideon to smash up the altar and image of Baal. By divine command Achan and family were smashed. God would not give Joshua victory until this was done. Saul was commanded by God (through his prophet Samuel) to utterly destroy the Amalekite's nation, and all their substance. He was disobedient and saved the king. Samuel hacked or smashed up Agag, although Saul was the regularly appointed one. This is a case directly in point. The officers in Kansas were oath-bound to do what Carry A. Nation did.

Our Savior's mission on earth was to "break (smash) every yoke and set the captive free." Upon two occasions he made a scourge of small cords and laid it on the backs of wicked men who were doing unlawful things. He came into this world "to destroy the works of the devil," to "bruise" or crush the "head of the serpent." We are told to "abhor that which is evil, " to "resist (or fight) the devil and he will flee." We are not to be "overcome with evil but to overcome evil with good." How? Resist the devil. God blessed the church at Ephesus, because they "hated the evil workers, tried them and found them liars." The hatred of sin is one mark of a Christian. Just in proportion of your love for God will be your hatred of evil.

I will here give you a Bible reading on the subject. These are some instances of smashing. The ten plagues of Egypt and the overthrow of Pharaoh were smashing. The death of the first born also ...

If I could I would turn the key on every church in the land, so as to teach some preachers to go out, and not stay in, and compel poor sinners to stay out. I yield no territory to the devil. Let us take every saloon, every house of prostitution of men and women for God. "There shall not a hoof be left behind." "The kingdom of heaven suffereth violence, and the violent take it by force," which means that where the evil is aggressive, we must be more so, and take, compelling surrender by the determination never to yield.

I feel that I have been peculiarly favored to go into these places, to "cry aloud and spare not and show my people their sins." I find this class so hungry for something better. These poor actresses, who dress in tights and sing indecent songs, are a weary, tired, heart-sick lot of slaves. I mingle with them as a sister. When I can say a warning word, I say it. I call them affectionate names and mean it. God will judge both of us. He knows who loved much; he can forgive much. Christ said to a lot of men who took the amen pews: "The publicans and harlots will go into heaven before you." Why? They "repented when they heard." "How are they to hear without a preacher?" I never see a man or woman so low but as a sculptor said of the marble: "There is an angel there." Oh, God, help me to bring it out!

Jesus received sinners and ate with them. He left a command that Christians should invite these to feasts in their homes. Oh! what a revival of religion there would be if the homes of Christians were opened to the lost and sinful, who are dying for some demonstration of love. If the Son of God, the lovely, the pure, the blessed ate with sinners, ought it not to be a privilege to follow Him? We are commanded to "warn, rebuke, and reprove with all long suffering and doctrine." People will work in a revival to get sinners saved, and will pass them day after day on the street and not a word of Scripture do they use to remind them of God's judgements. Jesus said: "The world hateth me because I testify that the words thereof are evil." I have had men to swear at me, call me names and threaten to knock me down. At first this caused me to feel mortified but that passed off. These very men have afterward told me I was right and they were wrong. The devil "threw some on the ground and they foamed at the mouth" before he was cast out. I have often taken cigars and cigarettes out of men's and boy's mouths. I wished to show them the wrong and that I was a friend. Would you let one you love take a knife to open a vein or cut himself? Oh! the sweetness and force of that promise: "Your labor is never in vain in the Lord." This covers all cases, if you, for the love of God, do anything. I often say to myself, after rebuking for sin: "You made a mistake in the way you did this or that, and are you sure it was done for the love of God and your neighbor?" "Yes." Then "your labor is never in vain in the Lord." It is not what we do that prospers, but what God blesses ..."He that planteth is nothing and he that watereth is nothing, but it is God that giveth the increase." And it matters not how awkward the work, if it be done from love of God, it will prosper. Like other things, the more you do, the better you can do.

All the Christian work I ever did seemed to meet with severe opposition from church members. This is a great stumbling-block to some. The church crucified our blessed Christ, that is, it was the hypocrites; for the church is the light and salt, the body of Christ. "If I yet please men, I should not be the servant of Christ." There is no other organization but the church of Christ that persecutes its own followers. The hierarchy in the church told Christ "He had devils," but they could not meet the argument when He said: "A kingdom divided against itself will not stand." If I, by the spirit of Beelzebub, cast out devils, by what kind of a spirit do your children cast them out." The devil never destroys his own work. If the saloon is of the devil, the power that destroys it is the opposite. If a mother should see a gun pointed at her son, would she break the law to snatch the gun and smash it? The gun was not hers. It may have been worth a thousand dollars. The saloon is worse than the gun which could only destroy the body.

It is a great blessing to know your mission in life. I know why Christians are waiting with folded hands, not being able to see their mission. They are not willing to pay the great price for their commission. The rich young man could have been a follower of Jesus, the greatest honor in earth or heaven, and could have had eternal treasure in heaven for the transient gain of earth. He would not pay the price. You must give all, to get all. The effect of smashing has always been to cause the people to arouse themselves. The Levite that severed his dear concubine and sent parts of her body to the different tribes of Israel was to cause the people to "consider, take advice and speak." Then they acted and four hundred thousand men presented themselves to redress this wrong.

The smashing in Kansas was to arouse the people. If some ordinary means had been used, people would have heard and forgotten, but the "strange act" demanded an explanation and the people wanted that, and they never will stop talking about this until the question is settled. Let us consider the character of Moses. It is said this man disobeyed God but once, and he was the "meekest of all men." We are first attracted to him peculiarly because he "refused to be called the son of Pharaoh's daughter, rather suffering afflictions with the people of God than to enjoy the pleasures of sin for a season." Rather be counted with the poor despised, afflicted slaves under the taskmaster's lash than be a king or an absolute monarch. This brought out his characteristic prohibition of sin -- the renouncing of every wordly ambition. He here made the choice, at the time when the temptations were greatest, for all that the world could offer was his. He gave all and paid the price it requires to get all. On the banks of the Nile he sees one man oppressing another. That spirit of prohibition of this great wrong caused him to strike (smash) the oppressor.

Here is a lovable trait of this great man. Moses, could not look on and see the helpless suffer at the hands of another, even though it brought death to himself. Forgetful of his own safety, defying the absolute power and authority of this despot, so far as it lay in his power, against all these odds he redressed the wrong of a fellow creature. God saw in Moses a man whom He could use. From the golden throne he sought a retreat, and for forty years was an humble shepherd, learning the lesson of caring for the flocks of Jethro, before he could be called to take the oversight of the flock of God. "He that is faithful in that which is least is faithful also in that which is much." God called this man out of the wilderness to go to the greatest court on earth as His ambassador. Not one compromise would he make, still true to his prohibition principles. God never used or blessed any man or woman that was not a prohibitionist. Eli was one of those conservatives and said only, "Nay, verily my sons." And he got his neck broke and both of his sons killed in one day because he "restrained (or prohibited) not his sons in the iniquity which he knew." Moses, although the meekest of all men, he said to Pharaoh, "There shall not a hoof be left behind." True to the uncompromising spirit of a great leader, when in the Mount, seeing the idolatry, smashed the two tablets of stone. Why? He would not deliver the holy laws to a people who were insulting God. This smashing was demonstration of Moses' jealousy for his God. After this I can see him striding down to the place of this "ball" or "hugging." The round dance of the present day is but a repetition of those lascivious plays, and with his ax or hatchet he hacked up that malicious property, shaped into a golden calf. This did not belong to Moses. It was very valuable but he smashed it and ground it to powder and then, to further humiliate these rebels, he made them drink the dust mixed with water; then to absolutely destroy and stamp with a vengeance this insult to God, he divided the people and those who were "on the Lord's side" fought with these rebels and slew (smashed) three thousand men. In one of the canonical books of the Catholic Bible, we have the story of the holy woman Judith who cut off the head of Hollifernese to save God's people. Esther, the gentle loving queen, had the wicked sons of Haman hanged. Our supremest idea of justice is a regard for the good and a punishment for the wicked. We amputate the arm to save the body. David says: "I will not know a wicked person; he that telleth lies shall not dwell in my sight."

The devil has his agents in the churches, and among those who are doing his work the best, are a class of professors who testify that you must not speak ill of any one, not even the devil. They are the "non-resistives." The devil is delighted to be respected, and not fought. He gets his work in just as he wants to and he can imitate true conversion, if he can place in the church those who hinder a warfare against sin. Paul said: "I tell you even weeping they are enemies of the cross of Christ." They are the devils in light. "But there must needs be heresies among you that they who are approved may be manifest." Persons often propose to do something. I may not see the advisability, but because there is action in it, I never object. Oh! for somebody to do with their might what their hands find to do." "Well done" is the best commendation. Faith is like the wind, we cannot see it, but by the quantity of motion and commotion. There are workers, "jerkers" and "shirkers," but through much tribulation and temptation must we enter into the kingdom of heaven. The counterfeit proves the genuine dollar; counterfeits are not counterfeited. So hypocrites prove the genuine Christians. If there were not a genuine there would not be a hypocrite. Our mother and grandmothers who went into saloons praying and spilling the poisoned slop of these houses of crime and tears were blessed in their deeds. Oh! that the W.C.T.U. would do as they did, what a reform would take place. I love the organization of mothers. I love their bold impulses, but I am heart-sick at their conventionality, their red tape. This organization could put out of existence every drinking hell in the United States if they would demand it and use the power they have even without the ballot. I intend to help the women of the Kansas W.C.T.U., but not one that has any respect for either Republican or Democratic parties shall ever be called on to aid me in my work, women who are not wise enough to know that the rum voting parties are traitors, can be nothing but a hindrance to the interests of mothers. One said to me, "You will cause many women to leave the organization." I said: "Good riddance to bad rubbish, the quicker they get out the better." As Nehemiah, that grand prohibitionist, said: "What have you to do to build the walls of our God?"

I have a great benediction on my work. Wherever I go the dear mothers shake my hand and kiss my face, saying: "God bless you. I want to help you. You did what I wanted to do." It is the heart of motherhood running over with love. "The gentle are the brave, the loving are the daring."

I got a telegram from a man saying: "Your article in *Physical Culture* on the use of tobacco has cured me of the vice." One man from Omaha, Nebraska, wrote: "Three years ago I was a drunkard. I had a drug store. I was losing business and going to ruin generally. When I heard of what you did, I said: 'If that woman can do that to save others, I ought to do something for myself.' So now I am a changed man. My wife is a changed woman. I have to thank you and Almighty God. My business is growing every day."

Upon several occasions I have had people to put five dollars in my hand. While I was lecturing in Pasadena, California, for the Y.M.C.A., one young man put in my hand what I thought was a silver dollar, but, on looking, it was a twenty dollar gold piece. I said: "I will lay that up in heaven for you." And so I have. I never learned his name but he will certainly find that twenty dollars in the bank of heaven with interest.

When I first started out in this crusade I was called crazy and a "freak" by my enemies, but now they say: "No, Carry Nation, you are not crazy, but you are sharp. You started out to accomplish something and you did. You are a grafter. It is the money you are after." Jesus said: "John came neither eating or drinking and ye say, Behold a wine bibber and a glutton." So it is the world never did understand an unselfish life. It is a small thing to be judged by a man that withers as grass. "If I yet please man, I should not be the servant of Christ."

There have been, from the first time I started out, persons who understood that God moved me. These were students of the Old Scriptures. Jesus told the people before the New Testament was written to "search the Scriptures -- these are they that testify of me. All Scripture is given by inspiration of God and is profitable for doctrine, for correction, for instruction in righteousness, that the man of God may be thoroughly furnished unto every good work." To be thorough, one must know the old as well as the new. In all the sermons of Paul, Peter and the rest, they quote from old Scripture. So did Jesus. Read Peter's first sermon on the day of Pentecost. There is a tendency to study the New Testament more than the Old. It is not possible to understand the New, unless we first study the Old. One of my favorite books is Deuteronomy, the dying words of Moses. Here he repeats the great mercy, consideration and power of God's dealings with his people. Tells the kind of characters God will bless. How God loves the pure and good. How He hates the wicked. We here see that God creates good and evil, and holds us responsible for the choosing. While God rules in all things we have the power to bring on ourselves blessings or cursings. This book declares the man or woman invincible that abandons himself or herself to do God's will.

> *True merit lies in braving the unequal.*
> *True glory comes from daring to begin.*
> *God loves the man or woman, who reckless of the sequel,*
> *Fights long and well, whether they lose or win.*

In the seventh chapter of Deuteronomy, God commanded the children of Israel to "destroy the images," "break down" the altars and "burn the graven images" of the Gods of the heathen. This was smashing. Also said to them: "If you do not drive them out, they shall be thorns in your sides." God gave them power and ability to do this, then he required them to do it. God supplies man's "cannots," not his "will nots." In Numbers, twenty-fifth chapter, Phineas was given God's covenant of peace and the priesthood, because he slew the woman and man that were committing sin: "Because he was jealous for his God and made an atonement for the children of Israel." This was smashing. God himself smashed up Sodom and Gomorrah. In the seventeenth chapter of Deuteronomy, God says: "The idolator and blasphemer shall be stoned with stones till he die. So shalt thou put away evil from you." This is smashing. I could write a book recounting the incidents recorded in God's Word.

"What is in thine hand, Abel?"

"Nothing but one wee lamb, O God, taken from the flock. I purpose offering it to thee a willing sacrifice."

And so he did. And the sweet smell of that burning has been filling the air ever since, and constantly going up to God as a perpetual sacrifice of praise.

"What is it thou hast in thine hand, Moses?"

"Nothing but a staff, O God, with which I tend my flocks."

"Take it and use it for me."

And he did; and with it wrought more wondrous things than Egypt and her proud King had seen before.

"Mary, what is that thou hast in thine hand?"

"Nothing but a pot of sweet-smelling ointment, O God, wherewith I would anoint thine only One called Jesus."

———————————————————

(The selection does not end here but this is typical of her oral style. Typically she did not have a conclusion; rather she ended when she felt urged to do so.)

CHAPTER XII

LAURA CLAY
(1848-1941)

Laura was one of ten children of the colorful Cassius Clay and his wife, Mary Jane Warfield. She was born February 9, 1849, at White Hall in Madison County.

As a child, Laura enjoyed many advantages because of the comfortable economic status and emphasis on education in the Clay family. She and her brothers, Brutus and Cassius, walked to classes at Foxtown Academy near White Hall, where a major emphasis was placed on writing and public speaking. All the Clay youngsters followed their father's example and decided to become orators. [1] Laura also attended Sayre Institute in Lexington, where she was graduated in 1865, followed by one year at Sarah Hoffman's Finishing School in New York City for training in the social graces. [2]

She felt Mrs. Hoffman's was inadequate for what she wanted in life, and that it was necessary for women to be as well educated as men. "I am amazed," she wrote in her diary, "to see how wide a gap there is between the education thought necessary for young women and that which is necessary for a young man to enter college, which is almost the beginning of his." [3]

In 1879, she was able to enroll in the University of Michigan where she studied for one year. Her formal education was completed when she studied one year at the Kentucky Agricultural and Mechanical College, now the University of Kentucky, when that school first admitted women.

Early in her life, Laura demonstrated a sensitive nature as is shown in her diary entry of April 13, 1864:

> *This evening I have been reading a book called "Historic Incidents and Life in India" -- The people are degraded beyond anything I ever imagined. It makes me sad to feel that human beings are so low. I would like to be a missionary, and help raise them from this degraded state.* [4]

A short time later she wrote regarding the differences between men and women, an early intimation of the theme which would dominate her life's work. On May 15, 1864, she wrote:

> *I feel rebellious sometimes about the differences in intellectual power between men and women. I do not care for the difference that exists between us while we are on earth, but only think of the future in heaven. I console myself thus -- If I were a man, I would not complain if I were inferior to marry an intellect. I am a woman but I think I have a mind superior to that of many boys of my age, and equal to that of many men. Therefore, when we get to heaven we will be equal. If I am not perfectly submissive hereafter, I will pray to God to make me so. Except for this feeling of inequality, I think I would prefer being a woman to a man.* [5]

By nature a religious person, Laura felt called by God to the cause of Women's Rights. "To do what I can to help on the great cause of Women's Rights seems to be that sphere of activity in his service to which God has called me." [6] She was not jealous of men, she wrote, but rather had a desire "to see women awake to the higher life which God, through the advance of Christian civilization, has opened to them." [7]

In 1879, Laura had a chance to become personally acquainted with Susan B. Anthony, who was to have a major influence on her life. Miss Anthony came to Richmond from

Massachusetts to organize a suffrage society.[8]   These two women remained friends until the death of Miss Anthony.   Letters in the Laura Clay Collection at the University of Kentucky reveal the esteem with which Susan B. Anthony held Laura Clay.

In 1881 the American Woman Suffrage Association met in Louisville for the first gathering south of the Ohio River.[9]   Twenty-five members chartered the Kentucky Woman Suffrage Association and elected Laura Clay its first president.

Miss Clay became active in the Kentucky Equal Rights Association in the 1880's promoting the admission of women to the previously male colleges in the state.   In June, 1888, she chaired a committee on the college petition of the state Equal Rights Association which appealed to the Curators of Kentucky University (now Transylvania University).   Minutes of the Equal Rights Association record that she presented the petition for admission of women to the Curators with a speech which was "short, earnest and to the point."[10] Eight months later, news was received by the Association that when the fall term opened women would be admitted to the university with equal privileges with men.[11]

It was in the 1890's when Laura Clay began to achieve national prominence as a spokesman for women's rights.   In 1894, Miss Clay, along with Carrie Chapman Catt, began a lecture tour of the South in Lexington, Kentucky.   For the next several years, newspapers throughout the country reported the successful speaking engagements of Miss Clay.   One reporter, in describing her, wrote: "Miss Clay is an unusually attractive speaker. She has a full, clear voice and speaks very evenly, varying only a few notes between her highest and lowest tones."[12]   On the same tour, another writer was more effusive:

> The address of Miss Laura Clay of Kentucky was a revelation of the possibilities of success in public speaking on the part of women; and while many left unconvinced of the expediency of necessity of encumbering women with the more than doubtful blessing of the ballot, those who "came to scoff" were full of

admiration for the fair speaker's power of argument,
interspersed with pleasant sarcasm, and brimful of
information, historical, sociological, and scientific.

Miss Clay is a middle-aged woman of striking personal
appearance, and in whose face character and superior
intelligence are unmistakably written ... Her earnest-
ness and evident sincerity of thought and purpose
make their impression upon everyone.[13]

Another writer in South Carolina described her speech as "beautiful in language, strong in argument and full of logic."[14]

According to newspaper accounts of her lectures, the audiences were usually large, and Miss Clay was able to hold their attention for the duration of a long speech. The idea of women's rights was a new political issue for most of her listeners, and they were eager to hear her thoughts on the subject. Most male statesmen and editors highly respected her and she knew she must keep this respect and support if her goals were to be realized.

Laura considered suffrage an issue best handled at the state level. In 1919, she wrote to the *Lexington Herald*: "I stand for rights with men for women of every race and section. Many women of Kentucky would rather trust their speedy enfranchisement by the state method to the good faith of Kentucky men than to the uncertain fortunes of a federal amendment."[15] In the closing years of the campaign for women suffrage, Laura Clay broke with Carrie Chapman Catt and the national leaders in the movement over the issue of states rights.

During the summer and fall of 1912, the Equal Rights Association formed a lecture bureau of Kentucky speakers to give free lectures on women suffrage, school suffrage, and civil service reform and kindred subjects. Laura, one of the principal speakers for the bureau, appeared under the auspices of the Equal Rights Association, the Federation of Women's Clubs and Women's Christian Temperance Union, conducting a highly successful tour of fifteen cities throughout the state.[16]

One biographer wrote that she reached the peak of her influence in national suffrage affairs between 1904 and 1910.[17] In 1913 a reporter called her the "pioneer Suffragist" of Kentucky.[18] Another said she was the most prominent figure in the South in the suffrage movement.[19] At the national level she served sixteen years as auditor for the National American Woman Suffrage Association.

As a speaker, Miss Clay was not without humor. On one occasion she kept silent while a well-known reporter gave information during a discussion on woman suffrage. His closing argument was, "Women are not strong enough physically for the strain of politics." He felt that women were clinging vines and men were the sturdy oaks. Before he could leave the podium, Miss Clay appeared beside him and "towering above the speaker, replied laconically, 'Oh, I don't know'." The laughter which swept the room proved she had won her point.[20]

In 1919, the women of American were enfranchised, but it was a bittersweet time for Laura Clay, because the victory was through the federal amendment rather than through the states. Her continued prominence in the state is indicated by the esteem in which she was held by the Democratic Party. She was selected as one of the eight Kentucky delegates to the 1920 National Convention in San Francisco. There she heard her name placed in nomination for President of the United States -- the first woman to be so honored by a major political party. During the balloting she "got a nice complimentary vote."[21]

Her political activity continued through the 1920's when she was often a speaker for Democratic Party gatherings.[22] In 1923 she was an unsuccessful candidate for the state senate. Continuing her interest in politics she traveled the state in 1928, speaking on behalf of presidential candidate Al Smith. In 1933, at the age of eighty-three, Laura presided at the Frankfort Convention which ratified the 21st Amendment in Kentucky.

During her lifetime three great issues were faced, the abolition of slavery, the emancipation of women and the temperance movement. On all three her stand was "courageous and unequivocal."

Almost thirty years after her death, on the anniversary of the right to vote for women, a writer summarized the career of Laura Clay:

> *Miss Clay brought to her life work -- the immense prestige of the Clay name, her own high intelligence and thorough education, and a skill as a speaker attained by few women. She was to exhibit through a long life, political acumen of the highest order, combined with a distinctively feminine tact.*[23]

Laws Of The States Affecting Women

Circa 1894

Speech to Women's Club Of Central Kentucky

This previously unpublished speech of Laura Clay is from the Laura Clay Collection at the University of Kentucky.

Perhaps on seeing my subject on the programme for this department some of the members may have felt that it was one in which women could take only a passive, intellectual interest, because though laws affect them directly, they have been in the habit of accepting the decrees of legislatures very much as they accept the decrees of providence, with the thought that it is out of their province or power to alter them. But to my mind, my subject is an intensely practical one, as my experience of some years leads me to believe.

To obtain a really intelligent comprehension of the laws, it is essential that, along with a hearing of the facts of the law, there shall be a measurement of them to see how nearly they conform to the objects of the law, that is, to promote the welfare of the people, and to maintain justice in the relations between individuals.

The laws of the state relating to women as wives, mothers, and property holders are modifications of more general laws, so as to apply to the particular relations involved; and to rightly judge of the essential.

What is most needed to elevate our laws, and raise them up to a high standard of justice of both sexes, is clear, broad, careful, feminine thought. Men need nothing so much as the aid of womanly judgment upon the difficult and knotty problems of how to adjust the laws so as to promote the welfare of the whole people, and to maintain justice between individuals, and, more particularly, in the relations between men and women, where at the complexity of the interests involved make an apparent conflict in the rights of the sexes.

Qualities of the law require a continual judgment of them by two standards, one of general equity, and one of the rights of women as compared with men. For instance, the law affecting women as mothers immediately is to be judged as good or bad. Is the law good as it affects rights and duties of parentage? And again, as it affects the rights and duties of motherhood in contradistinction to fatherhood?

Beginning with the laws affecting marriage, the laws of Kentucky forbid the marriage of blood relations nearer than first cousin. Some states forbid the marriage of first cousins and attempts have been made from time to time to have legislation forbidding it in this state, but so far without success. Marriage is forbidden in the following cases: (1) with an idiot or lunatic; (2) between a white person and a Negro or a mulatto; (3) where there is a husband or wife living, from which the person marrying has not been divorced; (4) when not solemnized or contracted in the presence of an authorized person or society; (5) when at the time of marriage, the male is under fourteen or the female under twelve years of age. Such marriages are prohibited and declared void.

Besides, Courts having general jurisdiction may declare void a marriage obtained by fraud or force, or at the instance of any next friend, where the male was under sixteen or the female under fourteen years of age at the time of the marriage, and the marriage was without the consent of the father, mother, guardian, or other person having the proper charge of his or her person and has not been modified by cohabitation after that age.

This difference of two years in age in the female and the male in these cases is the only difference the law recognizes between the sexes in the right of contracting marriages. This difference is founded upon the supposed earlier physical development of the female, though I believe such earlier development is not an accepted fact among physiologists.

The statistics which define the offenses which permit the marriage contract to be dissolved by divorce, classes them in four categories. The first category enumerates the two causes for which divorce may be given to both parties; and the second, six causes to the party not in fault; the third, three to the wife, when not in like fault; and the fourth, three to the husband, two of them whether he is in like fault or not.

The first is to the husband, when not in like fault; habitual drunkenness on the part of the wife of not less than one year's duration.

The nearest parallel of this for the wife's protection is, to the wife, when not in like fault; confirmed habit of drunkenness on the part of the husband of not less than one year's duration, accompanied with a wasting of his estate, and without any suitable provision for the maintenance of his wife or children.

The second in the category is; to the husband, whether he is in like fault or not: "Adultery by the wife, or such lewd, lascivious behavior on her part as proves her to be unchaste, without actual proof of an act of adultery."

The wife has no protection against the similar unfaithfulness of the husband; though from more aggravated forms she is protected as well as the husband by two provisions in the second category; to party not in fault; living in adultery with another man or woman; and, concealment from the other party of any loathsome disease existing at the time of marriage, or contracting such afterward.

When we come to the laws relating to women as mothers and note the utter disregard of the rights of motherhood, I confess that I find difficulty in expressing myself with moderation; and perhaps I should not care to try to do so if I were not thoroughly convinced by communications I have had with intelligent men, lawyers, and legislators during some years past, that in these laws our legislators have erred far more through their ignorance of the maternal heart and their inherent inability to take a feminine view of the subject, than through carelessness for the misery of women or selfish love of power.

That the laws stand as they are is the fault of women equal with men, because women have been far too apathetic and negligent in expressing their disapproval of laws unjust to their sex.

As this subject is worthy of very careful study, I shall state the theory of the law, as exactly as I can, and then how it is carried out in practice.

The theory of the law is that the State itself is the guardian of every child born in it, and is charged with the duty of proper care and its safety.

These duties it performs through its courts of law, and their exercise of the supreme right of the state over children is evidenced in the case of destitute orphans, or of neglected or vagrant children, for when such cases are brought to the cognizance of courts, they take measures to remove them from such destitute or demoralizing surroundings, and place them in homes, asylums, reformatories, or similar institutions. For obvious reasons, this duty of guardianship must be delegated and placed upon individuals. The law, therefore, regards natural ties and devolves the custody, nurture, and education of the child, upon its parent. I say its "parent," because ordinarily the law recognizes but one parent and that the father, but only and always excepting the poor, despised mother whose offspring is the sign of her shame. Though legislators have had ample opportunity to do so, they have never shown any disposition to set aside, they ignore, the natural rights of unmarried mothers in favor of un-married fathers, but unmarried mothers are invested with the same rights of guardianship as married fathers. With married mothers it is different. I cannot so forcibly express the insignifi-cance in which they are held as by reading extracts from the statistics concerning Guardian and Ward.

"The father of the minor, if living, or if dead, the mother, if suited to the trust, shall be allowed by the court to have the custody, nurture and education of the ward." Think of this, women, you who have been in the habit of supposing that women were honored by the state from their office of motherhood. "If suited to the trust," she may have the custody of her own child. But not in all cases, however, even if the father be dead, and the mother is suited to the trust. For a dead father has more rights than a living mother, as is seen by parentage tracts; "Any father may, by will, appoint a guardian to his infant child during its minority or for any less period, and may appoint the guardian-ship of the infant's estate to one, and the custody, nurture, and education of the infant to another."

Further, we read, "In appointing a guardian, the court shall pay proper attention to the following order of precedence, in sight, and not depart therefrom, unless it deems that prudence and the interest of the infant so requires: First, the father or testamentary guardian of his appointing; secondly, the mother, if unmarried; and thirdly, the next of kin, giving preference to males.

Notice this provision, also, under the chapter of "Wills": "No person under twenty-one years of age can make a will, except in pursuance of a power specially given to that effect, and except, also, that a father, though under twenty-one years of age, may appoint by will a guardian to his child."

Surely, this is the culmination of the injury to a mother. "The law strains a point to extend a father's so-called precedence in right." If a man dying under twenty-one possesses a calf, he may not dispose of it by will, but if he is a father, his immaturity may not prevent his appointing a guardian whose right to the custody, nurture and education of the child is superior to and may supercede that of the mother.

In the exercise of this right of guardianship, undivided with the mother, a father has the sole direction of his child's life, the mother's wishes being consulted only so far as he pleases. If he is in humble circumstances and hires out or apprentices the child, he alone decides the employment and surroundings, as to whether they are moral or healthful, or happy for the child, and he alone receives its wages. If in better circumstances, he alone may direct the education of the child, choosing its residence, its school and the moral training and religious, his mind shall receive. It is always within his legal right to remove the child at his pleasure from the custody and nurture of the mother, and to place it with whomsoever he chooses; and if he will, he is permitted to depute all these rights to a guardian of his appointing. It is terrible to think of the sufferings mothers may have to endure from the exercise of these unrestricted powers by misguided husbands.

The protection the law affords to mothers against the abuse of these powers by fathers is inadequate and hard to obtain in every case and in many of the worst instances, wholly unavailable. As long as the husband and wife remain together, without either legal separation or divorce, there is no clear provision for the defense of the mother, though perhaps a lawyer might find some of the intricacies of the law in some aggravated cases. An instance in point last spring, in Lexington ... was that of a respectable but poor woman in this city, whose husband, without any intimation of his intention to her, took one of the children, a boy between five and seven years of age, and placed it in the care of his mother in Texas; while he, leaving his family here, lived in Cincinnati with a worthless woman. The mother was in a distracted state over the loss of her child, but as she did not wish to take legal steps to separate or divorce herself from her husband, it was not evident what relief she could obtain. The sequel was that the grandmother notified her to come for the child. The mother had to collect the money for the trip from every sympathizing family and now has the child -- until the father chooses to take it away again.

When husband and wife are legally separated or divorced, the court decides which parent shall have the custody of the children, regarding the interest of the children in the decision. But the presumption is always in favor of the father, and if he resists the court's assigning the children to the mother, a clear case must be made out of his moral or financial unfitness for the charge of the children before the mother's superior claim is allowed, no matter if she is wholly "suited to the trust."

The inadequacy of this proves the protection of the mother appears in the facts that no security of the mother's right is given at all, except through an appeal to the court, which is a relief practically out of the reach of the women who most need it. When proceedings for legal separation or divorce are begun or threatened, if the father has all the presumption of the law on his side; and if he has the reason to anticipate that this will not suffice, he can, in many instances, easily defeat the law by removing the child from the custody of the mother and transferring it to another state before the court has taken action. After the child is once out of the state (and his legal right to take it where he pleases is unimpeachable until there is a decree of court to the contrary), it would take years of tedious and expensive litigation to compel him to return it. Practically, therefore, the mother has no right guaranteed to her by the law.

It is no excuse for these iniquitous laws to say that there is little temptation for men to abuse these powers, and that they rarely don't. Law is meant for the restraint of the bad and there is no cruelty by law too awful for some bad man to practice. A position to say such power is rarely abused for since relief is so precarious and delayed, there is every reason for women to keep their sorrows secret, and yet, from time to time society is shocked by a revelation of heart rending misery endured by a mother under the threat of the husband to use this oppressive power and her mother's wretchedness was never made public until, perhaps after years of suffering, either it became beyond endurance or some circumstances occurred to enable him to throw off his tyranny with impunity. Women are reduced to pitiable straits to escape the cruelty of these laws. I have observed the instances reported in the papers, such as a woman denying that she had ever been married to the man who was trying to rob her of her child; of another, perjuring herself as was believed by the neighbors who accounted her a virtuous woman, by swearing in her desperation that her husband was not the father of her child. When I was in South Carolina, these laws giving the children's earnings exclusively to the father were mentioned to me as one reason why the Negro women were too lax about marriage. It is a too common occurrence for the Negro husbands to leave the children with the wives as long as they were small, probably deserting her in the meanwhile, and when the children were large enough to work, to assert their rights to their hire and, under the law, and as the laws of that state do not permit even the miserable relief of divorce, the Negro women were not so willing to risk the bonds of matrimony, as they might be otherwise. This struck me as an unexpected outcropping of the demoralization caused by an unjust law.

Let no woman "lay the flattering unction to her soul" that if, a law became unjust to her sex may not force its evil consequences upon her or in her circle of acquaintances, that it is perhaps not very harmful. She may be sure that somewhere, secretly or openly, it is doing its deadly work of carrying undeserved misery and degradation to her sister-woman.

The remedy for all this injustice and misery is a comparatively simple amendment of the law; of which the principal features are: granting to the father and mother equal or co-guardianship of children, making their rights equal, and forbidding, under a penalty, either one or the other from winning a child from the custody of the other, without due process of law.

In happy and well-regulated families the extent of the law would never be perceived, for equality is the rule of conduct now. Where there is not perfect unity between the parents, and the father would be more conciliatory in his requirements, knowing that in the last resort he would have to justify his actions to a judge other than himself, and the wife would be more patient, secure in the assurance that her rights could never be seriously infringed, because, when necessary, she could be protected by law. Too, co-guardianship would remove causes of dissension between parents, rather than produce them, as is sometimes asserted. The principal thing needed, as I believe, to effect this wholesome change in the Kentucky law, as has been the example in some eight or nine other states, is an enlightenment of the public minds upon the subject, and such an expression from the women as will convince our legislators what is their intelligent wish. It is interesting to club women to notice that in Colorado, the Denver Women's Club, consisting of six hundred women, have a legal department which spent the whole of last season studying three bills which they wished presented to the Legislature. That is a pretty effective way of bringing their opinions to bear upon the legislature, and one which our Woman's Club of Central Kentucky lacks.

I believe legislators will cheerfully accept assistance from women on such points or concede to their petitions, when they are convinced that their suggestions are given after acquiring a fair knowledge of the subject, and proceed from an honest desire to promote justice and not win personal ends. With this conviction in my mind, and in the assurance that this Club can make valuable contributions to this much needed feminine thought, I have willingly accepted what might otherwise be a dry subject.

CHAPTER XIII

AUGUSTUS OWSLEY STANLEY
(1867-1958)

A. O. Stanley's inclusion in a collection of famous Kentucky orators may strike some celebrity-conscious readers as questionable, if not wholly unsuitable. After all. his public speeches were never nationally acclaimed, his political achievements rarely made the news, he never ran for President, and it's even been said he drank too much. However, the exclusion of one who has been called "among the last and best of the old-fashioned Kentucky orators" would seriously weaken the scope and variety of this work. In addition, even a cursory look at his life reveals a colorful, flamboyant figure, and a reading of his speeches suggests flights of eloquence that may verge on greatness.

Research indicates that Stanley's outstanding personality trait was his outspoken individuality. [1] He insisted upon personal liberty for himself and for everyone and most of his speeches are thematically tied to this demand. But his outspokenness led many to shout back, and his share of antagonists is enormous. The Anti-Saloon League accused him of intemperance, the anti-German radicals of World War I accused him of festering treason, the Ku Klux Klan accused him of disloyalty to his state, and the anti-Al Smith group accused him a being a papist. In spite of the controversies, a reading of his speeches makes it clear that he was an independent thinker, grounded in the workings of the Constitution, adamantly for civil rights and freedoms for all. In short, he demanded the upholding of the foundations his country was built upon, regardless of the risk to his personal reputation.

Christened Nudicut Owsley Stanley, this future Kentucky

politician disliked being called "N. O." Stanley and, at the age of ten, persuaded his mother to rename him in honor of his grandmother, Augusta. His parentage may have presaged his future. Stanley's mother was a niece of the former Kentucky governor, William Owsley, and his father, William, was a Confederate Captain, an associate editor of the *Shelby Sentinel*, and, finally, a minister of the Christian Church. Stanley was to become a governor, a fighter, a writer, and an orator of the old-fashioned camp meeting school.

A. O. attended Gordon's Academy near Nicholasville and the Agricultural and Mechanical College in Lexington, where he joined the Union Literary Society and won prizes in oratory. He transferred to Centre College when his father became a minister in Danville and received his Bachelor of Science degree there in 1889.

His first political exposure was as a candidate for county attorney. He lost to his Republican opponent, but four years later he was designated a presidential elector for William Jennings Bryan, and three years after that he was elected to the fifty-eighth Congress.

Stanley's first four years in Congress allied him with the "progressive camp," and he supported state regulation of insurance companies, a federal income tax, an eighteen hour day for railroad employees, and an investigation of the huge American Tobacco Company monopoly and its affiliates. It was his association with the last cause which brought him both notoriety and endearment in his home state. He was praised by tobacco farmers throughout the region for his part in repealing the six-cent tax, which newspapers referred to as the "Stanley Bill." He remained in the House of Representatives, fighting against the amassing of wealth by large companies, for twelve years. It was during this period, too, he developed his rhetorical style.

An excerpt from a speech on the passage of the Pure Food and Drug Act, delivered to Congress in 1906, shows early signs of the wit and irony which would continue to mark his technique.

Holding up a bottle of John Barleycorn, Stanley said:

> *Here is a quart of alcohol, 100 proof strong. It will eat the intestines out of a coyote. It will make a howling dervish out of an anchorite. It will make a rabbit spit in a bulldog's face.*

Stanley delighted in the repeat of parallels or contraries and in his later years became a master of the art.

After his defeat for a U. S. Senate seat in 1914, Stanley campaigned for Governor against Edwin P. Morrow, nephew of Kentucky's first Republican governor. While the two gentlemen were actually very close friends, their public performances scarcely displayed it, and this campaign has to be mentioned as one of the most dramatic in Kentucky politics. One particular event is worth highlighting.

This incident took place as both men were sharing the same platform and Morrow was thrilling the gathering "with his brilliant oratory." While Morrow was speaking, Stanley managed to sit quietly, though he had consumed far too much bourbon before the appearance. However, when his turn came to speak "his head swam and his knees buckled." Somehow he staggered to the back of the platform and there he vomited. Then, embarrassed, he returned to the speaker's stand where he said: "Gentlemen, I beg you to excuse me. Every time I hear Ed Morrow speak, it makes me sick at my stomach."

During this same campaign, Stanley rode a mule into Knott County "complete with saddle bags and a jug of corn liquor" to show that he wasn't too superior to do so. Morrow later said, "Owsley has gone into the Governor's mansion on a mule." Although the *Lexington Leader* accused Stanley of stealing the election, he won a close victory.

At the age of forty-eight, Stanley took the Governor's oath on December 7, 1915, in a "frock coat, gray trousers, and a tall silk hat," without the mule. To the surprise of many of his friends and enemies, he vowed to abstain from liquor during his term of office and, as far as is known, he kept his promise.

As Governor, Stanley naturally delivered many speeches, but one which demonstrates his delight in historical and classical allusions, and his enormous range of knowledge, was entitled "Liberty -- Its Substance and Its Shell," in which he referred to the Hapsburgs, the Hohenzollern, the Marne, the Light Brigade at Balaklava, Tacitus, Von Moltke, Bismarck, George V, Nicholas, Constantine, the Sultans, the Emperor of Austria, the Kaiser, Tiberius, Deormitian, Caligula, Nero, Frederick the Great, Henry Beauclere, Henry I, and Charles I.

While in office, Stanley was attacked from all sides. His positive addiction to freedom and liberty caused him much anguish, but he refused to retreat. One zealous group wanted him to outlaw the teaching of German in public schools, war hysteria having made this an extremely sensitive time. Stanley's veto of this measure caused some to say he "countenanced and aided the speed of disloyalty, sabotage, and treason." His counterattack was to grow a victory garden at the mansion, buy War Bonds, and make over a hundred speeches for war drives.

One of his major achievements as Governor was to create a tax levy bill, the first legislative redistricting bill in twenty-five years. This allowed a state budget system whereby the state schools -- University of Kentucky, Eastern and Western State Normal Schools -- shared a portion of the state's tax levy for the first time. The turning point of the state's educational development may well be attributed to this period.

Considering all the pressures he faced in office, it is not surprising that when he resigned as Governor to become a Senator on May 19, 1919, Stanley said he was happy to "lay aside the multitudinous and harrassing cares of this pestiferous job."

While campaigning for Senator, his theme of individual

freedom was stressed and re-stressed. Some samples from his speeches during this period will underscore this preoccupation:

Servitude is impossible to men who prefer death to oppressions.

To secure the inestimable blessings of liberty for themselves and their posterity, was the mighty task of our discerning and intrepid fathers.

The sole purpose of Civil government is to make all men free, not a few men rich. This is the cardinal principle of Democracy. Government, having no power to create wealth, has no right to bestow it; forced to exact from each citizen a portion of his estate or his earnings for its own maintenance, every dollar is impressed with a solemn trust that it will be economically expended for the good of all, not the aggrandisement of a few.

For our prosperity, our gratitude is due not to the Republican Party, but to Him 'whose loving kindness endureth forever,' who directed the frail barks of our Pilgrim Fathers across the trackless main to the shores of an industrial Eden -- to the stout hearts and brawny arms of the eager and tireless toilers, who explored the mountain passes, crossed the plains, tilled fields, felled forests, dug mines, established great industries, erected populous cities, opened highways across continents and canals between oceans, making this land of the free in wealth, beauty and power, the envy and the admiration of the world.

One single fundamental idea, sublime in its severe simplicity, is the very soul of the Declaration, it is the body of the Constitution of the United States.

> We are told there are a few rates in this temple, and
> blind fanaticism, wild in its disregarding of the sanc-
> tity of the organic laws of the land, boldly proclaims
> its willingness to wreck the temple to kill the rats
> that invest it.

Having served one term as senator, Stanley was defeated by Frederick M. Sackett by more than 24,000 votes in his bid for re-election. Combatting both the dry forces and the Ku Klux Klan, which Stanley held in contempt, proved to be more than he could handle and his home county went Republican.

After he returned to private law practice, Stanley was often invited to be a guest speaker. One of his most important public appearances was before the business community of Chicago, with five hundred leaders of commerce and industry in attendance. The *Cincinnati Enquirer* called this speech "one of the master arguments in support of the Federal constitution" and "as an historical analysis of American government it ranks as a classic. ... a 'Philippic' against the invasion of personal rights ... he hurls his matchless mind and eloquent voice against the despots." A sample follows:

> The mastery of the world passed with the fall of the
> Roman Empire from the shores of the Mediterranean
> to the Baltic, and for a thousand years and more the
> arbiters of human destiny have sprung from the loins
> of a Scandinavian warrior. Whether as Franks or free-
> men upon the banks of the Seine, as Saxons and Angles
> amidst the green hills and dales of Old England, or
> marauding pirates from the wilds of Schleswig and
> Friesland, their activities in peace and their valor in
> war have been dominated and inspired by one master
> passion, the maintenance inviolate of their personal
> independence, a jealous and eternal love of liberty.
> In savagery or civilization he has little known nor
> long endured the sway of a tyrant or the presence of
> a master.

Stanley also occasionally campaigned for other politicians, though his hopes for election had dimmed. And, to be expected, he continued his attacks on prejudice. While speaking for Roman Catholic Al Smith, he said he dared "any damned fanatic to deny him the right to worship as he pleased..." He also campaigned for Albert B. Chandler in 1935 during the gubernatorial contest, but later campaigned for Alben Barkley against Chandler in the 1938 Senatorial primary. His reasons for this may have been purely political, and not altogether altruistic, as his biographer suggests he hoped to fill Barkley's two-year term when the latter was elected Vice-President.

Stanley remained active in politics for twenty more years, following President Herbert Hoover's appointment of him to the International Joint Commission, a U. S. - Canadian agency, in 1930. He was Chairman of the American section after Franklin Roosevelt's inauguration in 1933. Dwight Eisenhower's election, however, ushered in the end of Stanley's appointments, and he retired at the age of 87 in 1954 because "the administration is hard up for jobs."

Stanley's success as a speaker lay in his mastery of the old art of the 19th century with its ornate embellishments. And while he was never a really prominent politician, the speech which follows should show to what degree he was able to charm, to sway and to captivate his audiences. The force of his words, the flow of the language, the syntax, the ironic tone, the incredible knowledge, surely rank him with Clay and Barkley in the art of oratory.

Address In Honor Of Robert E. Lee

by

Hon. A. O. Stanley

Delivered before the Hamilton Club, Chicago, 9 April 1907.

Upon the Virginia heights, overlooking the Nation's Capital, its white and stately columns rising amid the wealth of foliage and flowers that embower it, majestically reposing upon its lofty terraces, in Arlington -- its very walls hallowed by a hundred proud and tender memories -- inseparably intertwined with the private life and public services of the Father of his Country -- such was the once ideal mansion of an ideal man. A wife, illustrious even among southern matrons, for her worth, her devotion, and changeless fidelity, had blessed him with her love and made him the father of many children. Like Washington, the great warrior was wont to turn from public cares and scenes of carnage to the purer and serener joys of his home. Here, with his children, and his children's children at his knees, surrounded by wealth, culture, and idolatrous love, he found his highest and holiest delight.

No man felt more earnest desire for the maintenance of the Union; no man watched with keener regret the passionate out-bursts of intense partisans, North and South, and, at last, none beheld with more poignant anguish the fierce appeal from the forum to the field.

Could Lee have been actuated by aught save an iron and invincible devotion to duty, as he saw it, he would never have resigned his position of prestige and power in the Federal ranks.

Long and active service had convinced his cool, clear, and discriminating intellect of the character of the impending struggle. In answer to the earnest appeal of Gen. Scott to use his best endeavors to avert the inevitable arbitrament of the sword, he replied: "If it comes to a conflict of arms, the war will last at least four years. Northern politicians do not appreciate the determination and pluck of the South, and southern politicians do not appreciate the numbers, resources, and patient perseverance of the North. Both sides forget that we are all Americans, and that it must be a terrible struggle if it comes to war. Tell Gen. Scott that he must do all he can to avert war, and if it comes to the worst, we must then do everything in our power to mitigate its evils."

To espouse this forlorn hope of the seceding States, with their sparse population and limited resources, without a navy, without manufactures, and almost without munitions of war, and lead its meager and ill-accounted bands to ultimate victory, was a task which must have appalled even the grim determination of Lee, and appeared to his prophetic vision as beyond the utmost bound of genius or valor.

Avarice and ambition alike would have deterred him from such a step. His magnificent estate lay within the environs of Washington. Whatever the issue, it must inevitably fall into the hands of the Federal forces. His long and distinguished services, his high place in the Army, and the exalted opinion of his skill and capacity entertained by Gen. Scott -- now too old for active service -- all assured him a high and responsible commission, and every opportunity to display those transcendent talents which were soon to command the unstinted admiration of friend and foe alike. Seldom has ambition beheld a more tempting vista -- a victor's laurels, a conquering nation's acclaim, and possibly that most radiant prize that ever dazed a soldier's vision so often in this land, the reward of martial prowess.

Never has mortal man turned his back upon such a prospect since the mighty Israelite, refusing to be called the son of Pharaoh's daughter, left the alluring glories of a palace and the scepter of a king to become a wanderer in the wilderness, the leader of a band of despised bondsmen in life, and, in death, an unmarked grave on Nebo's lonely top.

Through it all Lee thought not of himself, his fortune, or his fame. Turning for the last time from the hospitable portals of his stately mansion, and speaking of the mere property rights involved, he declared, "If I owned 4,000,000 slaves I would give them all for the Union."

To-day, southern in every fiber, the son of a rebel captain, I declare that, from the depths of a grateful heart, I reverently thank the God of Hosts that there is not a manacle or a chain on one mute and cowering slave under the protecting folds of my country's flag.

Right or wrong, it matters little now. Robert E. Lee believed in the sovereignty of the Southern States; he modestly offered himself to his countrymen and his Commonwealth. His espousal of the cause of the Confederacy was hailed with delight; he was showered with honors and intrusted with high command. He accepted the sword tendered him with the terseness of a soldier, the ardor of a patriot, and the humility of a Christian.

How well and how long he defended the beleaguered cause of the Confederacy I need not relate; history has yet to do full justice to the miracles of his genius and the prodigies of his valor. McClelland, Pope, Burnside, and Hooker, each in turn, hurled his mighty and puissant hosts against that grim, gray line, known as the Army of Northern Virginia, and each in turn reeled, staggering and bleeding, from the deadly encounter. I need not speak of Second Manassas, Harper's Ferry, Fredericksburg, or Chancellorsville -- those mighty monuments to his prowess and his glory are deathless and eternal as the red annals of war. In the flush of triumph, in the wild tumult of victory, the conqueror still loomed towerlike above his conquest.

How that subtle and deadly elixir -- victory -- has seared the soul and fired to delirium the reeling brain of all the world's conquerors.

The imperial Roman majestically wraps his mantle about him and rebukes the sullen sea with the profane boast; "You carry Caesar and his fortunes." Drunk with the blood of 60,000 slaughtered Nervile, he lifts aloft his reeking blade and shouts, "I came, I saw, I conquered."

With Wagram, Jena, Ulm, and Austerliz inscribed upon his flaunting banners, his dauntless brow encircled with an iron crown, and the purple upon his shoulders, the French Emperor forgets the obscure Corsican and the students of charity at Brienne. Grim, solitary, and defiant, bedecked with diadems and garters and titles of nobility, he talks of his star and vainly fancies he holds in his puny hand that Nemesis, which to-morrow shall mock him, called destiny.

None of the world's great captains ever had more reason for exalting in the hour of supreme success than Robert E. Lee. Sprung from an ancient and illustrious line -- his father, the friend, confidant, and companion in arms of Washington -- fortune and fame alike view to do him honor. A paragon of physical strength and majesty, tall athletic, and graceful -- the front of Jove himself.

His countrymen regarded him with unexampled reverence and devotion; his soldiers hailed his presence in the camp with huzzas of admiration and delight, and in battle, on his white charger, he thrilled them like a god. In their eyes the invincible apotheosis of war. Yet in all his triumphs no word of boasting escaped his pure lips, and calumny has not attributed to any act of his a selfish purpose or an ambitious design. At Chancellorsville, and with the wild acclaim of twice 10,000 victorious veterans drowning the din of battle, he meekly ascribes the glory to the God of Hosts, and with tear-dimmed eyes seeks to soothe the dying agonies of his great lieutenant.

Great in victory, he was greater still in defeat. Behold him after the three days fight at Gettysburg, where first he faced disaster, with untold magnanimity assuming all the responsibility for that fateful day -- attributable to another's error or another's fault -- smiling and tranquil, he rides among his shattered and disordered columns, rising above the terror and turmoil around him, sublime, serene, undaunted; they halt at his command and rally to the magic of his call. Chaos becomes order and the Army of Northern Virginia wheels about in serried array, its spirit unbroken and its faith in its mighty chief unaltered and unalterable.

In the meantime there had arisen in the West a soldier, broad in conception, patient and capable in action, rigid and changeless as fate in his invincible purpose. He had twice bisected the Confederacy. Sherman, leaving desolation in his wake, was marching unimpeded toward the sea. On all sides, obedient to his masterful design, there was converging about the doomed Virginians a sinister and rigid cordon, bristling with bayonets, indifferent to slaughter and indomitable in its purpose. Through the southwestern mountain passes, through the gates of the lower valley, from the battle-scarred vales of the Rappahannock, from the Atlantic seaboard to the waters of the James, came the serried hosts on field and flood.

Lee rallied the wreck of his gallant army for the last encounter, but neither genius nor valor could avail.

The rebel lines, extending for 30 miles, thinned and attenuated, clutched the earth like a wild beast, and, in the teeth of impending doom, fought on, fierce and determined. At last, surrounded in the open plain, barefooted, tattered, pinched with hunger, gaunt from famine, staggering from sleeplessness, its last ration consumed and its last round of ammunition exhausted, bowed to the inevitable.

Less than 8,000 ragged veterans dropped their bright muskets from nerveless hands, and Lee tendered his stainless sword to the most determined foe and the most magnanimous conqueror of the age.

I rejoice that to-night, upon the anniversary of that fateful day, the South contemplates the scene without shame and the North without exultation.

The modest magnanimity of the Federal chief made of Appomattox more than a surrender -- it was reconciliation. Even in the flush of his great triumph he remembered with tender consideration the vanquished foe. All salutes and demonstrations calculated to wound the pride or harrow the feelings of the fallen Confederates were forbidden, he reminding his veterans that their foes of yesterday would be their countrymen of to-morrow.

Nor shall the South forget that when a Federal grand jury sought to disregard the soldier's parole and to stain that sword, the trophy of his valor and his prowess, he defended the honor and the life of his mighty captive with the same grim determination with which he had maintained the Union, and neither Senates nor Presidents could shake or alter his fixed resolve. At the bier of Grant a reunited Nation stood with uncovered head, while veterans, blue and gray, with tear-dimmed eyes and tender hands, laid him to rest.

After the lapse of half a century, its cruel wounds all healed, its battle-scarred plains covered with verdure, and 500,000 graves embowered in flowers -- North and South alike -- we look back upon that mighty and fraternal strife with a feeling of sadness and a sense of infinite regret.

222

CHAPTER XIV

ALBEN W. BARKLEY
(1877-1956)

In the tradition of another famous native Kentuckian, Alben Barkley was born in a log cabin. And, although he did not reach the ultimate political achievement of his precursor, an achievement predicted by his early teachers, Miss Girtie and Miss Lizzie, he came close enough to implant a new word in the American vernacular -- *Veep* -- a sobriquet which the thirty-fifth Vice-President said gave him "a warm feeling" whenever he heard it. Warmth well may be the distinguishing feature of this amiable, witty and endearing personality whose service to his state spanned almost half a century, a record unequalled only by Henry Clay a hundred years before. [1]

In order to avoid becoming, in his own words, "too enthusiastic about my 'creator'," "The Veep" denied that he was a self-made man, and yet in many respects he was -- he even remade his own name. He was christened Willie Alben Barkley but, in what was perhaps his first aggressive act of political sagacity, he renamed himself Alben William Barkley as soon as he was old enough to assert himself on the subject. He later said of the decision that he doubted "anyone called Willie Alben could have been elected assistant superintendent of the county poorhouse," and he considered, as "one of the graver short-comings" of his long career, the fact that he was never able to introduce a bill making it obligatory for parents to forebear naming their children until the children were old enough to name themselves.

Barkley was born on his grandfather's farm in Graves County, Kentucky, November 24, 1877, in unpretentious circumstances. His father, John Wilson Barkley, a tenant farmer, eventually owned fifty acres near Lowes, Kentucky, and became an elder in the Presbyterian Church, but when Willie Alben was fourteen he worked in the wheat fields nearby for the $1.00 a day he could add to the family income. However modest his early environment may have been, Barkley's ancestry was not.

His mother, Electra Eliza Smith, was the daughter of a Confederate soldier who died of wounds while serving with Morgan's cavalry during the Civil War. Grandmother Barkley was the cousin of James A. McKenzie, one-time state representative from Kentucky and later United States Minister to Rome. She was, in addition, the great-granddaughter of William Stevenson, the first ruling elder of the Fourth Creek Presbyterian Church, who was called "Little Gabriel" because he could sing and pray so loud. Stevenson was also the great-grandfather of the first Adlai Ewing Stevenson, Vice-President under Cleveland, and grandfather of the more recent Adlai E. Stevenson. In an ironic twist of genealogies, these combined lines turned the most renowned of the offspring into adversaries, as both Stevenson and Barkley vied for the Democratic nomination for President in 1952.

It was in Lowes that Alben William made his speaking debut, and an inauspicious beginning it was. Barkley, in his memoir, *That Reminds Me*, relates the incident:

> *I was on the program to "orate" the annual Children's Day celebration at the local Presbyterian Church. I had wanted to do my best, not only because my father was an elder in the church, but because I had a crush at the time on the pastor's daughter, Sadie Ward, who had pretty auburn hair. The day before the event, Mr. Joe Dunn, who operated a farm next to my father's, saw me, and said, "Boy, I'll bet you're going to forget your speech tomorrow!" When I got up to speak, I saw Joe Dunn sitting there in the middle of the front row,*

grinning at me. Immediately everything I had memo-
rized went out of my mind. I was so mortified that I
could not even face Sadie when the box lunches were
opened.

Barkley entered Marvin College in Clinton, Kentucky, where he was nicknamed "Monk" for his frequent "monkeyshines." While there he entered the annual Oratorical Contest, determined to win a medal, possibly in expiation for his earlier fiasco at Lowes. He was "dressed to the teeth for the event," with his hair plastered flat, wearing a black suit and a new striped shirt with the fashionable "snap-on celluloid cuffs." Proceeding smoothly, he suddenly noticed that one of his cuffs had come unsnapped. Once again, he completely forgot his prepared speech, but this time he didn't falter. He blithely readjusted his cuff as though its undoing were the most natural thing in the world, and proceeded to win the gold medal.

At Marvin, Barkley followed a classical curriculum and became a member of the Periclean Debating Society. At that time he was a practiced "stump speaker," reciting his orations to the unprotesting pines, which reminded him that Henry Clay had rehearsed his speeches to the pigs, and that "the pigs couldn't talk back either."

Barkley attended Emory University for one year and later taught the intermediate level at Marvin for $25.00 a month. He resigned after six months, however, having discovered that he had no great gift for teaching, and at 21, went to Paducah, where his father had found employment in a cotton mill. In 1898 it was still possible to be admitted to the bar by reading law in an attorney's office and then passing an examination. Barkley chose to read under Representative Wheeler and also served as Wheeler's clerk. His salary was "exactly nothing per month," but he had set into motion a destiny which would earn him more than money could buy.

After reading law for two years, he entered private practice and simultaneously began a career in Democratic politics. He was prosecuting attorney for McCracken County from 1905 to 1909, and during the next four years he served as judge of the County Court. He married Dorothy Brower, who was to be his wife for the next forty-seven years and the mother of his three children, David, Marian, and Laura Louise.

Barkley's entrance into politics was, to him, inevitable. He later said, "I was a Kentuckian and a lawyer, and I had, in those days, a natural inclination to stop whatever I was doing and start making a speech any time I saw as many as six persons assembled together." His first public duty did not, however, come as "natural." The very day he was sworn in as county judge he was asked to perform a wedding ceremony with over a hundred guests in attendance. Among the guests was Judge Richard Lightfoot, his immediate predecessor, who was long accustomed to the form of the ritual. Barkley's painful recollection of that day belies the eloquence he was later to attain:

> I began to choke up so I could hardly speak the words of the ceremony. I grunted, sneered, coughed, swallowed, bit my lips, blew my nose, wiped my eyes, rubbed my brow, and shook at the knees. Finally I undertook to lecture the hapless couple on the seriousness of the step they were taking. I got all bogged down in a wordy and windy sermon. At last, in desperation, I stopped short, blurted out "You're married!" and fled ...

In 1912, when Barkley was not quite thirty-five, he ran his first race for the House of Representatives and won. He became a member of the 63rd Congress on the day Woodrow Wilson was inaugurated, and remained a fervent supporter of the policies of that administration. During this period he met William Jennings Bryan, Wilson's first Secretary of State, whom Barkley referred to as "the greatest orator" he had ever heard. It is unlikely, however, that Barkley's speaking style was influenced by the classical and puristic Bryan, for Barkley had little tolerance for formal rhetoric in general. One of his favorite anecdotes on the subject concerns the definition of an orator:

> ... *if you meet a man and ask him how much is two and two and he says it is four, he is not an orator. But if you ask ... how much is two and two and he responds in the following manner, viz., namely, to wit: 'when in the course of human events, it becomes necessary to take the second numerical and superimpose it upon the figure two, then I say unto you, and I say it without fear of successful contradiction, that the consequential results amount to four,' then you (have) an orator.*

By 1926, Barkley felt prepared to run for the United States Senate, having served seven terms in the House. His campaign was successful and he served in the Senate for twenty-three years, from 1937-1947 as the Majority Leader. In that capacity, Barkley displayed his sharp sense of political strategy and became a leading spokesman for the Roosevelt administration.

There is little question that Franklin Roosevelt held Barkley in high esteem. At one point during his administration, it had been suggested that Barkley be appointed to the Supreme Court and there was pressure upon the President to take action. Declining to do so, Roosevelt offered Barkley his reasons in a letter: "You are a sort of balance wheel that has kept things moving forward all these years -- and that's that. I had come to the conclusion that there are nine Justices but only one Majority Leader in the Senate -- and I can't part with him in that capacity."

Barkley campaigned with Roosevelt for the first time in 1932. His spontaneous wit, and his ability to capitalize on any immediate situation, charmed audiences everywhere. He developed and refined the earthy, home-spun, yet occasionally sharp and biting oratorical qualities that were to endear him to the whole nation. Illustrative of his style is the following excerpt from a speech he delivered to introduce FDR from the rear platform of a train which was whistle-stopping through Kentucky:

> *My friends, it has been four years since I spoke in Corbin, so naturally I cannot call every individual in this great crowd by name. But I can recognize that you are the same people I addressed here four years ago. The reason I know you are the same people is that, after four years of Hoover, you are all wearing the same clothes that you had on four years ago!*

According to Barkley's account, the crowd roared "Amen!" and "That's the truth!" Roosevelt thereafter referred to the introduction as "a choice example of pertinent political satire."

During the campaign of 1936, Barkley again utilized the clothes imagery to good effect. He was making a speech in St. Cloud, Minnesota, when he noticed that his audience was beginning to laugh. To his horror, he saw that perspiration was trickling through his ice-cream colored trousers. He responded as follows:

> *Ladies and Gentlemen, I notice that you are amused by the fact that my trousers are becoming somewhat damp. Let me explain that four years ago this could not have happened. Under the Hoover administration, all I could afford was thick cotton underwear which would have absorbed the perspiration. But after four years of Democratic prosperity, I am wearing silk underwear, and, as all of you good people know, silk is just no good at all for soaking up sweat.*

On the floor of the Senate, however, Barkley's speeches were not always delivered in the rustic, lightly ironic vein. Sometimes he was charged with invective and was harshly satirical. Referring to the "political immorality" of the Harding administration, he said, "In the past eight years we have witnessed in the United States of America a series of political crimes so nauseating and revolting as to make grand larceny sound like an announcement of a hymn or golden text at Sunday School." And, during the Keynote Address of 1936 at the Democratic Convention, he responded in the following way to charges that the New Deal had harmed the farmers:

> They have wept over the slaughter of a few little pigs as if they had been tender human infants nestling at their mothers' breast. They have shed these tears over the premature death of pigs as if they had been born, educated and destined for the ministry or for politics. But their bitterest tears are not shed over the fate of the little pigs. Their real grief comes from the slaughter of the fat hogs of privilege and plunder which they have fed on the people's substance. They are not weeping because we plowed under a few rows of corn. Mr. Hoover started that. Their real sorrow springs from the fact that we have plowed under the sordid conception of Old Deal government and its chance to be restored to the control of American life.

Using this same tone and figurative language, Barkley delivered the Keynote Address at the 1948 Democratic Convention. He referred to the New Deal as "this cankering, corroding, fungous growth which every Republican orator, save one, denounced with unaccustomed rancor" and then "in their adopted platform hugged to their political bosom as if it were the child of their own loins."

It was at this convention that Barkley was first seriously considered for the Presidential nomination, and it was this address which inspired the enthusiasm. The *St. Louis Post-Dispatch* said the speech had "swept the Democratic Convention off its feet" and that "it was no secret that many of the delegates would have preferred" Barkley "as head of the ticket in place of Truman." Barkley was, instead, selected as Harry Truman's running mate, and the duo astounded many pollsters by winning the election.

During the campaign, Barkley made what he called "the first full-dress prop-stop campaign in national political history." He chartered a plane, *The Bluegrass*, and, in six months, gave 250 speeches in 36 states, covering 150,000 miles.

Barkley seemed to enjoy an easy friendship with Truman, whom he liked for his "humanness." Truman once brought him a gavel made of White House timber. Barkley responded "that since I had disappointed my early teachers by not going to the White House, it was very kind of the President to bring a piece of the White House to me." Barkley's continued desire for the highest office in the land was no secret. In the interim before the next convention, however, he had other thoughts on his mind. He met his next wife.

Widowed almost three years, he later noted that "the society columnists had been marrying me off with monotonous regularity to almost every eligible widow in the country. If I had entered into matrimony with every charming lady with whom my name was linked in print, I would have made Brigham Young look like a woman-hater." When, however, he met Jane Rucker Hadley at a Washington party at Clark Clifford's, he didn't dally. He swept Mrs. Hadley, a widow for five years, off her feet. Within four months of their introduction, they were united in a marriage which would last until his death seven years later.

In 1952, Barkley sought the top spot on the Democratic ticket, but withdrew from the running when some spokesmen for organized labor made it clear that they thought he was too old to be president, though they thought his record was good. He returned to the Senate in the 1954 elections.

In his role as an elder statesman, Barkley was often asked for advice by young Congressmen. Perhaps his most humorous, if not soundest, counsel was delivered at the "Congressional Night" party at the National Press Club of Washington, which is a traditional event in honor of the newly-elected Congressmen. Some of his instructions were:

Never act as a judge at a beauty contest or a baby contest. It is impossible to be impartial. If it is a beauty contest, you may have designs on the beauty. If it is a baby contest, the chances are that the unsuccessful babies will become voters before you quit running for office, and you will have built up a block of opposition which may prove disastrous.

Do not ride in any Government-owned or operated car ... unless you are willing to seal your lips against the practice on the part of others, which you do not intend to do.

When giving constituents your Washington address, do not fail to spell out in full "Senate Office Building." If you give him the abbreviation -- S.O.B. -- he will not know whether you are calling him one, or expect him to call you one.

Do not permit yourself to go on junkets, if it is a waste of time and it costs money that comes from the taxpayers. Avoid all such excursions, unless your remaining in Washington in the usual performance of your duties would involve greater waste of time and the people's money.

Barkley's particular oratorical technique has been described in polar terms as "the greatest hog-caller who ever came out of the Blue Grass State" and "a silver-throated orator, who, by comparison, would make Patrick Henry seem like a tongue-tied man suffering from chapped lips." Of the art of oratory itself, Barkley is characteristically self-effacing when he equates it with a bull calf: "a point here and a point there, and, in between a helluva lot of bull!"

Alben Barkley brought to oratory a subjective, personal dimension that did not rest on argument alone. It was more than a persuasive technique -- it was an extension of himself and, because it was grounded in his own personality with its particular humor, humility and geniality, people identified with it and with him. In her book, *I Married the Veep*, his widow recalled her first impression of Barkley: "I liked his mouth especially. It seemed touched, nearly always, with a smile in the making. Or echoing a smile that had just passed. His face was mobile. When he spoke, his whole face talked."[2]

The Veep's life ended in Lexington, Virginia, on April 30, 1956. As his funeral train passed through Kentucky on its way to Paducah, the people who stood by the tracks were seen dropping to their knees. Senator John Sherman Cooper remarked at that time that "They knew that a fellowship and understanding which had been a part of their lives had gone."

Record Of Democratic Party Keynote Address

By Alben W. Barkley, United States Senator from Kentucky, delivered before the Democratic National Convention, Philadelphia, Pennsylvania, July 12, 1948.

Our claim upon the confidence of the people rests upon a consistent, constructive and farsighted record of devotion to the people's welfare; a record which rescued the American economy of free enterprise from a collapse we did not foster; a record which four times the American people have overwhelmingly endorsed. In humility, but profound sincerity, we trust they will endorse it again.

There has never been greater need in the world than now for the sort of leadership which, from its origin, the Democratic Party has given in the development and fortification of democracy in America.

This leadership has not been sectional. It has been national. It has not sought to advance one class to the unjust detriment of others.

The unprecedented challenge, which beckons us to service in these uncertain times, demands that we look beyond the metes and bounds of states or nations, or partisan political organizations, to survey the obligations resting upon the democratic process, which we espouse, in rebuilding the hopes of a devastated world.

In the midst of such a summons, and on the basis of our record, we meet here today, and shall meet our opponents, all and sundry, in this contest and on the day of election next November.

What is this record of which I speak? What is the sum total of these accomplishments which we have wrought in the sixteen years now drawing to a close?

In spite of the chronic noise of this program's enemies, the American people will not willingly surrender the great gains which they have made under it.

> *The moving finger writes; and having writ,*
> *Moves on; nor all your piety nor wit*
> *Shall lure it back to cancel half a line*
> *Nor all your tears wash out a word of it.*

But, I call attention to the following items in our bill of particulars, of which we would remind the American people as evidence of our good faith with them and our service to them:

A farmer's agricultural and price support program, which, in sixteen years, has increased farm income by 800 per cent, substantially reduced interest rates on farm credit, reduced farm mortgage indebtedness by more than 50 per cent, and farm mortgage foreclosures by 95 per cent.

A soil conservation program, which has arrested the wasting processes of soil erosion, by which we propose to hand this land of ours down to other generations capable of their support.

A rural electrification program, which has lifted from millions of farm women the drudgery of exhausting housework and brought to millions of farmers the boon of electric power for their homes and barns and farm equipment.

A prosperity enabling the American people to indulge in personal savings of more than $100,000,000,000 since 1939.

A prosperity that has enabled the Treasury of the United States to discharge, in a little more than two years, more than

$27,000,000,000 of the national debt inherited from the great expenditures of the war.

Let us ask, and let the American people ask, those who spray this forest of superb accomplishment with the froth of their vindictive lips, which tree will they cut down with their mighty ax or their puny hatchet?

In 1946 the Republican party secured control of both branches of the Congress and has been in control ever since.

The people did not really mean to elect a Republican Congress. They were voting against irksome and irritating annoyances which the war had required and which many of them thought should have been already eliminated. But, whatever the motive, the result was the same.

What has been its record? How has it dealt with the monumental problems of the American people?

During the war, under the administration of President Roosevelt, occurred probably the greatest discovery in the history of science or invention, the discovery and utilization of atomic energy.

This fantastic element of nature has always existed, just as the rays of the sun always held the mystery of electricity long before Franklin flew his kite, but it had not been brought under control of man until the emergency of war produced it, at a cost to the American people of $2,000,000,000 or $3,000,000,000.

The problem which faces the world now is how, and by whom, it shall be used, and whether for the destruction of mankind, or for his greater advancement in developing and producing the means of greater happiness and prosperity.

The Eightieth Republican Congress refused to confirm for the terms fixed by law, the members of the Atomic Commission, which has been engaged in profound research into this new force of nature. But, it shortened their terms to a period of two years, so that, if successful in the coming election, they might secure political control of the Commission and its functions.

Judging from the proceedings of the recent Republican Convention, you would not have known that atomic energy had ever been discovered or dreamed of.

This Republican Congress claimed to have had a mandate from the American people. It began the discharge of that mandate in 1947 by seeking to destroy the Rural Electrification Administration, by denying to it adequate funds for its extension to the farmers of the nation.

Though lacking in courage to repeal directly the soil conservation program, they have sought, both in 1947 and 1948, to restrict or destroy it by denying it the funds necessary for its administration.

While lacking in courage to repeal the labor relations act, and their fair labor standards act, they have sought so to modify the basis upon which these enactments were predicated, as to destroy, in part, the rights enjoyed by labor in the collective process. They have done this by the enactment of a statute which had its inception in a desire to destroy the right of American labor to organize, portions of which enactment have already been declared null and void by the Supreme Court of the United States.

The American people have the right to demand that the Republican party and its candidates take them into their confidence regarding their intentions on this great program, which they condemn out of their mouths, but indorse in their platforms.

If we are to assume that they propose to abolish it from the statute books, let them so advise the American people. They cannot talk out of both corners of their mouths at once nor reincarnate the spirit of a mythological Janus, either in their platform or in their public utterances.

What, may I ask again, is the record of the Republican Eightieth Congress, upon which the candidates and platform base their claim for support?

When it first assembled in January, 1947, the new Speaker of the House of Representatives, who was the permanent chairman of the recent Republican Convention, announced that they would open each session with a prayer and close it with a probe.

They have been in control of this Congress during its entire existence. If their prayers have been no more effective than their probes, they did not rise above the heads of the Congressional inmates. The mandate, upon which this Congress claimed to have been elected, was supposed to have called for the undoing of nearly every thing that had been done since they folded their tents and departed from Washington in 1933.

There is more to this record than appears upon the surface. There is more to it than found its way into the law books. There is the record that is written in committee hearing and in floor debates. There is the record of things promised and not accomplished. There is the record of attempted sabotage of some of the greatest programs ever inaugurated by the American government.

So far as the Eightieth Congress is concerned, the evidence of things seen is no reliable guide to things unseen.

You do not see a housing bill in that visible record. What became of it? Notwithstanding repeated recommendations by the President urging it to enact adequate housing legislation, not only for the veterans of our latest war, but for millions of people in the lower income brackets, this Republican Congress did nothing. Word came down from Philadelphia, where the platform committee was in session, in the closing hours of the last confused sessions of the Congress, demanding that some sort of housing bill be passed. Anything with the word "house" in it would be sufficient. They had to see it written across the horizon. Where is that housing legislation? It is not on the statutes. It furnishes no roof over the veterans, workers or farmers. It is just another "gone goose."

Repeatedly, the President recommended the enactment of legislation to improve and conserve the health of our people. The Eightieth Congress fumed and fretted and dickered. But where is the health legislation which the Republican party and the Republican platform have promised the American people? It is another "gone goose."

Repeatedly, the President urged this Congress to enact legislation to improve the American educational system, to assist the states in providing better schools and better teachers and better school facilities for the education of our people, and found deplorably deficient during the administration of the selective service law in the last war.

The American people have the right to ask Republican leaders of the Eightieth Congress, and the platform makers at Philadelphia in June, and the candidates nominated at that convention, to explain why the Congress, which they endorse, failed utterly in the enactment of legislation to improve our educational facilities. They have the right to ask to what extent they may rely upon present promises in regard to education, made either by a platform or by candidates, since they have been unable or unwilling to honor their commitments in the past. Where is the Republican educational program?

If you ask me where all these measures now repose, I answer that they have gone to the home of lost causes. If I may quote a recent distinguished authority on the subject, they are a part of the flock of "gone geese," put to flight by the Republican Congress which has just adjourned.

Why did these measures remain unacted upon? It may be because they bordered too much upon the hated and despised theory that government should place its powers and its facilities at the disposal of the people, to be used by them to advance their welfare.

If you doubt this diagnosis, ask the Republican Speaker of the House of Representatives. Ask the Republican chairman of the House Rules Committee, which did not even permit the housing bill to come to the floor of the House for consideration or debate. Ask the Republican Majority Leader of the House of Representatives. Ask the chairman of the House Banking and Currency Committee. Ask the chairman of the House Ways and Means Committee. Ask the junior Senator from Washington, the junior Senator from Missouri, and the junior Senator from the state of Wisconsin.

Repeatedly, the President of the United States called attention to the increase in the cost of living, which, since 1945, notwithstanding periodical increase in wages, has reduced the wage earner's buying power by more than 16 per cent.

It was upon this issue, in part, that the Republicans won control of the two houses of Congress in 1946. But this Republican Congress was content to pass a milk and water voluntary price reduction measure, in spite of which prices have continued to soar. Production, they said, was the remedy to the high cost of living. Repeatedly, the President urged Congress to take definite steps to halt this spiral of increased prices and consequent lower take-home wages. Production has exceeded war-time levels. But prices have continued to rise while Republican Congress continued to dawdle.

Today the retail food price index is standing at 211 per cent compared to the average of 1935 to 1939. It is higher than it has ever been in the history of this country. Food prices are 12½ per cent higher than they were a year ago. They are 126 per cent higher than they were in August, 1939, and 45 per cent higher than in June, 1946, when price regulations were allowed to lapse.

The consumer's price index covering food, clothing, rent, fuel, electricity, ice, house furnishings and other necessities of the moderate income group now stands at 171 per cent higher than in August, 1939, and 28 per cent higher than in June.

But the Eightieth Republican Congress contented itself with the untruthful assertion that the President has all the powers he needs to hold the banks against the inflationary flood, and refused to take further steps in the war against inflation.

In the platform in 1944, the Republican party criticized the dispersion of the agencies dealing with labor subjects away from the Department of Labor, and pledged themselves to consolidate them all under the Secretary of Labor.

The Eightieth Congress not only deliberately refused to carry out that pledge, but has literally stripped the Department of Labor by transferring from it agencies already existing under its jurisdiction, such as the Conciliation Service, and refused to approve a reorganization plan sent to Congress by the President, which would have brought about a more central jurisdiction within the department on matters dealing with labor.

Following the enactment of the Smoot-Hawley tariff law of 1930, and the inauguration of a Democratic administration in 1933, Congress enacted a program for reciprocal trade agreements, in an effort to soften the inequities and exorbitant tariff duties provided in that law, and open up the doors for the resumption of international trade.

This is a tragic betrayal of our obligations, not only to the American people, but to the world. In our legislation providing aid for the recovery of Europe, we required every nation receiving this assistance to enter into similar agreements with other nations, to level off, in part, the barriers to trade that have stifled commerce, thrown labor out of employment and contributed to the frictions which have brought war and devastation to the world.

In the enactment of the Smoot-Hawley tariff law of 1930, I recall the influence of the Pennsylvania Manufacturers' Association. I recall the dominating influence of Mr. Joseph R. Grundy, then head of this association. He came to Washington and did his work. He did it well. He succeeded in procuring the enactment of the highest tariff barriers ever raised against international trade in the history of this or any other nation.

After accomplishing the creation of this legislative straight-jacket, he apparently disappeared like some sunken river from the surface of the earth, until the assembling of the recent Republican Convention, when he reappeared with all his power, influence and skillful manipulation in behalf of candidates, platforms and policies. He so dominated that convention that it has been designated by some of the press as the "Grundy convention."

The new Republican chairman insists that it must be a government of the best people, by the best people and for the best people. This is a resurgence of the ancient Hamiltonian doctrine that only the rich, the well educated, and the well born are qualified to participate in government in these free United States. Obviously, this will be the pattern of the Republican appeal to the American people.

> *All hail the power of Grundy's name.*
> *Let candidates prostrate fall,*
> *Bring forth the Republican diadem,*
> *And crown him boss of all.*

It would be a futile process to waste time seeking to analyze the newest Republican national platform. It was appropriately described by the Senator from Massachusetts, who was chairman of the Republican resolutions committee, when he said: "It is a tent big enough for anybody to get under."

But soon after he was nominated upon it, the Republican candidate for President announced that he would inaugurate the greatest house cleaning ever seen in Washington, if he should be elected.

We have, from time to time in the past, been promised or warned of other house cleanings, and the American people will recall in some recent Republican history the type of house cleaning they got.

The Republican nominee has also announced, with characteristic finality, that he proposes to clean the cobwebs from the government at Washington, as he has cleaned them from the government at Albany, following long tenure of Democratic administration at both places.

I am not an expert on cobwebs, but, if my memory does not betray me, when the Democratic party took over the government of the United States sixteen years ago, even the spiders were so weak from starvation that they could not weave a cobweb in any department of the government in Washington.

However, whatever the platform may or may not promise, whatever the candidate may or may not stand for, we have, in all this confusion and vague atmosphere of promises and threats, one clean true clarion call. They are going to eliminate all the bureaucrats in Washington.

Congress creates a bureau in some department, like the Bureau of Internal Revenue in the Treasury, or the Bureau of Reclamation in the Interior Department, or of Soil Conservation in the Department of Agriculture, or the Bureau of Foreign and Domestic Commerce in the Department of Commerce, or the Bureau of Yards and Docks in the Navy, or the Federal Bureau of Investigation in the Department of Justice. Some able and sincere American is appointed as the head of one of these bureaus, and he is immediately denounced as a bureaucrat, and the Republican politicians swear by all the gods of justice and economy they will eliminate him from the payroll as a barnacle upon our ship of state.

What is a bureaucrat? A bureaucrat is a Democrat who holds some office that a Republican wants; and the only sort of house cleaning you will get in Washington, in the event of a Republican victory next November, will be the changing of the political complexion of those who hold the offices.

The fourth article of the current Republican platform quotes Abraham Lincoln. The Republican politicians and leaders have not been closer to Lincoln in two generations than to quote him. But they did quote him in their platform where he said: "The dogmas of the quiet past are inadequate to the stormy present. The occasion is piled high with difficulty and we must rise with the occasion. As our case is new, so we must think anew and act anew."

This is a precise description of the conditions which faced this country sixteen years ago, when the Democratic party accepted the responsibility of charting a new course for our domestic and international economy.

We found that the dogmas of the quiet past were inadequate to the stormy situation which then confronted us. The occasion was piled high with difficulties, and we sought to rise with the occasion. As our case was new, we thought anew and acted anew.

Let us apply this principle to our present international situation. There can be no question that the unaccustomed remedies which the Democratic party applied to this new situation in America contributed largely to the ability of our government, and our people, to mobilize the moral, spiritual and economic forces of this great people to bring about the success of the Allied nations in driving back Hitlerism and its particular form of totalitarian tyranny.

We had not wished to be drawn into the great conflict which he precipitated. For more than two years we sought to avoid involvement, just as nearly a generation before we had sought to avoid involvement in World War No. I. But notwithstanding these efforts to remain aloof from the conflict, the question constantly arose, before we became involved, as to the extent of our preparation and our readiness for the conflict, if it should be forced upon us. This involved selective service, the repeal of embargoes and the arming of ships. It involved lend-lease, in aid of those who were fighting for liberty across the seas.

I do not wish now to dig up the dead bones of past history, but if the American people will refresh themselves by referring to the record of Republican votes in both houses of the Congress on all these measures, they will find a revealing consistency in opposition to every measure calculated to prepare our country for the blow and to soften its impact if it should be inflicted.

We were drawn into the Second World War because of events familiar to us all. We mobilized every element of our population and of our economy, and in this mobilization Republicans joined with Democrats, high and low, in the service of their country. We claim no partisan credit or merit because of this universal all-out crusade against world enslavement. But, it is the truth of history to say that these efforts were guided by an administration headed by a great American who inspired his countrymen to total devotion and total sacrifice in behalf of our country and a democratic world.

This man rests in the peaceful atmosphere of a quiet grave at Hyde Park. Some Republican orators of questionable taste seem to fear his spirit now, as they feared the force of his personality when alive. Neither their prejudiced minds nor their forked tongues can rob him of the eminence which he will occupy in the history of America and of the world.

It has been three years since the end of hostilities. In these circumstances, we have been compelled to assume the leadership and the greater responsibility for the preservation of peace, the occupation of conquered territory, and the inauguration of the processes by which a peaceful world might be restored to mankind.

Unfortunately, these three years have not brought peace. We have neither peace nor war. The world situation has reached a posture where intensity of feeling and spontaneity of conduct might easily precipitate armed conflict.

Our government, through the President and the Secretary

of State and all other responsible agencies, including a majority of the Congress, has sought to adjust the differences and adopt a foreign policy that would preserve our own integrity, guarantee our own security and ultimately bring peace to a distraught world.

In this effort, eminent and able and patriotic Republicans have shared the responsibility, and have aided us in keeping our foreign policy out of the mire of partisan politics and upon a solid basis of justice and equity in world security.

It was through the initiative of our government that the United Nations was established. We have sought to strengthen it, and pledge ourselves to continue the effort.

It was through our initiative that the World Bank and the World Monetary Fund were created to stabilize monetary currencies and stimulate reconstruction among the devastated nations and economies.

It was through our initiative that various international organizations, subordinate to, but a part of, the United Nations setup, have been inaugurated to further these indispensable objectives.

I rejoice, and we all rejoice, in the great contribution made to this universal purpose by these men who subordinated their partisanship to the welfare of their country and of the world.

But this achievement has not been accomplished without obstinate obstruction on the part of responsible men in the Congress of the United States. This is particularly true in the House of Representatives. I need not repeat the efforts of the Republican leaders of the House of Representatives, and their allies, to whittle away the recovery program until it should become a mere shadow of its original self, and descend to the level of a mere relief measure.

I need not refer to the actual sabotage of this great program by the reduction of 26 per cent of the amount which Congress has set as a practical minimum in the requirements for the first year of its administration. Fortunately, in the Senate, Republican leadership helped to retrieve most of the losses sustained in the efforts of the House of Representatives to break faith with our people and with people of the world, and in this accomplishment we may all rejoice without regard to political affiliations.

But this program has only begun. These same men will be in charge of that branch of the American Congress in the event of Republican victory. The American people must make up their minds whether they wish to take the chance of greater success on their part in the days to come in their sabotaging enterprise.

The American people must decide whether they wish to take the chance and assume the responsibility of denying our influence and power of resources, made available not only to win the war but also to win the peace, in holding back and driving back the forces of a new totalitarianism, which may be more ruthless and sinister than that which we defeated on the battlefield of the world in 1945.

The Republican platform undoubtedly attempts to repudiate the efforts of this wrecking crew in one of the branches of Congress, but, if they are successful, will the new Administration repudiate their efforts in the coming sessions of the Congress and during the four-year period covered by the law which Congress overwhelmingly adopted?

We rejoice to believe in this great venture we are actuated by no selfish motive, except that which consumes the breast of every liberty-loving human being to live in peace, to advance in moral stature, intellectual breadth, economic freedom and political equality throughout all the nations of the world.

We seek no territory. We seek no unjust economic advantage. We seek no dominion over the peoples of other countries. We do seek to enable them to restore the liberty for which they have fought for generations, and which many of them have lost.

We know that our nation cannot long remain free, if the rest of the world is in bondage.

We do know that our people cannot long remain prosperous, if the balance of the world is prostrate.

We know that the liberty-loving nations of the world must ultimately rise or fall together.

We do know that whether we wished it or not, the leadership in this great enterprise has been thrust into the hands of our people and of our government.

Shall we hold the torch and move forward with it, or shall we march back down the hill and blast the hopes of peoples everywhere, including our own country, and allow the world to sink into a long dark night of barbarism, brutality and godless overlordship from any source in any part of the world?

This question the American people must answer. May we hope that they will answer it in the language and the spirit of Thomas Jefferson, the founder of American democracy to which we have been devoted for more than a century and a half.

No genuine believer in the Jeffersonian philosophy is at liberty to deny the world-wide application of this immortal proclamation, born of the conditions which were the foundation of American independence. No true follower of Jefferson is at liberty to withhold from our own people, or the people of the world, the hope that they may enjoy that life, liberty and the pursuit of that happiness, upon which our own and all free institutions have been, and must be, founded throughout the world.

Surely the great Democratic party, assembled here in the midst of a great crisis that confronts mankind, assembled here at the end of a decade and a half of unparalleled achievement in the moral, economic and social life of our own country, in the midst of a world upheaval unprecedented in the annals of history, assembled here in the shadow of the historic hall where Jefferson wrote those things, surely, in these conditions, neither the great Democratic party nor the American people can foreswear their obligation to march forward on the highway of human advancement, both here and throughout the world.

This is no partisan call. This is no appeal for the lusts of office. This is no panoply of sophistries made to perpetuate or deny power to any political party. It is the swelling of human breasts with pride that God in His wisdom has given us the power and the opportunity to inaugurate a better world and a better society.

In the twentieth verse of the third chapter of Revelations is to be found a superb call to service, which has come across the centuries from the lips of the son-crowned man, who walked his way into the story of humanity: "Behold, I stand at the door and knock. If any man hear my voice and open the door, I will come in."

May we emphasize the meaning and the significance of this call in the present posture of world affairs, in the present obligations of the American nation, in the overwhelming challenge that comes to American leadership?

May we not apply this call to our present relationship to the world?

Behold, civilization knocks at the door!

Behold, the assembly of unnamed and unnumbered men and women who yearn for peace knocks at the door!

The validity of Christian principles of human society knocks at the door!

The rap of countless dead, who died on battlefield, in every sky, on every continent, on every island and every sea, to perpetuate these principles of equality and justice, of which I have been speaking, is heard knocking at our door of opportunity!

The knock is heard of countless women throughout the world, whose locks are blown over their shoulders by the wind of adversity!

The gentle touch of tender hands of millions upon millions of children, who long for happiness and education and the full life, can be heard upon the door!

Destiny itself knocks at our door in behalf of all these and more!

Shall we hear the voice and open the door, or shall we slam it in the face of an appealing world, turn our backs upon a divine obligation and refuse to lead the children of men out of the bondage of fear and slavery into a free world and a free life?

As one who, for a generation, has watched the ebb and flow of human hopes and aspirations, and has seen civilization upon the brink of the precipice and the crumbling away of the liberties of the people in many lands; as one who has lived and served through two world wars, and the aftermath of both, and the interim between them; as one who has stood by the side of Wilson, of Roosevelt and of Truman, to make his humble contribution to rescuing the things by which men wish to live, and for which they are willing to die, may I utter this humble prayer:

God of our fathers, lead Thou us on. As a nation, as a people, and as an assembly of people, give us wisdom to see the path of our duty, and courage to keep our feet upon it.

Amen.

CHAPTER XIV

A.B. "HAPPY" CHANDLER
(1898-   )

Forty years ago Happy Chandler said, "I was born under a lucky star. It will take care of me," [1] and today, one can still see that star twinkling in his eyes, sparkling in his voice, as he continues his active interest in Kentucky politics. In a recent interview, Chandler exhibited the appropriateness of his nickname, which he acquired as a student at Transylvania College: his laugh is quick and often, he recalls lovingly his childhood experiences in Corydon, his memory is sharp, his face expressive. One has the feeling that life is still not passing Happy Chandler by.

It is perhaps not unusual that this outgoing, ebullient man first wanted to be a football coach. Educated at Transylvania and later the Harvard Law School, Chandler's interests were more athletic than cerebral, and he still gleefully recounts the day he hit a grand slam homer for Maysville in the Blue Grass League. He later coached freshman football at Centre College, and his great desire was to be appointed head coach. He credits his entrance into politics to his ability to get this post. The two professions were later to fuse again, as he became two-time governor of Kentucky, a United States Senator, and Commissioner of Baseball. [2]

Born July 14, 1898, one mile north of Corydon, in humble circumstances, Chandler marks his years there as those which developed his language and oratorical gifts. In his high school, there was no debating society, but Miss Laura Harris, his English teacher, helped him to appreciate the reading of poetry. He can still recite some of his early lessons, and most of his campaign speeches were sprinkled with poetic quotations.

At Transylvania, his talent as an actor was tapped, and he took part in *Fanny and the Servant Problem*. Histrionics and a speech course under Dr. Saxton also helped to form his oratorical style.

In 1935, following terms as a state senator and Lieutenant Governor, Chandler became the youngest governor in the United States. [3]   He reports that he made over 900 speeches during his campaign, and that "the wags said I made the same speech 900 times." He spoke from the back of wagons, at courthouses and crossroads, sometimes giving as many as sixteen speeches a day. With his wife, the former Mildred Watkins, whom he married in 1925, Chandler courted his public by remembering their names; by singing "Gold Mine in the Sky" and "Sonny Boy;" by getting his audience to talk back to him; and, as he says, by never "saying anything in a speech that was vulgar or low or mean or calculated to hurt."

Chandler proved to be one of the most popular and successful governors of Kentucky. [4]   When he took office, the state was six million dollars in debt, and he reorganized the government from top to bottom. He said at the time, "What you own is sometimes of doubtful value, but what you owe is monstrous," and he decided the state was not going to spend more than it took in. At the end of four years, the debt was virtually paid off.

Part of Chandler's success in his first major political race was attributed to J. Dan Talbott, an influential politician, known as a "kingmaker." His goal was to give Kentucky the best political pattern in the world, [5]   and Chandler used this theme in his inauguration address:

> *I commenced the campaign in Kentucky this year with high hopes, with a smile on my face and a song in my heart. I bear no ill will or malice toward any man or woman in Kentucky who, for reasons best known to themselves, supported the candidate of their choice in the elections of this year. I owe the success of my campaign to the people of Kentucky.*

*I owe my allegiance to the people of our state. I shall
not permit ambition, or the hope of future preferment
or advancement, or the ambitions of my friends to
divert me from the firm resolution that I have made
in my heart to restore the government of my state
to the hands of the people ... I entertain the cherished
hope that when I shall have finished the course that
you may be able to say that I have, with entire devotion, kept faith with my fellow Kentuckians and that
the state shall not have suffered because of the confidence our people have resided in me.* [6]

He was true to his word. He consulted tax experts and
studied finance and taxation until he was an authority on the
subjects. [7] He appointed a committee of eighteen prominent men
to make recommendations for reorganizing the state government.

Chandler's tax plan, passed by the state senate without a
single dissenting vote, created thousands of jobs for Kentuckians
with public works projects involved in the addition of new public
buildings and highways. The complete reorganization of the
government produced notable and far-reaching results. Many
states sent representatives to Kentucky to examine the more
efficient organization and to borrow ideas. [8] Following the
passage of his reorganization law, Chandler told the legislature,
"You have fixed it so I can be a good governor and you've taken
away any excuse that I might have for not being."

In 1938 Chandler set his sights on the United States Senate.
However, in order to accomplish this, he had to defeat the incum-
bent, Alben Barkley, a formidable task. Rejecting the advice of
his friends, he entered the race and embarked upon a vigorous
campaign.

This contest was an intensely heated one, and it appeared
for a time that Chandler might win. However, President
Roosevelt saw the possible Barkley loss as a serious threat to
his power and took a personal interest in the election, making

several appearances in Kentucky for "my dear friend, Alben W. Barkley."[9]   In addition to campaigning for Barkley, Roosevelt used his influence to give thousands of jobs to WPA workers and he appointed five judges in Kentucky. Today, Chandler says, "I ought to have won that .... I was born too soon."

During his campaign against Barkley, Chandler used much the same strategy that he had used in his bid for governor. As a speaker, he had a knack for adjusting his style to fit the occasion. He appeared with a grin, spoke in a folksy manner, and attempted to relate himself to his audience.   One writer characterized Chandler's style as, "He can go corny or classical and make 'em jump from the rafters."[10]

A speech delivered during the Barkley contest illustrates Chandler's distinctive approach:

> *Folks, I am where I am because I asked you to put me here, and I agreed to, and I did. I did my own talking and most of you believed what I said. I've done what I said I would, and you know it. I'm doing my own running. I haven't got President Roosevelt to do my campaigning for me. I haven't got the White House burning electric lights all night thinking up ways of electing me, although from what I hear they're spending some of that time thinking up how to defeat me -- me, Happy Chandler, who used to sell newspapers, shine shoes and sing to the barber for haircuts.*[11]

Chandler described his opponent in the senate race: "Barkley was the most over-rated fellow I ever encountered in my life; he was bombastic ... couldn't find a grain of wheat ... all chaff ... I was on the ground. He was in the clouds most of the time. He had a big, booming voice; I usually spoke quietly and softly ... "

Although Chandler lost this chance for a senate seat, he was able to become a senator without a fight. Mills Logan, the junior senator from Kentucky, died shortly before Chandler's term as governor expired. Chandler then resigned, swore in Keen Johnson, his Lieutenant Governor, as Governor, and Johnson appointed Chandler to Logan's senate seat. Chandler subsequently was elected to complete Logan's term and was re-elected in 1942 for a six-year term.

One of Chandler's major contributions in the Senate occurred in 1942, when, as a member of the Truman Committee and the Military Affairs Committee, he volunteered to fly to the Aleutians to study Allied defense against the Japanese. During the trip, he had an opportunity to discuss the situation with General Douglas MacArthur. Immediately upon his return to Washington, Chandler went to the White House with his report and, MacArthur's recommendations, after which defenses in the Aleutians were strengthened.[12]

In 1943 Chandler took a trip around the world to get first-hand information about the war situation. This journey gave him influence in regulating lend-lease programs, and it allowed him to bring back information regarding the true picture of the relationship between the United States and its Allies.[13]

Chandler remained in the Senate until October 12, 1945, when he resigned to become Commissioner of Baseball. Some authorities thought Chandler left the Senate because of boredom. He did not get the attention he enjoyed as Governor, he did not have the comfort of the Governor's Mansion, and, worst of all, he was always in Barkley's shadow. He complained, "I'll always be a very junior Senator as long as Barkley is here."[14]

His departure from the Senate brought to an end eighteen years of service to Kentucky, beginning as Master Commissioner of Woodford County and ending in the United States Senate.

However, in 1955, Chandler returned to the political scene as the Democratic candidate for Governor. Again, he traveled across the state conducting his uniquely personal campaign. He found several changes had taken place since his first campaign for Governor twenty years earlier. The increased use of radio, and the introduction of television, reduced his speaking engagements from 900 to between five and six hundred. His success in this election was called by some "an unbelievable comeback."[15] And one writer, commenting upon the reasons for Chandler's victory, said:

> There are juices in him that appeal strongly to those who watch him and hear him. They like his vaudeville show. They like to hear him sing "Gold Mine in the Sky" today as much as they liked to hear him render "Sonny Boy" twenty years ago.[16]

Another writer compared Chandler to an old-time medicine man creating the atmosphere of an old-time camp revival meeting.[17]

When the results of the election were final, Chandler made a short victory speech to his supporters in Louisville:

> I have won other elections. I have known moments of victory before, but none approaches the present one. It is one thing to win a high political office under ordinary circumstances unlike those which surrounded the campaign this year. Few candidates for public office and few nominees have ever been the object of slurs and slanders which were aimed at me during the campaign this year. The fact that Kentuckians rejected -- refused to believe -- the unkind things that were said -- the fact that our majority was a record majority -- indicates confidence, the like of which few men have ever enjoyed.[18]

A few months later, Chandler was inaugurated Governor of Kentucky, the third man in the state's history to win a second term. In his inaugural address, to a crowd of more than one hundred thousand, he indicated his intention of supporting a better highway system and programs in education. He pledged to expand the state park system and to bring new industries into Kentucky.

Chandler later made two unsuccessful attempts at the governorship, in 1963 and 1971. For those campaigns he resorted more to radio and television, although he states that he spoke in the same way: "I spoke the issues .... "

In 1974, Chandler was still very much the orator and one of the last of the great Old South politicians. On January 19, he addressed the United Daughters of the Confederacy in Louisville. A reporter described the event:

> *Much of the politician still remains in Chandler. He still loves to press the flesh, to hug, to give and receive compliments. He also is quick to bring up facts about his various tenures as governor and U.S. Senator.*[19]

Happy Chandler may well be Kentucky's last great political orator. He, more than any other Kentucky governor, bridged the gap from the big political rallies to the advent of television as a medium for campaigning. In 1936, speech critics were comparing him with Abraham Lincoln and Franklin Roosevelt.[20] His abilities as a speaker have been summarized as "His real attractiveness as an orator stems from his ability to generate warmth, his technique of blending into any atmosphere, and his enviable ability to project enthusiasm."[21] And this zest for living still abounds as he carries out his daily tasks at his law office in Versailles. As one writer has noted, Chandler seems to project that "God's still in his heaven whether or not all's right with the world."[22]

Text of Chandler's Address

To The General Assembly

Frankfort, Kentucky, April 20, 1936

I very greatly appreciate the opportunity which you give me to come here upon this occasion and discuss, not only with you, but with our fellow Kentuckians all over the state, the condition of the Commonwealth. I want you to know at the outset that the revenue session in which we are presently engaged does not bring up propositions that are personal in either their nature or character, and for that reason I trust that, while we shall consider these very important questions during the next two or three weeks, it will not involve in any instance the loss of personal friendships which all of us enjoy.

These measures are not political; they are not personal; but somebody must assume the burden of suggesting to you men revenue measures that will solve the financial difficulties of the Commonwealth of Kentucky. I entertain the hope that my fellow Democrats who are members of the House and Senate, who either agree or disagree with me, will maintain their good humor; and I also earnestly hope that my Republican members in both Houses will conduct themselves the same way. It seems that nothing can be gained by losing one's sense of humor; and I even very greatly appreciate the presence of the gentleman from Knox who, I understand, said he would not be here if I made this speech. And I don't know of any reason I may not be able to tell what I have in mind, maybe not much, but I will try to tell you during the course of the afternoon some of the things to which I hope you will give your careful and most earnest consideration before this session shall have adjourned.

At the commencement of this session I suggested the raising of $12,000,000 or $12,500,000 of new revenue to meet the state's expenses.

As a candidate for public office before all the public, before the people of Kentucky, I gave definite assurances; and I challenge them today to show a single instance where I have not kept faith in regards to the program enunciated by me for the people of Kentucky. I said that we would consider certain measures that we thought would be for the good of all our people. I said that we would provide adequate support for the sensible administration of the State Government and its different departments. I said that we would endeavor to fix the state so that it would live within its income and not go deeper and deeper in debt each year as it has heretofore for the past twenty-five years. I said that we should cut the expenses of administration, and I warn you now that a perusal of the expenditures will show that we have cut the expenses from 20 to 25 per cent from an administrative standpoint, during the next biennial period.

I asked you to prepare a budget which would meet the new conditions. That budget is roughly twenty-two million dollars. It is the best budget of its kind that was ever prepared for the people of Kentucky, notwithstanding the fact that we have two million five hundred thousand dollars in that for the old age pension system; seven hundred and fifty thousand dollars for the rehabilitation of the state charitable, penal and eleemosynary institutions, and one million two hundred thousand dollars for the retiring of warrants and for the payment of interest on warrants.

By way of economy, by way of operating the State Highway Department and keeping it within its income, we paid a four million dollar debt and approached the biennial period on April 1 without any debt in that department, except a million dollars on contractual obligations which will only become due in the future as the work is completed.

You have men who have been willing to contribute to this result. They have performed the most constructive piece of legislation in the history of Kentucky.

This thing is certain; there are no popular tax bills; but I promised the people of Kentucky that if elected I would advocate the repeal of the general sales tax. That was done within a few days after we met; you repealed that tax, and it shall not, with my help, be imposed upon the people of the Commonwealth again. I promised the people of this state that I would not advocate an increase of the tax on real estate. I shall keep that pledge.

With that in mind, with the idea of presenting a balanced budget for the first time in twenty-five years, I came before you and presented certain revenue measures as being fair, equitable and just, and as being adequate to meet Kentucky's financial problems.

The first bill was calculated to raise about three million or three million five hundred thousand dollars in revenue from whiskey, and this bill was passed in the House and in the Senate with only a single vote cast against it.

I want to refute the statement made in the House that there was a deal made by me with the whiskey people. I never took a drink of whiskey in my life, and never intend to, but if they manufacture it, they should pay a fair amount of taxes to maintain their part of the functions of the State Government. Under the present law they pay seven million five hundred thousand dollars, approximately, as their part of the total tax burden. I said if they would agree to pay these taxes I would recommend to you that that was a fair proportion of the taxes to be paid by them.

I made certain other statements with reference to tax programs, and suggested that you spread the taxes among our people on those who are taxable subjects, on those who are able to pay taxes. I told you that I favor putting a reasonable amount of tax on those who are able to pay, and not shouldering the burden of taxes on those least able to pay, at a time when they are least able to pay it.

Living in the heart of the tobacco district as I have since 1922, I suggest that it would be fair if you gentlemen would pass a law to tax cigarettes; and I suggested, in view of the fact that we were trying to spread the burden of taxation generally, that the great business of raising tobacco should not object to paying $1,400,000 to help care for the public health, the public schools and public institutions and to rehabilitate the state charitable, penal and eleemosynary institutions of the state.

I want to say to you that for the entire year of 1910 only 8,000,000 cigarettes were consumed in the United States. Since that time twenty states have placed a tax on cigarettes. New Jersey placed a tax on them just the other day, which is a consumer's tax. They cannot put it on the farmers because it is paid by the man that goes to the store and puts down his money for cigarettes; 1 cent on an 10-cent package and 2 cents on a 15-cent package. It will raise altogether $1,500,000; and it is my opinion that the people of Kentucky ought to agree to raise that amount for the benefit of all the people of Kentucky.

They say it limits the consumption of tobacco. I think you have over-estimated how much of Kentucky's tobacco is consumed in Kentucky. My good friend Joe Robinson could grow almost enough tobacco on his farm, if made into cigarettes, as is smoked in Kentucky in one year. I don't think you men should permit any crowd of fellows from the Brown-Williamson and the Axton-Fisher Tobacco Company to come down here and stampede you against voting for the revenue that is so much needed.

I don't blame you if you voted against giving the school people twelve dollars per capita and if you want to vote against the thousands and thousands of helpless unfortunates who are confined in Kentucky's institutions; who have inflicted them, in physical and mental helplessness, the tragedy of being compelled to live in the type of buildings in which they are now confined and crowded; that is for you to decide. But if a fire should break out and many of them should be burned to death, I would have you remember that you voted not to raise the revenue to provide adequate and decent housing facilities for these poor, unfortunate wards of our state.

I am willing to lead this fight and I am right in the front. I want to recall to your mind that two years ago, in order to prevent the passage of a sales tax on the necessities of the people of Kentucky, I signed my name to a minority report advocating that this tax be placed on cigarettes. And I carried every county in this district and every precinct in every county except in Fayette County. I carried Fayette in both primaries, but in the general election my Republican opponent, who lived in the county, carried it.

I want to say to you, gentlemen, that if you vote for this and balance this budget, I am going to call you into extraordinary session and ask you to refinance the state's debt. You can provide for its payment over a period of years. We can refinance it at 2½ or 3 per cent, and it now bears 5 per cent per year.

It would be a shame on the Legislature of Kentucky if you neglect the distressful conditions that exist in the charitable, penal and eleemosynary institutions. I want you to know that Kentucky will stand No. 1 if all of you will agree to vote for this measure; if you will join with me in voting this tax for the next two years, we will build a model prison in Kentucky and a model insane asylum and a home for these little kiddies upon the hill without crowding them into impossible conditions.

Today I have had the promise of forty-four members of this Legislature to vote for this cigarette tax. We will get enough votes to pass the bill, because it ought to be passed; and then we will adjourn speedily. We have wasted time. We adjourned two or three days last week and went home in order to prevent the orderly processes of legislation from going on. I am going to ask you to stand by for the next two or three weeks, and let us finish this job.

There is enough credit to go around. It is not just a Democratic proposition; it is a proposition for all the state. It looks like among these men big enough to be elected by the people of the state, there should not be any low and mean enough to take advantage of any proposition and thereby plunge the state into a deeper financial situation than it already is involved in.

I know you could suggest many things better than I have suggested. The job is a big one, and I will say to you this afternoon that never in the history of Kentucky have so many of our fellow Kentuckians had the opportunity to achieve the results needed to put our state on a sound financial basis.

I went to Louisville the other night and made a speech to the Kentucky Education Association. I could have suggested some things to those people, but I didn't want to make a demonstration and didn't even ask them to indorse the tax on whiskey. I said, "as an individual citizen, interested in a per capita of twelve dollars, interested in the great university at Lexington, interested in the four great teachers' colleges of Kentucky, and interested in these little barefooted children of Kentucky that I have heard so much about and have gotten so little for, I want you to urge your representatives to vote for these taxes, and when you do, we will spread out the burden of taxation."

Why, nobody wants to pay taxes. There are no popular measures, and everybody who is about to be taxed is going to object and will suggest somebody else that it will suit better. Professor Martin was recommended to me by the President, and those in the United States who know tax matters say that he is the best man in the United States when it comes to figuring out a fair and just system of taxes.

This afternoon I talked to some of the men of northern Kentucky. Some of them object to the payment of an income tax and a corporate tax on property. I said to them, "Gentlemen, I know you realize the situation that we have in Kentucky. You realize that year after year the state has continued to spend money and to go deeper and deeper into debt, without reckoning upon a day for payment. I know that you want this Legislature to provide for the settlement of Kentucky's just debts and for the maintenance of the state's credit." These men said to me, "While this will hurt us, we wish, Governor, that you would provide that this tax will not be effective longer than two years from the present date." And I told them I was agreeable to that.

I went before a great group of labor the other night. These boys want to make their contribution to good government in Kentucky, and they sat by and said that they would back the Governor and the Legislature in this program.

I said to some of these people (legislators) the other day, "I don't know whether they scared you the other day, but if they scared you into killing a bill, it looks like the people could scare you into passing one."

I went into politics in 1929 and I am still here, and I have done more running than any of you. This job of running is a hard job, but I have never apologized for my actions or failed to vote; and I am up here charging you to assume the responsibility; trying to influence you to do the correct thing and the manly thing. The burden of the fight is on you; and a little bit later on I am going to advocate the passage of a bill here that will keep the tobacco companies from guessing at what the farmers are going to make.

I started down in western Kentucky as a barefooted boy, worming and suckering tobacco. I put the trenches in the barn and cooked potatoes and chickens and did all those things while we were firing the tobacco. I have gone day after day down the tobacco row. I want to say to you fellows who are really interested in Kentucky and the tobacco situation, that I am going to co-operate with the President of the United States. I am going to co-operate with this great program of his to get the farmer a fair price for his tobacco; and in the future I don't want you to let the tax in Tennessee -- the Tennessee farmers' three or or four or more dollars a thousand on tobacco affect you, but I won't stop there.

I don't want you to let the tobacco companies stick you on your prices and take your profits away from you, so that they will have so much money like one of them did one year when it paid the president of the company a million dollars bonus in addition to his salary. Where do you think that bonus money came from? We are asking for this money for the children of Kentucky, for the schools of Kentucky, and for the charitable, penal and eleemosynary institutions of Kentucky.

The going is not always pleasant; it is rough sometimes; but I want to warn you against making a combination to defeat the Governor's program without offering something in its stead. Don't just agree to beat a tax bill because it will give some temporary trouble.

I have gone to the people of Kentucky on every important issue in my lifetime. This afternoon I am speaking directly to you, but I am also speaking to every man and woman in Kentucky who is listening in, and who is interested, and who wants to know how you are doing here in Frankfort, and wants to know whether you are representing them or not.

I am giving you a true story, making a plea to the man who thinks more of Kentucky than he does of his own selfish interest or of greed.

It has been said to me, "Governor, you will make yourself unpopular if you advocate this taxation, and if you continue it, it will put you out of politics and defeat you." That ought to be popular with my Republican friends. I challenge you to join me in passing this bill and making me unpopular. I don't have to have another office. But I believe it depends on whether or not the people have a right to believe that they are represented in this House, that their Governor has the courage to come right out and tell the people what he is for and why he is for it.

Of course, if I didn't have anything better to do than to sit in an office and write an editorial column, in the *Lexington Leader*, which says that people of the state need not expect to get anything out of the present Administration (and they say that with the motto they have at the head of their paper) it might be different; but they are doomed to disappointment, Mr. Buckley.

A great deal of good will came from this Administration, and it is not because I am a Democrat; and I want to rejoice and thank sincerely those newspapers of Kentucky who are unaffected, who are uncompromising, who won't sell out, who are not afraid, because this is a time when it takes a courageous man to take the gaff.

You are not worthy to occupy a seat in this House if you let anybody make a demonstration that will prevent you from not doing your duty. Some of my dearest and closest friends entertain the idea that this will be hurtful to them. I have never asked a man to do anything that I would not do myself; I never ask a man to do anything that causes him to break his obligation, his word to his people; but I submit to you, gentlemen, that Kentucky has the most glorious opportunity that it has had in the last twenty-five years, to put into power an honest Governor and to keep in operation a Government that will be careful to guard finances and the lives and the health and the property of all the people of the state.

If I were a member of the House and Senate I would like to have an opportunity to see into the future, what would result, and, with that in mind, I just deliver this plea to the men and women of Kentucky. Just give me an opportunity to have some of the money that I am asking for now; just give me the opportunity to balance the state's budget; just give me an opportunity to refinance the state's debt. When you do, that will make available a million dollars for the general expenses of the state government which we have not heretofore had. I reiterate my pledge now, to all the people of Kentucky, that the highest ambition I have is to do the sensible, just, honorable and fair thing.

I have a right to believe that you will help me, join with me in bringing it about.

I would not, for anything on the face of the earth, be under the intimidation of any group of people that might come here to place themselves on exhibition, and bring a group of people with them and "demand their pound of flesh" and demand that you kill that bill. I would not be just if I did not say that every one of my fellow Kentuckians who came here asking to be heard on a matter of interest to him should be accorded the right to be heard.

I challenge the members of this House, Democrats and Republicans alike, to join in the passage of these bills from top to bottom. If you will do it, in two weeks this job can be completed. We have more work yet to be done.

There will be some objections, but there will be objections that can be met by taking these bills and making them meet reasonable objections. I never have insisted on a bill just being passed without meeting reasonable objections of people who had a right to object. But, this has not been a reasonable objection. It is a desire to kill and kill as quickly as possible.

I challenge you, men, to stay in session for the next twenty-four days. Just complete this job, and when you shall have done it, every man in this Senate and in the House will be called blessed by the people of Kentucky. And the objections that certain people of Kentucky may make, that will be made by selfish interests, will fall into a faint whisper; and you will balance the budget and arrange to pay off the debt over a period of years, and you will be able to say, "I am prepared to stand the test. As one of your Representatives, I didn't shirk my sworn duty when I took my oath of office." I will take care of the objections.

I am glad to have this opportunity to speak to you, gentlemen, again; and I thank you, and goodnight.

ENDNOTES

Chapter II

[1]Robert Davidson, *History of the Presbyterian Church in the State of Kentucky* (New York: Robert Carter, 1847), p. 134.

[2]William Garrett West, *Barton Warren Stone: Early Advocate of Christian Unity* (The Disciples of Christ Historical Society, Nashville, 1954), pp. 27-28.

[3]Elder John Rogers, *The Biography of Elder Barton Warren Stone,* written by himself, (Cincinnati: J.A. and U.P. James, 1847), p. 34.

[4]West, p. 29.

[5]Rogers, p. 36.

[6]Rhodes Thompson, *Voices from Cane Ridge* (The Bethany Press: St. Louis, 1954), p. 140.

[7]William P. Strickland, ed. *Autobiography of Peter Cartwright, The Backwoods Preacher* (Carlton and Porter, New York, 1857), p. 33.

[8]West, p. 33.

[9]Rogers, p. 38.

[10]*Ibid.,* pp. 39-42.

[11]West, p. 42.

[12]*Ibid.,* p. 49.

[13]Alonzo Williard Fortune, *The Disciples in Kentucky* (The Convention of Christian Churches in Kentucky: Lexington,1932), p. 39.

[14]Catherine C. Cleveland, *The Great Revival in the West 1797-1805* (University of Chicago Press: Chicago, 1916), p. 136.

[15]*A Concise Sketch of the Life and Experience of Isachar Bates, January 29, 1758-March 17, 1837,* Typescript Copy, Kentucky Lib-

rary, Western Kentucky University.

[16]W.E. Arnold, *A History of Methodism in Kentucky* (Herald Press: Louisville, 1935), VII, 93.

[17]Mss. in Kentucky Library, Western Kentucky University; The sermon was preached at Bowling Green, November, 1833.

[18]*Christian Messenger,* 6 (1832).

[19]Charles Crossfield Ware, *Barton Warren Stone: Pathfinder of Christian Union* (Bethany Press: St. Louis, 1932), p. 325.

[20]*Ibid.,* p. 326.

[21]Benjamin Lyon Smith, *Alexander Campbell* (Bethany Press: St. Louis), 1930, p. 314.

[22]Rogers, p. 11.

[23]Elder James M. Mathes, *Works of Elder B.W. Stone* (Moore, Wilstach, Key and Co.: Cincinnati, 1859), pp. 247-270.

[24]Evan A. Ulrey, *The Preaching of Barton Warren Stone,* unp. Ph. D. dissertation, Louisiana State University, 1955, p. 327.

[25]This is one of five sermons in Stone's handwriting known to exist. One is owned by Butler University, three are in a private collection in Oklahoma, the one printed here is owned and printed through the courtesy of the Disciples of Christ Historical Society in Nashville. The sermon was apparently prepared for a New Year's audience in 1841. Except for a few slight changes in punctuation, the sermon is printed as it was written.

Chapter III

[1]Barbara Mayo, *Henry Clay* (New York: Farrar Rinehart, 1943), p. 5.

[2]Bernard Mayo, *Henry Clay: Spokesman of The New West* (Boston: Houghton Mifflin, 1937), p. 15.

[3]Barbara Mayo, pp. 13-14.

[4]Clement Eaton, *Henry Clay and The Art of American Politics* (Boston: Little Brown Co., 1957), p. 5.

[5]Sources for most of the references to Clay's life, unless otherwise noted, are from the works of Barbara and Bernard Mayo.

[6]W.A. Clarke, *Monument to the Memory of Henry Clay* (W.A. Clarke, Cincinnati, 1857), p. 275.

[7]Clement Eaton, p. 65.

[8]Samuel Eliot Morison and Henry Steele Commager, *The Growth of the American Republic,* Vol. I (New York: Oxford Press, 1962).

[9]Barbara Mayo, p. 277.

[10]Observation of Harriet Martineau stated in Eaton, p. 152.

Chapter IV

[1]J.P. Barbour, "Ben Hardin," Lecture given before the Filson Club, March 26, 1885, MSS, Filson Club.

[2]Related by Alfred Allen, cited in Lucius P. Little's *Ben Hardin: Times and Contemporaries* (Louisville: *The Courier-Journal* Job Printing Company, 1887), pp. 150-151.

[3]Little, p. 555-6.

[4]*Ibid,* pp. 13-14.

[5]Barbour,

[6]Little, p. 54.

[7]William Cabel Bruce, *John Randolph of Roanoke 1773-1833* (New York: G.P. Putnam's Sons, 1922), p. 202.

[8]Little, p. 351.

[9]George Rawlings Roage, *Henry Clay and the Whig Party* (Chapel Hill: University of North Carolina Press, 1936).

[10]*Biographical Sketch of the Hon. Lazarus W. Powell,* Frankfort: General Assembly of Kentucky (1868), p. 20.

[11]Little, p. 294.

[12]*Ibid.,* p. 296.

[13]*Ibid.,* pp. 569-70.

[14]Frances Richards, "John Rowan," Unp. M.A. thesis, Indiana University, 1930, p. 42.

[15]Little, p. 285-286.

[16]Arabel Wilburn Alexander, *The Life and Work of Lucendia B.*

Helm (Nashville: Publishing House of the Methodist Episcopal Church, South, 1898), p. 17.

[17]Little, IX.

Chapter V

[1]Mrs. Chapman Coleman, *The Life of John J. Crittenden with Selections from Correspondence and Speeches,* 2 Vols. (Philadelphia, J.B. Lippincott, 1871). p. 13.

[2]Albert D. Kirwan, John J. Crittenden, The Struggle for Union (Lexington, University of Kentucky Press, 1962), p. 4.

[3]E.G. Swem, "Kentuckians At William and Mary College Before 1861," *The Filson Club Quarterly,* V. 23, July 1949, pp. 173-198.

[4]Kirwan, p. 16.

[5]Coleman, I, p. 15.

[6]Kirwan, p. 18.

[7]*Ibid.,* p. 21.

[8]Coleman I, p. 35.

[9]Kirwan. pp. 38-39.

[10]Coleman I, p. 22.

[11]*Ibid.,* p. 23.

[12]*Ibid.,* p. 25-26.

[13]John Savage, *Our Living Representative Men,* (Philadelphia: Childs Peterson, 1860), p. 131.

[14]Baltimore *Patriot,* Feb. 2, 1836, cited in Kirwan, 104.

[15]Coleman, I. pp. 96-97.

[16]Kirwan, pp. 134-135.

[17]Coleman I, p. 127.

[18]Speech of Mr. Crittenden of Kentucky on the Oregon Question, United States Senate, April 16, 1846.

[19]Coleman I, p. 287.

[20]Kirwan, p. 231.

[21]Brainerd Dyer, *Zachary Taylor* (Baton Rouge: Louisiana State University Press, 1946), 312.

[22]Coleman I, p. 332-333.

[23]Coleman I, p. 250.

[24]Kirwan, pp. 267-268.

[25]Coleman II, pp. 39-59.

[26]Trial of Matt F. Ward for the Murder of Prof. W.H.A. Butler, Hardin Criminal Court, April, 1854 (Louisville: Morton and Griswold, 1854).

[27]Kirwan, p. 286-287.

[28]*Ibid.,np. 288.*

[29]*Ibid.,* p. 323.

[30]Cited in J. Jeffrey Auer, ed., *Antislavery and Disunion,* 1858-1861, (Evanston: Harper and Row, 1963), p. 318.

[31]Speech of John J. Crittenden before the United States Senate, March 17, 1858, on the Question of Admitting Kansas into the Union.

[32]Savage, p. 140.

[33]Waldo W. Braden, ed. *Oratory in the Old South* (Baton Rouge: Louisiana State University Press, 1970), p. 264-265.

[34]The Union, The Constitution and The Laws, Speech of John J. Crittenden at Monzart Hall (Louisiville) August 2, 1860.

[35]Kirwan, p. 377.

[36]Auer, p. 322.

[37]Thomas C. Cherry, *Kentucky: The Pioneer State of the West* (Chicago: D.C. Heath and Company, 1923), p. 260.

[38]Coleman II, pp. 270-290.

[39]Coleman II, pp. 270-290.

[40]Kirwin, p. 420.

[41]E. Merton Coulter, *The Civil War and Readjustment in Kentucky* (Chapel Hill: University of North Carolina Press, 1926), p. 39.

[42]*The Courier-Journal,* May 30, 1909.

Chapter VI

[1]The information for this preface is originally in *Richard Hickman*

Menefee by John Wilson Townsend (New York: Neale, 1907).

Chapter VII

[1]Winston Coleman, Jr. "Cash Clay," *Rural Kentucky Magazine,* April, 1962, p. 19.

[2]Cassius Marcellus Clay, *The Life of Cassius Marcellus Clay, Memoirs, Writings, and Speeches,*(Cincinnati: J. Fletcher Brennan and Co., 1886), pp. 46-47.

[3]*Ibid.,* pp. 79-80.

[4]*Ibid.,* p. 84.

[5]*Ibid.,* p. 89.

[6]William Ritchie, "The Public Career of Cassius M. Clay," unp. MSS, Kentucky Library, (no date), pp. 195-6.

[7]William H. Townsend, *The Lion of White Hall,* (Dunwoody, Georgia: Norman S. Berg, 1967), p. 15.

[8]David L. Smiley, *Lion of White Hall* (Gloucester, Mass.: Peter Smith, 1969), pp. 152-3.

[9]William H. Townsend, *Lincoln and His Wife's Home Town,* (Indianapolis: The Bobbs-Merrill Company, 1929), pp. 190-1.

[10]Andrew Wallace Crandell, *The Early History of the Republican Party* (Boston: The Gorham Press, 1930), pp. 70-71.

[11]Photocopies in Townsend, *Lincoln,* p. 245.

[12]James Rood Robertson, *A Kentuckian at the Court of the Tsars,* (Berea: Berea College Press, 1935), p. 36.

[13]Cited in Ritchie, p. 166.

[14]*Cincinnati Daily Gazette,* September 1, 1862.

[15]Cited in Smiley, pp. 224-5.

[16]*Ibid.,* p. 229.

[17]Clay, p. 526.

[18]Speech of Clay at New Haven, June 28, 1887, in the *Clay Collection,* Eastern Kentucky University Library.

[19]Cassius Marcellus Clay, *Icarus,* Jan. 15, 1894, unp., Eastern Kentucky University Library.

[20]Ritchie, pp. 195-6.

[21]Clay, p. 209.

[22]*Lexington Leader,* December 17, 1894, clipping in the Kentucky Library.

[23]Cited in Townsend, p. 40.

[24]Joe Creason, "Cassius M. Clay: Kentucky's Grand Old Lion," *Courier-Journal Magazine,* August 19, 1962, p. 46.

Chapter VIII

[1]Unless otherwise noted, material is from a Master's Thesis by Lucille Stillwell Williams (University of Kentucky, 1934).

[2]Charles Kerr, editor, *History of Kentucky, Vol. II* (Chicago: American Historical Society, 1922), p. 843.

[3]Lewis Collins, *History of Kentucky, Vol I* (Kentucky Historical Society: Frankfort, 1960).

Chapter IX

[1]Source for information is Howard W. Robey's University of Kentucky Master's Thesis (1939).

Chapter X

[1]Joseph Frazier Wall, *Henry Watterson: Reconstructed Rebel,* (New York: Oxford University Press, 1956), p. 220.

[2]Henry Watterson, *The Compromises of Life,* (New York: Duffield and Co., 1906), pp. 24-25.

[3]*Courier-Journal,* July 3, 1872.

[4]Wall, pp. 126-27.

[5]Henry Watterson, *"Marse Henry": An Autobiography,* Vol. 1, (New York: George H. Doran Company, 1919), pp. 289-90.

[6]*Courier-Journal,* Feb. 20, 1877.

[7]Isaac Marcosson, *Adventures in Interviewing* (New York: John Pune Co., 1919), p. 35.

[8]Cited in Ray Stannard Baker, *Woodrow Wilson, Life and Times,* (New York: Harper Brothers, 1968), p. 57.

[9]*Courier-Journal,* June 13, 1911.

[10]Wall, p. 175.

[11]*Ibid.,* 177.

[12]Fannie Barlowe Gray, *Day in and Day out* (Louisville: S.L. Ewing and Co., 1879).

[13]Watterson, *Compromises,* p. 102.

[14]*New York Times,* Dec. 23, 1921.

Chapter XI

[1]*Carry Nation,* Unp. MSS, Louisville Literary Collection, p. 1.
[2]Herbert Asbury, *Carry Nation,* (New York: Alfred A. Knopf, 1929), p. XV.

[3]*Ibid.,* p. 169.

[4]*Register of the Kentucky State Historical Society,* Vol. 31, 1933, p. 176.

[5]*Nation,* p. 166.

[6]*Ibid.,* p. 105.

[7]*Ibid.,* p. 94.

[8]*Ibid.,* p. 137.

[9]Paul E. Isaac, "Prohibition and Politics," *Turbulent Leaders in Tennessee 1885-1920,* (Knoxville: University of Tennessee Press), p. 130.

[10]*Lexington and the Bluegrass Country,* (Lexington: The Commercial Printing Company Press, 1938), pp. 89-90.

[11]*Nation,* p. 30.

[12]*Ibid.,*

[13]Robert Lerois Taylor, *Vessel of Wrath,* (New York: The New American Library, 1966), p. 63.

[14]*Ibid.*, p. 73.

[15]*Ibid.*, p. 85.

[16]Asbury, p. XV.

[17]Taylor, p. 62.

[18]Asbury, XVII.

[19]Carry A. Nation, *The Use and Need of the Life of Carry A. Nation,* (Topeka: F.M. Steves and Sons, 1905), pp. 124-128. None of her speeches exist. Because of her extempore style of delivery she never wrote any speeches; however, this is typical of her oral speech style.

Chapter XII

Much information in this chapter came from the Laura Clay papers in the University of Kentucky Library.

[1]Paul E. Fuller, "Laura Clay and the Womans Rights Movement" (unpublished Ph.D. dissertation, University of Kentucky 1971), p. 7-8.

[2]Clavia Goodman, *Bitter Harvest* (Lexington: Bur Press, 1946), p. 14-18.

[3]Laura Clay Diary, July 15, 1874, University of Kentucky Manuscript Collection. Laura Clay Papers.

[4]*Ibid.*

[5]*Ibid.*

[6]*Ibid.*

[7]*Ibid.*

[8]Betty Lewis Balke, "The 50th Anniversary of the Vote for Women and a Bow to Laura Clay," *"Courier-Journal,* August 23, 1970.

[9]Fuller, *op. cit.* p. 56.

[10]Kentucky Equal Rights Association, Minutes of the Association for 1888.

[11]*Ibid.*

[12]*Greenville Daily News* (South Carolina) n.d., 1896.

[13]*Charlestown News and Courier* (South Carolina), n.d., 1896.

[14]*Lexington Dispatch,* n.d., 1896.

[15]Balke, *op. cit.*

[16]For more detailed discussion see Mary Gray Peek, *Carrie Chapman Catt* (New York; H.W. Wilson Co., 1944).

[17]*Goodman, op. cit.,* p. 44.

[18]*Knoxville Sentinel,* January 1913.

[19]*Knoxville Journal and Tribune,* January 28, 1913.

[20]*Owensboro Inquirer,* n.d., 1913.

[21]Fuller, *op. cit.,* p. 368.

[22]*Lexington* Leader, June 30, 1941.

[23]Balke, *op. cit.*

Chapter XIII

[1]Information is supplied by Thomas W. Ramage, whose master thesis, *The House Career of Augustus Owsley Stanley, Kentucky Congressman* (University of Kentucky, 1961) and doctoral dissertation, *Augustus Owsley Stanley: Early Twentieth Century Kentucky Democrat* (University of Kentucky, 1968), offer the only documented sources the editors could find.

Chapter XIV

[1]Unless otherwise quoted, The Source of Impression is Barkley's memoirs, *That Reminds Me* (Garden City: Doubleday, 1954).

[2]Jane Barkley as told to Frances Spatz Leighton (New York: Vanguard, 1958). p. 45.

Chapter XV

[1]Orval W. Baylor, *J. Dan Talbott, Champion of Good Government,* (Louisville: Kentucky Printing Corp., 1942).

[2]Unless otherwise noted, the information contained in this chaper was obtained from a personal interview with Mr. Chandler

at Versailles, Kentucky, September 25, 1973.

[3]Vincent X. Flaherty, "Life Story of Happy Chandler," *The Sporting News,* March 28, 1946.

[4]*Ibid.*

[5]*Ibid.*

[6]Ronald W. Beshear, "The Speaking of Albert Benjamin Chandler," (unp. M.A. Thesis, Murray State University, 1970), p. 5.

[7]Flaherty.

[8]*Ibid.*

[9]*Ibid.*

[10]Walter Davenport, "Happy Couldn't Wait," *Colliers,* July 16, 1938, p. 13.

[11]*Ibid.*

[12]*The Kentucky Standard,* August 11, 1938 (in the files of the Filson Club.).

[13]Flaherty.

[14]*Ibid.*

[15]J.B. Shannon, "Happy Chandler: A Kentucky Epic," *The American Politician,* ed. by J.T. Salter, (Chapel Hill: The University of North Carolina Press, 1938), p. 180.

[16]Robert L. Riggs, "Happy Chandler Rides Again," *Saturday Evening Post,* October 15, 1955, p. 155.

[17]*Ibid.*

[18]Beshear, p. 83.

[19]Billy Reed, "Happy Chandler Brings 'Old South Manners' to Meeting," *Courier-Journal,* January 20, 1974.

[20]Lew Sarett and William T. Fester, *Basic Principles of Speech* (Boston: Houghton-Mifflin Company, 1936), p. 21.

[21]Beshear, p. 6.

[22]Shannon, p. 191.

INDEX